©2003 by Lorraine Hart

Helen Morrison, M.D., is certified by the Board of Psychiatry and Neurology for general psychiatry as well as child and adolescent psychiatry. She is also a certified forensic psychiatrist. She is the editor or coauthor of four academic books, as well as the author or coauthor of more than 125 published articles in her field. Dr Morrison has worked with both national and international law enforcement, and has made presentations in more than fifteen countries. She lives in Chicago with her husband and children.

Harold Goldberg has written for the *New York Times Book Review*, *Vanity Fair*, and *Entertainment Weekly*. He lives in New York City.

MY LIFE
AMONG THE
SERIAL KILLERS

Inside the Minds of the World's Most Notorious Murderers

HELEN MORRISON, M.D.
and Harold Goldberg

WILEY

Published in 2004 by   John Wiley & Sons, Ltd, The Atrium, Southern Gate
Chichester, West Sussex, PO19 8SQ, England
Phone   (+44) 1243 779777

Copyright © 2004   Helen Morrison

Email (for orders and customer service enquires): cs-books@wiley.co.uk
Visit our Home Page on www.wiley.co.uk or www.wiley.com

First published May 2004.
This paperback edition published in February 2005.

Published by arrangement with William Morrow, and imprint of HarperCollins Publishers, Inc.
New York, New York U.S.A.

Other Wiley Editorial Offices

John Wiley & Sons, Inc. 111 River Street, Hoboken, NJ 07030, USA

Jossey-Bass, 989 Market Street, San Francisco, CA 94103-1741, USA

Wiley-VCH Verlag GmbH, Pappellaee 3, D-69469 Weinheim, Germany

John Wiley & Sons Australia, Ltd, 33 Park Road, Milton, Queensland, 4064, Australia

John Wiley & Sons (Asia) Pte Ltd, 2 Clementi Loop #02-01, Jin Xing Distripark, Singapore 129809

John Wiley & Sons Canada Ltd, 22 Worcester Road, Etobicoke, Ontario, Canada, M9W 1L1

Wiley also publishes its books in a variety of electronic formats. Some content that appears
in print may not be available in electronic books.

Library of Congress Cataloging-in-Publication Data
(to follow)

British Library Cataloguing in Publication Data
A catalogue record for this book is available from the British Library

ISBN 0-470-86978-X

Typeset in 11.75 on 14.5 pt Garamond.
Printed and bound in Great Britain by T.J. International, Padstow, Cornwall.
This book is printed on acid-free paper responsibly manufactured from sustainable forestry
in which at least two trees are planted for each one used for paper production.
10 9 8 7 6 5 4 3 2 1

FOR MY BOYS: GIII, GIV and GED

It is true. The intangibles of your love, caring, laughter, and hugs banish all the bad and evil that I see and experience in this research. My love to you.

—H.M.

For Mom, and for all those who listen and learn.

—H.G.

Now that I'm about to enter
Unmapped woods
I must shed all excess baggage
and like the backpacker
go light and essential,
leaving behind those luxuries
that have pseudonymed themselves
into necessities.

—JAMES IORIO,
"UNMAPPED WOODS"

CONTENTS

AUTHOR'S NOTE

During the course of my investigations as a forensic psychiatrist, I have profiled and/or interviewed more than eighty serial killers. When I speak to them or to members of their families, it is always my policy to have each of them sign a legal release form that allows me to use what they tell me for scientific purposes. Some of the letters and interviews from the people I have profiled appear in this book. They're presented here not for the purpose of titillation but to help the reader understand the theories that I put forth in this book.

INTRODUCTION

The downtown Chicago summer night was filled with the wind-spun perfume of nearby roses and freshly mown lawns. My children were in bed, the youngest sleeping soundly with dreams of magic and Harry Potter, and the oldest sleeping the hard sleep that comes after playing three periods of ice hockey. Across the street, a young couple walked hand in hand, and their laughter echoed as they passed out of view. My neighbors pulled up in their car and I waved to them. Dressed to the nines, they'd just celebrated their wedding anniversary, and they waved back as they moved inside their house. As their door closed and the neighborhood fell completely silent, I began to think about my own life and the fact that my children and my neighbors knew only in the most general terms what I do in my professional life. Our friends recognize that I am a psychiatrist who deals with very difficult cases, and perhaps it's better that they don't know any more than that. My two boys don't know why I sometimes leave for weeks on end, not yet. What I do is so very far removed from this thriving, affable neighborhood—the satisfaction we get from planting oak saplings with the community association, the occasional elegance of charity galas or the opera—that most everyone would be shocked to hear about it.

After a few minutes, I went inside our four-story brick house, a nearly perfect place that was my husband's grandfather's home and office where he practiced medicine for decades. In the back of the first floor is a former examination room that now serves as my work space when I'm at home. Its walls are coated with tin, still there from years gone by. It's the history here, the cheerful medical attention given to the neighborhood for over eighty years by the good doctors, that inspires me. I pulled from a beige-colored folder some pictures of a child, a girl not only murdered brutally but also battered nearly beyond recognition. Sometimes I don't think I can take the sight of one more photograph of an innocent whose life has been so senselessly taken.

In preparation for a keynote address to a coroners group, I jotted down some notes onto a legal pad about the number and location of each wound on her lifeless body. Nearby were wire mesh baskets, with reams of other notes, replete with the pictures of other girls and boys, all murdered. This is not uncommon work for me. It is what I do, and I believe it is what I was meant to do.

Admittedly, it is not the work that most would choose, but I am what people now call a profiler, three short syllables that have given my professional research life a determined focus and purpose. For the past thirty years, longer than I care to remember, I have been privy to the most devious inner workings of serial murderers, and I have been compelled to traverse both the country and the world in a kind of solitary, endless journey to discover who they are, where they are hiding, and why they kill. Sometimes I think I know too much about them, certainly more than just about anyone in the world. But even as my knowledge of multiple murderers increases each day, my great fear is that I will never know enough.

I am not a profiler in the way you've seen on television. A few years ago, Ally Walker starred as the smartly dressed Samantha Waters in the CBS television series *The Profiler*. Waters said she worked via "thinking in images," picturing killers through colorfully edited montages in her mind in a kind of extrasensory perception that helped her track down serial murderers. While she could never exactly control her visions, they always seemed to arrive at precisely the dramatic moment that moved the story forward into that most crucial element of primetime television—the commercial. As for me, I am not clairvoyant in any way. Unlike Sam Waters, I do not see detailed, cinematic flashes of what happened in the past or what will happen in the future. And although some people have called me "The Real-Life Clarice" because of the books and movies *The Silence of the Lambs* and *Hannibal,* Clarice Starling and Hannibal Lecter are the stuff of fiction. In Thomas Harris's novels, Hannibal develops an emotional bond with Clarice that belies a twisted, sick love, but love nonetheless. In reality, the caveat in working with serial killers is that they are completely, utterly inhuman.

As a forensic psychiatrist with a health law degree, my job is grounded in careful science and in reasoned theory. After speaking at length to more than eighty of them, I have found that serial murderers do not relate to others on any level that you would expect one person to relate to another. They can play roles beautifully, create complex, earnest, performances to which no Hollywood Oscar winner could hold a candle. They can mimic anything. They can appear to be complete and whole human beings, and in some cases are seen to be pillars of society. But they're missing a very essential core of human relatedness. For them, killing is nothing, nothing at all. Serial murderers have no emotional connection to their victims. That's probably the most chilling part of it. Not only do they not care, but they also have no ability to care.

With serial killers, I never quite know whom I'm dealing with. They are so friendly and so kind and very solicitous at the beginning of our work together. I've been swept up into their world, and that world, however briefly, can feel right. I've often thought, Is this person the right person? Is all the work I've done—painstaking research, scientific collection of data, complex theorizing—simply wrong? Maybe I missed something. They're charming, almost unbelievably so, charismatic like a Cary Grant or a George Clooney (although they rarely are as handsome). They treat me as if I am their kindred spirit.

However, when I sit with them for four to six hours at a time, solid, without interruption, everything changes. My interviews are crafted to seem like talks, easy conversations. I've learned that a serial murderer can't maintain his solicitous role for any period of time past two to three hours. At this point I can begin to strip away the superficial layer of affability to reveal a dark, barren core.

He begins to fidget, sigh, tsk, clear his throat, roll his eyes, look around. Small beads of sweat form on his forehead. Finally, he begins to become annoyed, begins to break down. What he'd rather I do is sit there patiently and become a repository for his endless thoughts and ramblings. Yet through a combination of indulgence, tolerance, listening, and constant indirect questioning, I will always get him to say more than he wants to say. It can take months for a breakthrough, and when it comes, there's nothing more electrifying, nothing more satisfying.

A good portion of the satisfaction I get comes from piecing together the facts that help me understand a case and then make it more cohesive. Each fact or datum becomes a part of a monumental puzzle, and I try to connect the information to other crimes that have been done. Along the way, I learn more and more about the serial killer— life story, personality, the attitude he has toward his victims—bit by bit. It is painstaking and difficult, particularly because it involves precious, innocent human life that has been snuffed out senselessly and horrifically.

From the more than a hundred files I sifted through in preparation for my speech, I could see the victims' struggle and pain in the photographs. The signatures of serial murderers emerged on the bodies of their poor victims—bites, cuttings, or knots they used to make their marks, as though they were marking their handiwork with some kind of misplaced pride.

Later today, I will drive down to Merillville, Indiana, a sleepy town of about 27,000 people. It's the very picture of American suburbia with its IHOP, Lowe's, and Costco. Inside the Radisson Hotel I will give the keynote speech to the annual meeting of the Indiana Coroners Association. As the coroners sip coffee and eat morning Danishes, I'll deliver my address, explaining my theories about why serial killers are compelled to kill. What signs of a serial killer should coroners hunt for at a crime scene? What triggers their actions? What makes them tick? Why do they continually hunger for murder? The popular perception is that they have been physically and/or sexually abused by their parents when they were innocent children. That is the stuff of fiction—a complete misconception. In the pages that follow, I'll explain my theories, some of which are controversial. But they are grounded in decades of research and science. In addition to my own ideas, I'll take the reader on a journey though these killers' brains, with transcripts from our psychiatric sessions and in their own words from their own letters.

Into my briefcase's front pocket, I placed a particular file, one bearing three names that may be familiar to you, John Wayne Gacy. Gacy, a paunchy fellow who often dressed as a clown with a huge, red-painted mouth when he entertained the sick and infirm at local Chicago hospitals, raped, tortured, and then buried many of his victims under the floorboards in his house. The case would soon become a staple of the press, which depicted Gacy as the very incarnation of evil, the devil himself. It was 1980 when I first encountered this murderer of thirty-three young males.

It was close to Christmas when my husband and I returned to Chicago from our honeymoon, and we were excited about settling into our new apartment. Ours wasn't the most luxurious apartment in the world, but at the time it seemed the perfect nest for two doctors deeply in love. I had picked up the mail and sat down at the kitchen table to go through the bills, magazines, and Christmas cards that had accumulated. There were small packages, medical journals, and too much junk mail. But one envelope bore unfamiliar handwriting. Inside was a card with primitive handmade art, drawn with a pen and colored in with crayon, of Christmas trees and a snowman. Inside the card, the inscription read, "Peace on earth. Good will to men . . . **and boys**— John Wayne Gacy." It was obscene, bold, as though Gacy were celebrating his brutal murders of so many young men. There was no way that Gacy, who I was to interview shortly, should have had access to our unlisted address. But he had found it and sent the card directly from jail. Gacy's "greeting" made me realize once again the danger inherent in my work, not only to me but also potentially to my family. I had been threatened and taunted before, so I tried to put Gacy and his murders aside, but my husband took the incident hard. For some time, he couldn't stop worrying about it . . . and me.

I finished crafting my lecture for the coroners and put the speech, photos, and notes into the worn leather briefcase. I turned briefly to pat my green jade turtle for good luck, switched off the light, and quietly closed the door. As I walked upstairs to bed in the semidarkness, there were some things I felt I knew for certain. Serial killing can be explained and understood. There are intricate but knowable patterns that every serial killer maintains. And because of what we're learning regarding the patterns of DNA and genetics, the very phenomenon of serial killing may be preventable in the future. In this book, which is the story of a good portion of my career, I hope to begin to explain how.

ONE

BABY-FACED
RICHARD MACEK

In March of 1977, the old road to Waupun, Wisconsin, was some-how eerie and foreboding, not simply rural but isolated in the kind of way that makes you watch your back. About twenty minutes outside of Madison, the colorful, welcoming signs for homey diners and Wisconsin cheddar cheese vanished, and the whole world seemed devoid of life. The sleepy fields along the way were still brown, not yet tinged with green, and there was an uncanny quiet, made heavier by the gray, chilly day. To be quite honest, I was nervous. I was a young doctor about to step into a world brimming with horrible crime and serial murder. It was a world full of macho, hard-drinking law enforcement officials who'd seen too much, and I wondered if I would be accepted or even tolerated not only as a professional, but also because I was a woman. Occasionally, I gripped the steering wheel too hard, as if driving straight and steady on the highway would steady my thoughts. I glanced at myself in the rearview mirror, to make sure the anxiety didn't show. It was important that I appear calm and com-posed.

I was no stranger to challenges, to tough times. As a child living in a small town near Pittsburgh, I never knew my real parents. It's not that I didn't yearn to find out. It just wasn't part of the deal. My parents weren't that kind. Sure, six other children and I had a roof over our heads, and food, but when it came to the real security that love can provide, well, it simply wasn't present. It sometimes seemed that the reason six others and I were children to these people was due to factors not understood, even now. Our lives as children were often unremittingly dark, and we were very alone in the world the parents defined.

But in one way I was ahead of the game. I discovered an early passion for what I wanted to do. At the age of eleven, I watched as eight-year-old Beth, one of my favorite siblings, came down with scarlet fever. The rash of scarlet fever usually looks like a bad sunburn with unsightly but tiny bumps. I often felt like a mother to the rest of my siblings, so as her condition worsened, her chills and shakes, high fever, and vomiting had me worried. As she hallucinated, I was sure she was near death. I became frightened, full of the kind of all-encompassing terror that only children can feel. But when a doctor came to the house to treat her, she soon began to recover. In my young mind, I thought the doctor was a miracle worker. Amazed, I vowed right then to become a doctor. I was working by age twelve to bring in money, and I believed that if I worked harder and longer than anyone else, I could accomplish anything to which I set my mind—including becoming a doctor. It didn't matter if I had to deliver newspapers or if I worked as a waitress or a clerk in a grocery store to do it. Sometimes, I stood restless at the outskirts of our small town. And I imagined myself somewhere else, traveling to the more exotic places I saw in magazines or heard about on the radio. I could get out. I would get out. I had to.

As I drove, I kept thinking about what the FBI agent had asked me. "Have you ever seen anything like this before?" Special Agent Louis Tomaselli obviously had seen a lot in the course of his job, but the gruesome nature of the eight-by-ten black-and-white photographs he showed me had him mystified and concerned. Tomaselli was smooth talking, dark haired, and wiry. He had this way of talking with his hands. Careful but darkly animated, his hands moved not simply to express what he said but also gestured, twisted, and grabbed the air to help me picture the words. Early in our conversation, he said, "There's not much difference between me and the bad guys—except the FBI got to me first." The off-the-cuff comment startled me, but it made sense. If you're straight and narrow and you're going in undercover, you may be too conspicuous and your cover will be blown. Like a chameleon, you have to blend into the environment in which you're working. It never crossed my mind that people could go either way. I was young, from a town so small you might think it was just a bunch of nondescript wood frame houses at a dusty intersection. My sense had been that you were either right or wrong, that the rules in life were very black and white. This was just one of the myriad of core beliefs that would change radically for me in the months ahead.

Tomaselli approached me moments after a seminar I cotaught in 1977 called "The Use of Hypnosis in Criminal Investigations." At that time, law enforcement was intrigued with the possibilities of using memory-enhancing techniques like hypnosis, so the seminar was well attended. I told them that hypnosis is simply a state of deep, intense focus and has nothing to do with magician's wands. I myself was the subject, but it wasn't at all about strutting around onstage like a chicken. I was shown a photograph of a crime on a subway before and after I was hypnotized. The officials in the room were impressed that I was able to recall many more of the details within the picture when I was hypnotized. Everyone in attendance learned that memory could be improved but not manufactured through hypnosis.

Hundreds of investigators like Tomaselli had gathered just outside of Madison, Wisconsin, from around the state for a two-day confer-ence about investigating and solving homicides more effectively. Many of the seminars dealt with hard-to-crack cases. Crime scenes would be set up and the law enforcement professionals in the audience would try to piece together what had happened. In my short career as a resident specializing in child and adult psychiatry and neurology, the cases I'd dealt with were routine, and I knew I wanted a deeper level of in-volvement and understanding. As a doctor, but more as a human being, I was hungry for knowledge.

Tomaselli had come up against a seemingly insurmountable brick wall. He and the FBI could not find the perpetrator of the vile crime captured in the photo. Yet he was not about to quit, even though he had tinkered with just about every possibility he could conjure up. As Tomaselli spoke, I found myself captivated by all of it, the idea of an unsolved mystery, the idea that, in the world of crime and crime solving, there was, in addition to life-and-death drama, room for good, objective science. And perhaps room for me as well.

Tomaselli removed more photos from a manila envelope. The images were of a woman, brutally stabbed several times. She was left on her back in room 18B at the upscale Abbey resort hotel on the shores of Lake Geneva, about fifty miles southeast of Madison, Wisconsin. Violence was unheard of at the Abbey, and the crime shocked everyone within a hundred miles. At least for the moment, the lakeside resort could no longer be considered the "Newport of the West."

The photos didn't shock me—it wasn't as if I hadn't seen blood or violence before. After finishing undergraduate work at Temple University, I was a medical student in Philadelphia at the height of the riots in the late 1960s. Blood filled the hospital at the Medical College of Pennsylvania, and our ER looked more like a *M*A*S*H* unit, as though war had broken out in the streets. Those days will forever stay with me.

Tomaselli was still holding the photo, and he was focused on something the killer did to the woman's face. He had taken a penknife and made slits in her eyelids.

"Have you ever seen anything like this?" Tomaselli repeated. I looked closely again, especially at the slits. It almost looked like the kind of primitive, ritual cutting common to ancient cultures. If you look back in history, runic symbols were sometimes cut into the palms of Germanic women during labor and childbirth as early as the third century B.C. But it was clear this modern-day act had nothing to do with long-lost magical symbols expected to promote health, freedom, or valor. This wasn't about pagans and enchantment; this was barbarism. Here, as the woman lay lifeless on her back, it was clear there were also visible signs of strangulation. But Tomaselli said that according to the coroner and others involved in the criminal investigation, the murderer continued brutalizing her after she was dead. He stabbed her repeatedly. And then he slit her eyelids.

I said no, I hadn't ever seen anything like it. No longer darkly exuberant, Tomaselli stopped talking and stood there, waiting for me to say more. I looked him straight in the eye. "But if you ever catch him, I'd like to talk to him."

It was exactly what he wanted to hear. He said he'd be in touch.

I didn't obsess about those photos, but I thought it was somehow compelling to see that kind of violence and brutality. It's not just about the horrible idea of someone getting stabbed. It's the whole, unnatural disarray, the chaotic scene of someone's life cut short, and the intense awareness that someone, someone vicious, is still on the loose. What was he doing? Was he scheming, planning his next attack? Was he stalking someone in broad daylight even as I thought about him?

Instead of fear, I felt curiosity. What kind of person would be able to commit that sort of crime and then disappear? What drove him? What went on in his mind? Such foul crimes are most often committed by members of a victim's family, and most people who commit such a crime are caught very quickly. But these crimes were of a different sort, strangers. Here, law enforcement was trying to connect the wretched crimes of one geographical area to those in another area entirely. And it had become clear this killer was a complete stranger to his victims.

He was, as it turned out, Richard Otto Macek, a man alleged to have killed at least five women. As I drove northeast from Madison in my eight-year-old Datsun station wagon, I had no specific idea of what to expect. I only had Macek's name, his date of birth, and a general sense of the crimes for which he was suspected. Of course, I remembered the photographs of the brutalized maid, black-and-white photos that now had all the depth and brilliance of Technicolor as I thought about them. In my mind, I envisioned various fuzzy images of people who are violent and could cause destruction. I imagined that Macek would be dark, hulking, disheveled, and wild-eyed, intimidating in every way.

When I passed through the placid streets of Waupun, I noticed sculptures of pioneer women on the streets and in front of City Hall, the eyes of which looked up to the skies in a kind of hope. They had names like *Dawn of Day* and *Morning of Life,* a kind of expectant optimism that did little for the depressing place. I supposed Waupun needed anything that would cheer its citizens, since the town of ten thousand housed not one but three prisons, including Central State Hospital. I'm not sure why there were three jails; I only know they kept a lot of people employed.

While he awaited trial for the Abbey murder, they kept Richard Macek in a highly secure and heavily guarded room at Central State Hospital in Waupun, a place where the criminally insane received the help they needed. The authorities suspected Macek of five murders—including that of the maid and one in Illinois—but Macek claimed he couldn't remember the crimes. Both police and doctors were highly suspicious of his story, but at Central State, the best psychiatrists couldn't get much out of Macek.

The hospital was housed in an old stone building, ugly and standing low amid desolate, barren fields. The gulag-like place was surrounded by a barbed-wire high fence. After double-checking that my bag held a cassette tape recorder, extra batteries, some pens, and a notepad, I made my way to security, which was much tighter than I expected. The guards were off-putting and rude, like high school bullies. After the requisite metal detector, I was told I couldn't bring in my tape recorder. The thing that got me was that use of the device had been prearranged. The guards themselves were condescending and kept repeating, "You can't carry this tape recorder in. You don't have permission from the warden." And I said, "I do." And so it went around in circles. Sometimes I think the guards in these institutions are worse than the prisoners. These particular guards proved the cliché that power corrupts. This was their turf and it was their rules, petty as they were. And it would be their rules without exception.

They held me up for forty-five minutes before Agent Tomaselli arrived to whisk me through. I forced the confrontation with the guards from my mind as we walked quickly through a maze of halls. Tomaselli explained that police caught Richard Macek after a woman he attacked in a Laundromat fled. She freed herself from his grip and jumped from his car at a stoplight. When questioned, she explained to police that his car had a broken red taillight. Before I could hear more, a squeaky door with a wire-reinforced window opened into a small, airless meeting room with green walls. Inside sat the warden, an investigator from Illinois, and one from Wisconsin. As I looked around, I felt like I was intruding on a private old boys' club.

The warden, seemingly bored, sat in a Hawthorne chair, his bulk bulging through the oak slats. Staring past me, the warden blandly asked, "How can you help us?"

I said that through hypnosis, I might be able to bring out what Richard Macek had forgotten, especially the specific details of the murders he may have committed.

"Hmmm," said the warden as though he didn't believe me. "Hmmm," as if my response didn't merit even a word. Their nonchalance bewildered me. Did they want to get to the bottom of the murders for which he was suspected or not?

Throughout the meeting, they didn't look me directly in the eye, and they often spoke as if I weren't present in the room. It was quite clear that the law enforcement people had an agenda much different from mine. They wanted to use me as their agent to coax Macek into confessing to a crime in Illinois—to the murder of a teenager named Sally Kandel. On January 25, 1973, warehouse worker Richard Milone was jailed and later convicted of the murder, but Milone protested that he was innocent, and a group of people, including Tomaselli, believed Milone. A small but growing amount of public pressure made the supposedly closed case fester like an open wound. The murder of young Sally Kandel was particularly appalling because the killer had bitten her severely. It most likely was Macek, but he had pulled out all of his teeth before forensic odontologists got to her case. Since he now was without his real teeth (he now wore dentures), it would be far more burdensome to link Macek to the bite marks.

But I had my own agenda; I wanted to begin a scientific study, one that looked into what made a serial murderer take innocent lives repeatedly. I kept thinking this was a necessary and interesting research project. If things worked well, it might really reveal something important about the many unknown aspects of a serial murderer, from his childhood to plotting the act of killing. It might even be beneficial to other crime investigations in the future. But they kept thinking that hypnosis was an unusual way to get him to confess.

The investigator from Illinois, a skinny man with a snipe-like nose that was too long and ears that were too large, blanched at the prospect of a scientific study.

He cleared his throat. "Scientific study," he mumbled, tapping his pen on the table as though he were aggravated. I began to wonder why Tomaselli had invited me at all.

I felt an unspoken condescension in the room, one that asked, What is an attractive, probably not competent, woman like you doing here? I tried my best to alleviate the situation; to put them at ease and make myself less threatening, I smiled at them even though they didn't smile at me. Without Tomaselli's urging, I didn't think I'd be there. But one thing became clear as I listened to them talk—they felt that Macek had committed *many* more killings than the brutal stabbing of the maid. And that's why I was here. They were so baffled they might even let a young doctor still in residence into their cloistered world of criminology—if it helped to unravel the case. I would have to prove myself in these few minutes we had before Macek came into the room.

Bear in mind that it wasn't yet a great time for women in the workplace. These still were the early days of the feminist movement, and women generally were not treated like equals. The National Organization for Women was not yet a decade old, the first battered women's shelter had just opened, and *Ms.* magazine was considered to be radical, bordering on Communist. As recently as 1972, the Equal Rights Amendment had passed the Senate, but only twenty-two of the thirty-eight required states ratified it. Women then held slightly more than a dozen seats in Congress. It was thought to be a revolutionary time, but a difficult time as well. Women had to act either aggressively to change their circumstances or had to focus clearly to keep plodding away in the trenches. I was certainly not a burn-your-bra kind of feminist. I didn't attend protests or marches or meetings. Yet I was of a single mind—to be the best doctor I could be, and no one was going to stop me.

Therefore, I was determined not to become annoyed by the officials in the room, no matter how I was treated. My approach was assertive and workmanlike. I thought, I'll let the insulting behavior wash away like water off a duck, but let's get done what needs to be done.

When two guards brought Richard Otto Macek into the meeting room, I couldn't believe what I saw. He was nothing like what I had anticipated. He was a short man in his thirties with whitish hair that bore remnants of blond and an unmemorable, babyish face. He was dressed in a drab brown shirt and pants issued by the prison hospital. Macek himself was physically odd. He was powerfully built, short and stocky, and he struck me as having brawny arms and a massive torso, reflecting enormous strength. Paradoxically, he struck me as pudgy with a peculiar combination of male and female characteristics, including a roundish body and soft, almost delicate, features.

Although he had shackles on his feet, he was not at all the odious murderer I expected. He looked right at me, smiled brightly, and shook my hand with a manly grip. It was as though this were a social event and he was trying to play the part of attentive host. He smiled again, this time showing his somewhat ill-fitting dentures.

"How's the weather? How was the drive?" he asked. He put his hands on his hips. "Are you comfortable in that chair? If not, we could get another chair."

When he spoke, his manner was exceedingly friendly. In a way, it was almost like role-playing—as though someone had given him a script and said this is how you're supposed to behave. He minded his manners. He joked, laughed, and generally kept the conversation light and breezy. He seemed pleasant, someone you could talk with easily. It was absolutely puzzling—how could a cold-blooded murderer act so convincingly polite?

The law enforcement people left after Macek signed a release stating that any and all of his words to me could be used in any way, even for Illinois or Wisconsin to convict him. As we sat in the room alone, I continued to be struck by the overall impression that he appeared to be a nice man, that perhaps they had jailed the wrong guy. In the coming twelve months, however, I would speak to Richard Macek for over four hundred hours. I would get to know him better than most of his family ever did. It wouldn't take a full year to really get to know Richard Macek, however. Within weeks, what I found out about him would have stunned his closest relatives.

TWO

DANGEROUS TERRAIN: HYPNOTIZING A SERIAL KILLER

On March 8, 1977, the day we met, Richard Macek had written a letter to me about that meeting. The paper bore a coat of arms in the lower right corner, featuring two armed lions facing each other with their tongues sticking out. Under the lions' paws stood the motto *In hoc signo vinces*. It is a Latin phrase meaning "In this sign thou shalt conquer" and was adopted by Constantine after he had a vision of a cross in the heavens, a waking dream that occurred just prior to his victorious battle against Maxentius in A.D. 312. A popular and adaptable battle cry, *In hoc signo vinces* has been employed by everyone from the Catholic Church to neo-Nazi hate groups to advance their various causes. It was interesting that Macek used the coat of arms, since Macek was a man who had nothing and now had less. Whenever I spoke with him, it was clear Macek wanted to be more than he was. To pretend he had an important history full of adventure and blue-blood relations, he took to adding this coat of arms to his letters.

All prisoners write letters: it passes the time, and they have too much of that. The notes are always self-involved; they write about their days and nights—even when nothing much happens. Macek's two-page handwritten letter included the announcement that he was "a little insecure and scared around women." What a lie this was for a man who murdered women exclusively. What concerned me was not his revelation about being "scared around women." That was a ruse. How would I get to him? How would I break through and coax him into lowering his guard? In my heart, I knew I was in for a royal struggle to find out if this man, who often bit and chewed on his victims with feral intensity, fit any kind of diagnostic category of psychiatric disorder, any classification of murderer known to us throughout history. The rest of Macek's letter was uneventful and devoted to sucking up, as if he hoped that speaking to me would help his case. Yet I was glad he wrote, and hoped he would write more. The more I knew about him the better.

Because I tend to compartmentalize and focus acutely on the task at hand, I hadn't given the Richard Macek case all that much thought in the two weeks that had slipped by since our first meeting. When I was a third-year resident at the University of Wisconsin Medical Center, my life was a constant whirl of seminars, patients, teaching medical students, and generally working through the sometimes hellish duty of being on call.

To a young transplant, the expansive Midwest was full of a culture about which I knew very little. Though I could have chosen a residency on the more familiar East Coast, recruiters convinced me that the program was eclectic and well-rounded and that they really wanted women at Wisconsin. There had been on-campus protests by the students demanding that women become an integral part of the medical school and residency programs.

By the 1970s Madison was a progressive-minded city of 150,000 considered to be the Haight-Ashbury of the Midwest. Not only was it still full of the introspective culture and the patchouli-laced lifestyle of hippiedom, but it also brimmed with anti–Vietnam War rhetoric and wild experimentation with drugs . . . and violence. While a resident at the University Hospital, I lived in the shadow of the 1970 bombing of the physics building. Sterling Hall was attacked by four anti–Vietnam

War protesters who dragged six barrels of ammonium nitrate and fuel oil into a van, only to explode the vehicle and its dangerous contents, damaging twenty-six buildings. The explosion was earth-rattling enough to be heard twenty miles away.

Years later, the event still loomed large, and it seemed that a form of anarchy still reigned on campus and in town. Students who were depressed or who lost control after a night of drug-filled partying would walk off dormitory roofs. In the student union, I would often encounter one of my schizophrenic patients. If I made the mistake of ignoring him or not acknowledging his presence, his paranoia could lead to a confrontational scene that could grow inflamed and end in fury.

I sometimes escaped by going off and riding a light blue Schwinn ten-speed bicycle. North of Madison on a railroad bed long abandoned by any train was the thirty-two-mile Elroy-Sparta trail, which wound through rock tunnels and among pine trees and sugar maples, wood violets and speckled red granite. But when I returned, I often had to deal with hospital politics.

As one of four women granted residency that year, I was tolerated (though certainly not embraced) by the departmental and hospital administration that so actively had recruited me. After serving on various committees and working very diligently, I was elected president of the 280-person house medical staff. The hospital administration even sent a dozen long-stemmed roses in a pretty box to my office, which I cut and arranged in a vase. As I placed the flowers on my bookshelf, the first thing that crossed my mind was that they wouldn't have sent roses to a male doctor, and I wondered if they had an inkling of what was going on with the embattled and disgruntled medical staff.

On the next day, I began with my executive staff a process whose ultimate goal was to unionize the residents, primarily because one of the brightest young doctors was fired without due process. We were working a hundred hours each week—which we accepted wholeheartedly. But we wanted training, security, and various quality-of-life issues to be adequately addressed as well. Since our move for organization was chronicled in the local papers, administration officials must have rued the day they called the florist. Finally, after a fair amount of news coverage, the administration backed down and agreed to due process. We felt we had achieved our goals, and we dropped the idea of forming a union.

Despite working as a resident with not a lot of money to spare, I had moved into a charming apartment. I felt a rush of independence, as though I'd moved up in the world. Meanwhile, I was wrestling with the challenge of the child-faced Richard Macek, and how precisely to strip away those layers of congeniality. It was my job to reach an unprotected inner core that would lead me to learn much more about the murders he may have committed.

I'd already had Dr. Brooks Brennin, a psychologist specializing in aggression, interview Macek. After poring over the results of a Rorschach inkblot test (which was very much in vogue at the time), it became obvious to Dr. Brennin and me that Macek responded on an exceedingly basic oral level, seeing monstrous teeth with jagged edges in one of the black forms. The oral stage is a phrase coined by Sigmund Freud, who believed a baby's mouth is the center of his primary pleasure during his first few hundred days of living. Macek's interpretation of the images conveyed resentful and aggressive attitudes, possibly because he felt he didn't get what he needed as a child from those around him, especially his mother and father. It also indicated Macek's possible antipathy toward his parents (perhaps over feeling unloved) and toward children who seemed to have what he felt he could not. It was very likely that Macek was overwhelmed by the developmental demands of babyhood and had severe conflict in the oral period. For example, infancy is a time when the child has no physical power to use weapons, other than the act of biting, to be destructive.

Richard explained he was never the center of attention, and he reported that he felt inadequate and inferior. His decreased tolerance for frustration and rejection could have played a major role in the acts of voyeurism for which he was arrested when he was a younger man. In addition, his Rorschach test responses indicated a fear of his masculine identity, and the denial of the need for his mother and father. But Rorschach tests are just one indication for a psychiatrist. For instance, if you go to a family doctor and get a blood test, and that test reveals an elevated white blood cell count, that's not the end of the story. More tests need to be done. So it was for Macek, except my tests would take much more time to complete than any kind of test a family doctor might perform.

I picked up the phone and arranged for Dr. Roger McKinley, a reputable hypnotherapist, to put Macek into a trance. McKinley would help Macek remember events that he was unable to recall. At least Macek would perceive some of his memories more vividly through concentration and relaxation. Since it appeared that all of the murderer's crimes were against women, I didn't want to attempt the procedure myself and risk being perceived as a potential victim as we probed Macek's mind. After all, there was the chance that, in a trance, Macek would see me as someone he wanted to kill when he began to relive a killing. McKinley had an impressive depth of knowledge and was the same expert with whom I conducted the seminar where I met FBI Agent Tomaselli. We didn't socialize as friends, but we worked very well together. Because of all this careful planning, I was sure the procedure would go well.

The next few days passed quickly, and there I was, driving up to Central State in Waupun once again. As I turned into the parking lot of the depressing old prison hospital, I was eager to discover what grim memories lay buried inside Macek's brain and what thought processes were embedded in his mind. Most people think that when a subject is hypnotized, the doctor probes the unconscious mind, which Freud thought was the mind's repository of the weird and frightening memories with which a person just cannot deal. But you can never get into the unconscious; you can get to what's called the preconscious, where bits of information that border the unconscious can be found. But patients do need to be prodded for recollection to make it out of the preconscious.

McKinley had hauled from the trunk of his Mercedes a heavy reel-to-reel tape recorder along with a case full of other equipment, including cords, a microphone stand, and a microphone—all to be painstakingly inspected by the always suspicious guards.

McKinley and I set up the machinery in the same dreary, cramped interview room in which I first met Macek. The prisoner was led in, still affable, still exchanging pleasantries. There is no real preparation for hypnosis, no drugs, no pep talk, no blood tests. Macek knew he was going to be hypnotized, and he appeared ready. The baby-faced killer had agreed in writing to be hypnotized, but when we started he was somewhat anxious, worrying that people were stopping to peer into the cramped room at him through a small window. Macek didn't want to be stared at, and he didn't want to be the subject of hospital gossip, which was percolating due to a growing media frenzy that sensationalized Macek and his crimes. In addition, the low voices of those outside the door, including one of the guards, got under his skin. We pressed on, though. As the hypnosis began, McKinley suggested that Macek imagine himself in a field of fragrant clover, where the annoying voices he heard became the meaningless noises of a pleasant world that bathed and engulfed him. But an aggravated Macek said that he wished to be in the field by himself, alone and away from any human sounds whatsoever. Though his body relaxed and his breathing slowed, his mind was somehow still tense. Finally he closed his eyes and went into what seemed to be an absorbing hypnotic state.

The first words he uttered were simple but forceful commands that cried out gently, almost as a whisper.

"Stop me. Stop me," he said, his voice raised a bit in intensity, the two short syllables weighing heavily, mysteriously.

"What's going to happen, Rich?" McKinley frowned. He seemed concerned.

"Stop it."

"Will you tell me first what's going to happen? Are you going to choke?"

"Stop me, now!"

We had given him a key word, the word *release,* to help him relax, to warn us to remove him temporarily from the trance. But he either refused to utter the word or had forgotten about it all together. I took his pulse and saw Macek was beginning to calm. McKinley reasoned with him, his voice becoming a combination of soft yet strong tones. His words were unmistakably direct.

"Rich, you want to find out who you are, don't you?"

Macek nodded.

"Turn back the pages, you turn back the pages. What year are you in now?"

"Seventy-four."

Macek began to recount the details of one of his murders, the killing for which he was incarcerated and for which he would eventually receive a sentence of two hundred years in prison, the brutal knifing of Paula J. Cupit, the maid at the Abbey resort. He said he was standing outside the Abbey, that he saw the Abbey's driveway and cars parked there. After looking around, he strode inside the main door, wandering the halls. He poked his head into room after room, into door after open door, until he saw Paula. He said that merely gazing upon her was making him nervous, "uncomfortable," and "odd." He retreated from the room but returned shortly thereafter, feeling "hot," perspiring. Macek remembered that his heart was "racing." He lied to Paula, making up a story that he had lost his son, and the good-natured hotel employee offered help in finding him. He then avoided describing the murder completely. Dr. McKinley tried to jog his memory so that he would recall more vital details.

"What do you have in your pocket?" McKinley asked. Inquiring about minor objects or events tends to prod the memory more than questions about specific scenes or bold interrogations like "How did you kill her?"

"Comb. Key. Wallet. Ball."

"Where is the knife?"

"Threw it away."

"Why did you throw the knife away, Rich?"

"Blood."

"Do you know how the knife got bloody?"

"No."

"Do you want to find out?"

"Scared."

Macek hesitated but went on to explain how he bought a double-edged knife at a hardware store in the quiet town of McHenry, Illinois, the kind of town with after-work mixers at the local bank and Miss McHenry beauty pageants at the high school. Macek went to have a drink, to order two scotches and water at an unnamed lounge with a Hawaiian motif. (Richard wasn't an alcoholic, but an occasional social drinker; no serial murderers are addicted to drugs, drink, or even smoking.) After the drinks, Richard's afternoon still wasn't quite complete.

"I, I, I leave and get in the car. I'm driving to go home, but I didn't. The car turned and went toward the hotel."

He described the car as if it had a mind of its own, transmogrified and turned human, as if it controlled him. It is not uncommon for serial killers in general to believe that things have the characteristics of people, just as sometimes they believe people are things without feelings. Macek strolled back into the hotel, then hunted the rooms to find the maid. In the bathroom of one of the rooms, he found Paula still working, scouring the floor, perhaps her fifteenth of the day, and he confronted the poor woman, who was still on her knees. When she tried to leave, he blocked her way. When she tried again, he closed the door so there was little chance for exit and escape.

"I says, that's all right, that's all right. You don't have to worry. It's all right. Um-hmm. Then I touched her. On her chest."

Neither of us knew precisely what was happening. I sat within a couple of feet of Macek, monitoring him. I noticed that his right hand began to move, slowly rising off the desk, and then the left hand began to rise too. His face turned crimson and his breathing rate increased somewhat. Otherwise he appeared perfectly normal. At that point, Macek took the heavy microphone from its stand and into his right hand. Grasping it tightly, he lifted it high above his head. It was one of those surreal, bizarre flashes where everything seems to slow. I should have thought to jump up and move away, but I was trapped in the moment. Macek himself made no sound, but the microphone came crashing down. His right hand arced near my face and then away, settling hard on the small finger of his left hand. The sound cracked and echoed through the room. But Macek was not hurt and still remained in the trance. Everyone, from the guards to McKinley, believed Macek didn't need to be shackled, that he was an affable prisoner willing to cooperate with us. We felt that shackling would somehow impede Macek from recollection, and Macek really had advanced nicely under hypnosis, until this.

Dr. McKinley had never experienced such a reaction and he now looked concerned and puzzled. What happened with Macek plainly shouldn't have happened, no way, no how. During hypnosis, this sort of behavior is supposed to be far more controlled and less spontaneous. Clearly, there was turmoil occurring inside Macek's mind, and he could physically act it out.

We were taken aback, stunned even—but we had to maintain our composure. We continued almost by rote, our training taking over, until we took Macek out of the trance. Unfortunately, Macek hadn't spoken at all about biting, raping, and ritually cutting Paula J. Cupit.

As we left the facility, we looked at what Macek had done with the microphone as a mere aberration. But again, the image of Macek slamming down the microphone wended its way into my senses as I walked to the car. I played the scene again in my head. Before Macek threw down the mike, I was unable to detect any clue that there was something wrong. I mean, I am a highly intuitive person who has encountered plenty of really aggressive people in my day-to-day work in psychiatry. Most of the time, I will get some signal that things are not going well. When that is the case, I will change tactics or pose a question in an unconventional way, modifying the tone of my voice, employing words that are more soothing and appealing to the individual. When I'm working with someone, as I was in this case, I'd quietly signal to him to bring Macek out of the trance. But Macek's outburst came completely out of the blue. There was no warning, no change of inflection, no strange look on his face, absolutely nothing that would have indicated that this display of violence was about to ensue. Though I believed Macek's emotions would not flare up again, I decided to have McKinley bring along a smaller cassette recorder next time, one with an almost weightless plastic microphone—just in case.

As I parted ways with the discomfited McKinley, I hoped that Macek would not again become so unrestrained under hypnosis. On the way back home, driving past cornfields and dairy farms, I convinced myself to believe it.

I looked into Macek's criminal and family history dating back to 1967 and discovered he was not very close to his father, a gruff, successful, and self-made man whose ownership of a brewery lifted his family to an upper-middle-class existence. He was very strict, rarely permitting Richard to date and employing physical means of control and discipline with all family members. He hit. He slapped. He punched his sons and his wife until they lived in a good deal of fear.

Macek's crimes began early, according to Illinois police reports. As a young boy in grammar school in the suburban town of Elmwood, Illinois, Macek was arrested for stealing the panties from a neighbor's clothesline. Once he took them, he chewed on the crotches. Appearances notwithstanding, this was not a sexual act. Rather, it had more to do with the still babylike Macek enjoying the touch, feel, and smell of the softer cotton fabric the crotch was made of, avoiding the coarser cotton in the rest of the panty. This is something some serial killers like to do. John Wayne Gacy placed his mother's panties in a paper bag and hid them under his porch, often taking them out and caressing them for comfort. You might ask, well, why not touch or chew a T-shirt? A T-shirt just isn't as soft as panties.

In 1966, Macek's father died of a myocardial infarction in a hospital while being treated for hypertension. Not many months later, Macek was arrested for voyeurism, Peeping Tom incidents in which he'd perch by night near a window with a small handheld telescope, watching the sleeping woman inside. Over time, Macek's crimes became increasingly violent and included charges of beating up women. In 1974, the infant daughter of his girlfriend with whom he was staying was found dead on a heating pad, burnt to the extent that her poor body looked like a sausage that had burst through its casing. Macek was never convicted of this death, but I think he did it. By 1976, I believe that he had murdered eight women, although police had gotten him to confess only to the murder of the maid. In all of these cases, the murder or attack was sadistic, sexual, and violent, including incidents of stabbing, drowning, strangulation, mutilation, biting, and/or necrophilia.

On the following morning, we gathered again in Waupun, this time in a second-floor conference room, an immense, spacious room in which the five-foot-four, 192-pound Macek seemed inconspicuous, tiny. He sat, waiting alone at a long, polished oak table, again unshackled. With a guard outside the door, I felt comfortable, focused, and ready.

I resolved to use this session to probe the killings of Nancy Lossman and her three-year-old daughter, Lisa, found dead in 1974 in their Crystal Lake, Illinois, apartment. Nancy's body was discovered nude and battered. Macek had strangled her with the cord from a venetian blind. There were, gouged in her right breast, substantial bite marks, and there was evidence of necrophilia, according to the coroner's report. He drowned the little girl, Lisa, in a toilet bowl and, bizarrely, placed towels in the bowl as well. But he left Nancy's sleeping son alone. Macek never tried to kill a boy or a man. He preferred to kill women. Just as substance abusers have their drug of choice, Macek had his murder victims of choice.

As McKinley led Macek to recall these disturbing events, the criminal remained relaxed under hypnosis, and all seemed well. Within a few minutes, Macek began to remember more.

He stood there with lighter fluid in his hand, and he plotted to burn everything around him to cover his tracks. As Macek brought to mind the fire he started in the utility room in the Lossman apartment, he said he rummaged about to find a match to ignite the blaze. Inwardly, I found this strange, primarily because Macek was not a stupid man; surely he knew that a small can of lighter fluid would mainly cause a smoky fire that wouldn't last and wouldn't destroy the crime scene. But as I contemplated this, something changed.

"Ooooh!" Macek's groan was piercing.

"AHHHHHHH!" He was clearly uncomfortable, tense and sweating.

"It hurts. The fire!" Macek exclaimed that he was in agonizing pain, that he was immersed in the flames, that he could feel them lash at his skin. As I looked at Macek, I felt he was beginning to exist inside the past, a past that we might not be able to control with hypnosis.

"AHHHHH!" he roared. Hands that had been hanging by his side tensed into fists, and then he cradled his right hand in his left. It was happening again! McKinley looked alarmed and loosened his tie.

Macek had burned his hand in the fire, a flare-up that he saw and felt as lucidly as the terrible moments when the murders of the mother and daughter had occurred. I took stock of the room around us. Certainly nothing there had changed. No one had entered, not a guard, not anyone, and the temperature was the same. Then my eyes focused on Macek's hand. On his fingers, I saw red blisters, big as dimes, rise from the inferno he was experiencing in his head. I closely examined everything, looking all around to make sure there was no outside source—a hidden match, a pocket lighter, a cigarette—of heat. There was nothing. I was frightened at what seemed to be an almost supernatural event.

Something had to be done immediately. We interrupted the trance and said to Macek, "Let's take a break." I kept staring at the blisters that remained on his hand. At that moment, I chose to end any further hypnotic sessions. The whole process had disintegrated, and the risk of continuing was tremendous. Macek could lose control, and the cost could be a total erosion of his very tenuous state of mind. Or he could assault someone within the prison hospital, forcing authorities to put him in seclusion where he couldn't be seen, and putting an end to my scientific research just as it had begun. Then and there, I had to admit that Macek may never have been adequately hypnotized. For a moment, I wondered whether part of his brain was conscious and controlling *us* just as we believed we were exploring the depths of his mind. There in the confines of Waupun State Hospital, I began to understand that I was walking on a razor's edge as long as I worked with serial murderers. Because so many things could go wrong, I felt if I made one false move or slip, I could be shredded.

There was something going on that was completely out of the realm of what I had learned or had ever experienced. We were trekking into the unknown, and it was not safe to be there. I did take consolation in something Sigmund Freud wrote in 1905: "No one who, like me, conjures up the most evil of those half-tamed demons that inhabit the human breast, and seeks to wrestle with them, can expect to come through the struggle unscathed." I believe that what happened with Macek had to do with the suspension of the boundary of time. If you think about it, when Macek was focused and reexperiencing his past murders, time ceased to exist. Back in that traumatic moment where his life played itself over in three dimensions, Macek was capable of reliving his horrors as if they were happening in real life. Again, he didn't have a cigarette to burn himself. He didn't have anything. He was back there in the past, as if nothing had ever changed, and his hand was, for all intents and purposes, burned. I've already mentioned that there is a part of the mind called the preconscious, the place in the brain that stores mental contents that are not conscious but could be, like memories that can be recovered. But they aren't quite near enough for immediate mining. The preconscious can also include the hints of memories—traces, parts, pieces, rather than the whole memory itself.

As I mentioned, you can never get to the unconscious, according to theory. But is there something somewhere within the boundary to that wall that's so permeable that it seeps through into the consciousness of the patient? What part of the mind allows a human to go back and forth from the conscious to the preconscious occasionally as freely as one goes from the dining room to the kitchen? I think it is a boundary so fluid that you can't tell what is real time to the serial killer. So it was for Richard Otto Macek, and for many others too, who would talk about these bits of remembrances, but only after dozens of hours of probing.

For our own safety, we called two young guards to take Macek away. I recounted the eerie tale of what had just happened.

"What was really weird were the blisters that appeared on his hand. Take a look," I said.

One guard looked dumbfounded, but he did not believe what he saw. Convincing these people who saw everything as black and white, rather than in shades of gray, was next to impossible. After some confusion, an angry look fell over his face.

"What the hell do you think you're doing? You're just a faker! This is all fake. Fake."

The other guard said, "You did this to him yourself. You burned his hands. You want us to believe THIS? You're full of crap."

Some people have asked, well, if this really happened, where's the photo of his hand? But getting a camera past security would have been impossible. And I think the tape of the session speaks for itself.

Though I'm sure this information filtered up to the superintendent, I never heard a word from him or other prison officials. I'm sure they didn't want anyone on the outside to know we were talking to Macek, nor did they want this admittedly bizarre story to seep out into Waupun and beyond. I could almost hear them say, "Don't make my prison anything out of the ordinary. Don't you shake things up. But, hey, aren't you cute for comin' in with all of your investigations and all that science?"

THREE

BREAKING THROUGH
MACEK'S MIND

It was a dimly lit dive that reeked of malt, mildew, and cigarette smoke. My eyes took a moment to adjust. Along the dark old bar and at each one of the rickety tables was a tin bowl full of Wisconsin cheddar cheese spread and a plastic basket of Keebler crackers. I had walked into this watering hole on the side of the road to Waupun, Wisconsin, to meet with FBI Special Agent Louis Tomaselli, but he hadn't yet arrived. Somewhat out of place in my gray-blue skirt and dark blue blazer, I ordered bourbon straight up and sat at a small table. As the jukebox played a Johnny Cash song, Tomaselli, dressed casually in blue jeans and a plaid shirt, requested a whiskey and sat down.

I gave him the update. "We're making progress with Richard Macek. He's beginning to open up. In addition, he's sending letters almost every day. They're single-spaced and handwritten, up to twenty pages each. Sometimes he sends letters three times a day. I'm not sure I believe it yet, but he says he trusts me."

Tomaselli nodded, spread some cheese on a cracker, ate it in one bite, took a gulp of his drink, and informed me that Macek would likely be transferred to a prison in Illinois. "It'll be sometime soon. They have enough to warrant extradition for the Lossman killings."

"Do you know when?"

Tomaselli shook his head. He glanced around the place and stared at a neon beer sign. Then he tried to regale me with macho stories of his latest case, in which he was able to infiltrate a Wisconsin motorcyle gang, to ride with them and become accepted as an insider. A few minutes later, he boasted about his training exploits at the new FBI center in Quantico, Virginia.

He leaned forward and bragged, "It's got three hundred and eighty-five acres. Huge. It's completely wooded. Completely secure. It even has its own mock city to use for training purposes."

It was obvious to me that Tomaselli had his own agenda—getting a conviction—and that he wasn't interested in hearing much of a report on my progress with Richard Macek, let alone any details that didn't serve his own needs. He really wasn't listening to what I had to say about Macek. I felt most of the meeting was useless and was glad when it was over.

Still, I did learn that Macek was going to be extradited to a prison fifty miles northwest of Chicago in the McHenry County town of Woodstock, Illinois. While the timing was still up in the air, it was critical that I continue my sessions with Macek on an accelerated schedule. I wrote and phoned the prison hospital in Waupun and asked the superintendent to inform me of the date of the imminent transfer to Illinois for the killing of Nancy and Lisa Lossman.

But when it finally happened, I was the last to know.

Each day or so, Macek mailed letters to me. Once or twice they were typed—when he was angry with me and felt I somehow "didn't deserve" the intimacy of a handwritten note. The letters themselves centered primarily around three things. He whined about recurring aches and pains, including chronic headaches, which were likely psychosomatic, perhaps due to overwhelming, disorganized feelings about his crimes or worry about his forthcoming trials. He didn't regret his crimes; he just whined about his circumstance, writing, "I don't see how I could do this" and "Why did this happen to me?" The letters were also filled with the trite details of everyday prison life. He told me when he woke, what he ate, when he went to sleep, the song that played on the radio, about decorating the prison Christmas tree for the holidays. Even though I felt we'd have a breakthrough soon, many of his letters were full of complaining and banalities:

Dear Dr. Morrison,

I have just arrived to my room after our visit. Right at this moment, I feel very confused and frustrated. . . . Right now I have a very cold and empty feeling inside. And I feel very scared! My heart is racing! I have the feeling that I am being cheeted or pushed along. NO! NOT by you or any of the other Doctors. But by Louis (Tomaselli). Don't get excited or nervous but I feel at times I were dead. KEEP THAT TO YOURSELF, OK? But I'm so ashamed and fearful for what I have done, else where at other times. As I feel now I can say NO, I don't know anything or did anything, but at the same time, I'm not sure If I did do anything else! To me it doesn't sound good or so to say it sounds dumm . . .

I would like to help and please everybody. But what can I do. Now I feel like crying. And that is embarrassing. TO ME, IT IS EMBARRASSING! I just went into a black. And I feel like tearing up this letter. Becaues I feel dumm. Just like I did when I tried to write to (another doctor). I have to subsutute words becase of spelling, and then losing thought of what I want to say!! And the words or frases I want to use. I guess I'll end my letter for now. I feel tired and uncomfortable. You see feeling like this I have to keep to myself. Because the Doctors here are quick to put a patient on heavy medication and I'm not about to be turned into a ZOMBI! . . .

Thank you for your time and interest in my case and or me.

Respectfully yours,

Richard O. Macek

When he felt he had gotten more comfortable with me and that he considered us to be friends, he became demanding, asking me to bring him such things as "Coast to Coast deodorant soap, Efferdent denture tablets, Alka-Seltzer and Alberto balsam shampoo." The most telling characteristic of the letters was the fact that he did not really communicate in them: many of the sentences contained generalities mixed with clichés. The dispatches had little meaning, kind of like the babble you hear from a celebrity who doesn't want to express anything to the press but knows something must be said. Macek wrote what he thought he was expected to write, what he felt a prison official would prefer him to write. The letters were not vetted by officials because of the privacy laws surrounding the doctor/patient relationship, but they were more often than not impulsive rants with little punctuation and words with misspellings like *amagin* for *imagine*. Gradually, it became evident to me that they were intentional and may have reflected a need to be in the limelight: "Please look at me. I am different." Starved for attention for much of his life, Macek wanted more than to be known. He wanted to be famous. His dreams would include fantasies about riding in limousines and Cadillacs and living in mansions.

When he spoke to me, it was the same thing. Cognitively, he was disturbed when he attempted to communicate. He would use words in a somewhat awkward formal construction like "he had thought I was dumm." They were also interspersed with gross errors in syntax and the use of slang. The structure of Macek's sentences frequently disintegrated into annoying non sequiturs. If you asked Macek a question such as "How many days are there in a year?" he might say "Two hundred and five." If you asked him why, he might say, "The thought just flashed through my mind." It showed that Macek had very little internal self-control at times. He couldn't take that second or two to think before answering. He was not dim-witted; he had an above-average intelligence. But snap judgments dominated his chatter, so much so that his awareness, insight, and ability to discern were whittled down to sudden declarations that were full of mistakes. It's a kind of topsy-turvy way of being that stems from within, a chaos that eventually leads to the expression of uncontrollable fury. It's not frustration. In fact, the cause for such rage is not specific. It is nothing that we can yet pinpoint or know with conviction.

Macek became obsessed with worry about his life and health in these letters, but the strange syntax and spelling remained when he wrote:

I woke up choking. My heart felt like it was jumping or trying to jump out of my chest. Cold sweat all over. But my body felt warm. My face felt like of Billions of pins were sticking me in the face. I had a dream, or nightmare if anything. I just seen my life pass my eyes. I'm dead. And I seen how it happened. I dreamed after all of everything was finished in court, ect. I got old fast; I started deteareating from within. Every hour, day, week, seem to be racing by me. I can't keep up I'm alone. All alone now one to turn to, no one to hold and tell them I Love them! I look for help. But people walk past me and just look and keep on walking. My skin is just hanging on my bones. But my mind is still active. I see doctors coming at me with needles full of Drugs, liquid and pills poored down my throat. I see myself screaming, trying to tell them is is the wrong stuff.

Additionally in his letters, he began to flirt with me, doing things like calling me "Boops." Since he was safely behind bars, I gave it little notice.

It was appropriate, though, that I learned from Macek himself about his transfer to Illinois. He wrote a short note that simply said he had been moved and his address had changed. "When are you coming to see me?" he asked. Due to my workload I hadn't seen Macek for over a month, but Macek was right. It was now time to see him in Illinois. After calling and writing repeatedly, I received permission from the authorities in rural Woodstock, Illinois, to continue my meetings with Macek. The Woodstock in Illinois was part of McHenry County itself. Full of rolling, farm-filled countryside, it had 111,000 residents, and farmland there sold for $1.50 an acre—$1.80 if a farmer got lucky. Traveling down those old, empty roads, I rarely saw another car or another human. Though the sun shone, the lack of humanity for miles upon miles was, well, creepy. After making the trip from Madison, I slowed as I passed the bright, towering Woodstock Opera House, where a young Orson Welles and Paul Newman had once acted and which had just been renovated. Next to the courthouse in the pretty town square, I passed a run-down, shuttered jail next to the courthouse. Continuing on, I found the brand-new facility north of town.

While the county jail was just a few years old, it was minuscule, housing about thirty persons at the time Macek was a prisoner. In a nondescript meeting area, surrounded by thick, heavy, but not bullet-proof glass, I sat waiting for Macek. I wished they hadn't given him a job as a cook wielding a knife in the kitchen; after all, he had killed with a knife and made his ritualistic cuttings something of a hallmark of his murders. But that was the way the prison system worked in the town—it sometimes defied any semblance of logic or security. Macek walked in and seated himself at a small, gray metal table bolted to the wall. It took a moment to sink in, but I was stunned to see draped on his shoulder, almost as if it were a proud weapon of war, a white terry-cloth towel. The metaphor wasn't lost on me. Macek had strangled the maid at the Abbey with a white towel. And he had stuffed towels into the toilet . . . pushing them on top of three-year-old Lisa Lossman until her young life had ended, a crime for which he could receive an additional two hundred to four hundred years in jail. This gesture with the towel was a stratagem of power for him, as if to say, "I'm in charge here, no one else. I can take your life with a towel. At the very least, I can play with your mind whenever I want to." I wasn't afraid, but I was angry.

I went directly to the attending guard, who was relaxing and reading a newspaper. In no uncertain terms, I asked, "Can you please remove that towel?" Now, Macek was well known even in this rural area because of the many newspaper accounts about him, including those dubbing him "The Mad Biter," as if he were a vampire. There had even been some Hollywood inquiry into doing a movie about Macek's life and crimes. But I'm sure this guard was oblivious to the fine points of the particular murders, including the towel. He regarded me curiously, as if I were paranoid.

"You want what?"

"We have to get rid of the towel."

Macek himself looked at me as though he didn't understand why I would be upset by the towel. Yet he also knew games wouldn't work with me, so he handed over the towel to the guard without so much as a peep.

For hours, I sat near Macek, digging into his psyche. On the surface, he talked about how he viewed himself as a "good father" who "loves all creatures." He said he had "a lot of love for kids" and that he'd give his "right arm for them if there's anything that they needed." In reality, he never abused his kids or his wife, and he acted like a very caring husband and father. He made them presents, and he brought home a menagerie of pets for them. Most serial killers rarely abuse those very close to them because their family, the very idea of a wife and kids, is part of a structure that keeps serial killers "normal," at least while they're with them. Macek's family life was, as far as I could tell from speaking with his quiet wife, Sandy, generally unremarkable, and he doted on his three children.

As a child himself, Macek hailed from the Chicago suburbs and enjoyed a middle-class upbringing. He went to parochial school, where he tried to impress the kids in gym class with feats of strength. He once told the *Detroit News* that his mother and father had "two homes and fours cars and three boats. And not a penny in the bank." Macek did call his father abusive, saying his father hit him and didn't want him to date, but he wasn't much more protective and violent than a lot of fathers. According to Macek, his mother was never quite satisfied with him, but he did not harbor hate for either of them. He did indeed care for Sandy and the kids as best as he could, with jobs as a machinist, cook, and truck driver.

As we continued our talk, Macek appeared to be cooperative, helpful, and easygoing. But his charisma and seeming zest for life disintegrated once we got past the three-hour mark—especially when the interviews were uninterrupted. The breakdown was most apparent when I confronted him with his controlling manipulative behavior or his occasional lying. Macek's personality then became this kaleidoscopic mix of belligerence and guile. To throw things off-kilter, he demanded I get him things like water or toiletries or that I talk to the guard so he wouldn't stare at him. He would burst into a fit of rudeness or boorishness. It was vehement, and it came out of nowhere. "You're full of shit!" he'd scream. It was after an outburst that he might say something important.

And then, hours into the session, he sat forward, almost expressionless, and cautiously admitted, "I—I can't tell if people are alive or dead unless they stop fighting me."

About a week later in early September 1977, I prepared to visit Macek again. I finished work late in the day and drove to Woodstock in the evening. Soon it was black all around, and I had turned onto a two-lane back road to find the local motel at which I'd made a reservation. Since there were no street lamps anywhere along the twisting route, I switched on my bright beams. Wisps of ground fog hung over the road, forming recognizable shapes as I drew near, only to vanish as I drove through them.

When I found the motel, it was clear, even at night, that the two-story place was in disrepair. I paid for the room and picked up my keys. With my luggage in hand, I walked up two flights of creaky stairs. The motel was practically deserted, and its manager was certainly in no danger of having to get up from his TV viewing to click on its red neon NO VACANCY sign. Just a half dozen cars were stopped in the parking spaces, and it seemed as though they'd been there forever.

The door to the room opened with a whine. From the rugs to the bed, the room was furnished in a dull brown decor. On the headboard was one of those ancient massaging machines that cost a quarter to operate. On inspection, the room was anything but secure. The door seemed cardboard thin, and the picture window almost welcomed thieves. I pulled the drapes tightly shut. As I readied for bed, I had the constant feeling that something was wrong. I checked the closets. I bent over to peek under the bed. It was on a platform. Nothing there, nothing at all, I assured myself. After inspecting the bathroom, including the shower, I pulled aside the drapes to look out onto the parking lot. Nothing. Nothing there.

Then the phone rang, blaring. I hesitated, resisting the impulse to pick up the receiver. No one I knew had an inkling that I was in rural Illinois. Finally I picked up the receiver, thinking it must be the motel manager with some message about checkout time.

"Hello?"

"How are you?"

"Who is this?" I may have recognized the voice, that flat, soft voice, but it couldn't possibly be him.

"It's Richie."

"What— It can't be." I thought I would drop the phone. Instead, I sat down on the bed.

"Sure it is."

"Where are you calling from?" How did Macek deduce I was here, at this particular place?

"Well, if you look out your window, you'll see I'm down there . . . I'm right out there." I tried to think logically. How could I get help? "I'm in the phone booth. All you have to do is go to your window and look to your left and I'm down there."

We were both silent then. I didn't want to look. I wondered how close my car was and whether I would need to make a break for it.

"Go look. I bet you can't. Bet you won't. Go look." I was becoming really nervous, still struggling with my thoughts to believe that this couldn't possibly be real. But at the same time it was real. Everything was completely blurred, that fine line between reality and nonreality. I moved to the window and pulled back the thick curtain.

It was there, a shiny metal phone booth with a fluorescent light, flitting moths, and spiderwebs. The phone booth *was there*. He, however, was not.

"But you're not there." I had fallen for the ruse and I was angry.

"I bet I got you going, didn't I?"

"This really is not funny."

"I know it's not funny, but I decided to do it anyway."

"Well, first of all, how did you get to a telephone?"

"The guards let me."

"Where are you calling from?"

"I'm calling from the guard station."

"How could you be doing that? You're not supposed to have access to a phone."

"I kind of have access. I can get access whenever I need it."

"How did you find me?"

"Oh, I have my ways." It was so unpleasant. But I didn't get off the phone right away because I wanted to tell him his behavior was inappropriate.

"This is not comfortable for me. You know it's not comfortable. You know I'm scheduled to see you tomorrow. We're going to discuss this further tomorrow."

His was kind of a nonreaction.

"Well, what do you mean, you didn't like it? It's me calling. You should like that."

I got into bed and tried to work on my notes regarding the conversations we'd had recently. He had said that as a child he'd had horrible dreams of being attacked by a pink eraser. While trying to make sense of what this meant, I remained irritated with myself; I couldn't believe I fell for Macek's prank. Yet I was frightened because I'd never had that kind of experience before. Even after the phone call, I had to convince myself that he wasn't there. "He's not here," I repeated to myself. "He's not here." It was a reality check I had to make. I felt the need to inspect the closets again, all of the corners and the shelves above, and to find out what was inside the platform beneath the bed. I really wanted to do this. And I really wanted to look out at the phone booth again. I finally told myself I didn't have to.

"He's not here."

"Richard, we can't have this happen again."

"What do you mean?" he asked. He sounded a little hurt.

"You know what I mean."

"I guess I do."

"If something like that ever happens again, our sessions will end. I will stop trying to help you."

Again, he had a kind of nonreaction, but it sunk in, and his scary games came to an end. Despite his shenanigans, I was making progress in coaxing him to recall the details of one of his more horrendous crimes. It was one for which another, probably innocent man was being blamed. Not only was Richard Milone accused of the murders, but he stood trial, was convicted, and sentenced to 90 to 175 years in prison at the Menard Penitentiary in Chester, Illinois.

It was a repulsive crime because young Sally Kandel, a popular freshman at Glenbard North High School in Carol Stream, Illinois, was only fourteen years old when her life was taken. According to the case file, the fresh-faced teen with pretty long hair and a captivating smile was a five-foot-six member of the track team, an athlete who had won a Presidential Fitness Award for two years straight. On the evening of September 12, 1972, at about 6 P.M., Sally ate a dinner of broiled round steak, french fries, and banana cake.

"I'm going out for a bike ride," Sally said, after finishing her dessert. "But leave the dishes because I'll be in to do them by seven o'clock."

"You *better* be sure to be home by seven," said Cynthia, her mother.

"Even earlier, Mom, because *Bonanza* starts at seven."

The last time her parents saw Sally, she was wearing blue jeans, a white turtleneck body sweater, sneakers, and a blue windbreaker. At 5:50 A.M. the next morning, one of the DuPage County deputy sheriffs discovered the teen, lifeless, between the third and fourth rows of corn in a muddy, waterlogged field over two miles from her home—a distance she had never before traveled by bicycle. The muck there was so like quicksand that deputy Donald Schmitt complained he ruined his shoes as he surveyed the death scene. Next to the farm was a gravel road, wet, bumpy, hard to ride on a bike. Nearby, the bike itself was found, its front wheel bent and crooked.

Blood still seeped from the back of Sally's head when the police found her. After examination, the coroner stated that she had died from severe head injuries, a skull fracture and a gash that made its way into the brain. In his report, the coroner counted over twenty lacerations to her head. It was determined that Sally Kandel was beaten with a sixteen-inch grocery cart handle found near the road and upon which were discovered several hairs and much blood. There was a tear measuring fourteen and a half inches in front of her jeans and into the left of the crotch area. On her right inner thigh was a jagged 3.5-by-4-centimeter bite that cut through the skin, determined to have been created after Sally had died. Part of Sally's thumb had been cut off. And on her eyelids were two slits each about two centimeters long, also made after she died.

Richard Milone, a low-level warehouse worker scraping to get by, had never before been involved in any serious wrongdoing, although there had been some minor run-ins with the law. However, he had cleaned his car right after the murder, preparing to offer it for sale. He had indeed kept a grocery cart handle—the same one used in the murder—in his car for protection. He explained that he lost it while running in a cornfield. Nevertheless, the bulk of the case against him revolved around the testimony of dentists who felt that the bite mark on Sally Kandel's thigh matched Milone's cuspid tooth. However, Dr. Lowell J. Levine, a New York ondontologist, testified that the look of the teeth didn't really match. In fact, he felt that they were closer to an abnormality found in Richard Macek's teeth, an extremely long and sharp bicuspid tooth. Beyond this, the ritualistic cutting in the eyelids was the distinguishing symbol of Richard Macek, who had done the same thing to Paula J. Cupit, the maid at the Abbey resort. Macek had also hit women in the head before, such as twenty-four-year-old Sharon Kulisek, whom he jumped in a Laundromat. She remained in a coma for seven long days before reawakening to describe for police how she was beaten and to describe who attacked her.

Macek and I had traversed the varied planes of the Sally Kandel case as if it were a game of three-dimensional chess. Round and round, up and down, backward and forward, we went. Macek couldn't remember. Macek remembered a detail. Then he wasn't sure of the detail. Then he took back the detail he remembered. He hemmed, he hawed, he flirted, he changed the subject, he rambled. He whined about his wife, his case, his cell, the guards, the newspaper reporters, his lawyer, how he once struck fear into the Illinois state governor upon their meeting in the prison kitchen. He changed the subject constantly. At times he was adamant, inflexible, incorrigible. I plodded on during each four- to-six hour session, trying to stop his soliloquizing with questions of my own, then listening to him for long stretches, then trying to get him back on track. I would ask the tough questions, over and over again.

Through all this, he continued with his long letters, which had become increasingly, well, friendly. Once Macek wrote:

At different times, I've seen myself just pick you up and carry you into my cell. Put you on the bed, and we just layed there and talk . . . Yes, me laying on my back you laying on my chest just talking, anything that comes to mind. No kisses, not fondling nothing just good honest talking Why in bed? It's one of those few places where you can actually relax in privacy and talk without being uncomfortable at all. At least it's been one of my favorite places that and the couch also.

Overall, there were dozens of letters like this. I knew that Macek was not at all "falling in love" with me, not for one second. More, it was a combination of what he felt he was supposed to say. In his mind, a man should say these things to a woman. But he didn't mean them within his *self*. It was more like a child reading words from a book in class, concentrating on pronunciation and the sound of his words rather than feeling or absorbing the true meaning of the words. But unlike a child, he had no self.

Forty-five minutes past midnight on June 9, 1977, Macek sat down in his cell and wrote me a two-page letter that was, to say the least, disconcerting. He began with the usual "I want to see you very badly. More than you can amagin." He then went into a mixed-up rant that read: *My headaches are increasing. My tempers blows ski [sky] high . . . My strength seems to increase 3 to 4 times." Near the end of the page, after talking about his children and without a break to begin a new paragraph, he wrote, "Sandy I miss you so very much. I always love you always! I'm so very lonely without you. . . . Remember Daddy loves his little girl very much. Love Your Husband, Richard.*

As I read his words, I don't think I've felt anything eerier. No horror movie, no strange insect crawling over me in the night, no peculiar stranger at the door could have elicited a more visceral response from me. I seemed to have become his wife, and the two of us, the real wife and the doctor, were somehow indistinguishable to him. Sandy was a quiet, nondescript person with dark hair who doted on Richard, at least before he was put in jail. I was straightforward and had blond hair. We certainly didn't look or act alike. How could he have mixed up the two of us? But as I thought about it, I told myself that Richard had just forgotten to whom he was writing. Thoughts somehow had melded two people into one. Lucky me.

Spring turned to summer, which turned to fall. In Madison in late October, there were little ghosts and jack-o'-lantern cutouts hung throughout the hospital. On Halloween, excited children donned their masks and costumes. In my building, witches and goblins, unable to contain their glee, paraded door to door for Halloween candy.

But Macek had his own Halloween horror story to relive. When he told me how he killed Sally Kandel, his recollection was so lucid and startling that I suggested to him that he write it down in the presence of a prison official.

So, late in the evening of November 3, 1977, with the chief jailer standing nearby as his witness, Richard Macek began to write from his cell on lined paper. With his penmanship full of careful loops making words that were perfectly legible, he wrote:

> Late afternoon on the 12th of September, 1972. The weather was foggy and damp. I was driving and had to go to the bathroom. There was nothing close at the time and I stopped the car and got out and walked into the Woods to go.
>
> There was a girl walking with her bike.
>
> I began to talk to her. Then I hit her on the back of the head on the right side, with a black bar, like a grocery cart handle.
>
> I took her into the field and beat her further in the head area . . .
>
> She was wearing a wind breaker jacket and slacks.
>
> She was laying on her back. Her right leg was raised higher than the other.
>
> And I bit her on the right thigh . . .
>
> I had at one time an extra pointed tooth in the right hand side of my mouth.
>
> Along with the rest of my teeth, that extra pointed tooth was extracted with the others by Dr. Walsh an oral surgeon.

The small-town dentist himself explained that only a couple of Macek's teeth needed pulling. But Macek exhibited one of the primary traits of a serial killer: the conniving ability to get his own way, even without violence. He convinced Dr. Walsh to yank out all of his teeth.

William J. Cowlin, the state's attorney for McHenry County who was in charge of the Kandel case, refused to believe anything contained within the Macek confession. Unlike the small group of officials, including the FBI's Tomaselli, who believed in Milone's innocence, Cowlin was that tough-as-nails type who wouldn't give credence to a murder unless it happened in front of his face. Admittedly, Macek had toyed with prison and police officials, often saying something and then denying it the next time he was interviewed. He had done this so many times that Cowlin was certain he was crying wolf. And Cowlin already had someone in jail, someone who was convicted by a jury. He didn't want to spend any more of the state's money on a case he saw as finished. But I believed Macek. In that confession were three salient facts that Macek could not have gathered from newspaper accounts he may have read about Sally Kandel's murder. There was no way that Macek could have known she wore a windbreaker on the night of her death, or that she was lying on her back and her right leg was raised higher than her left leg, or that there were bite marks on her right thigh.

The sad reality is one that haunts me to this day: Milone languished in jail for decades, more than a quarter of his life wasted behind bars. I had done what law enforcement had asked me to do. I had gotten Richard Otto Macek to admit to the crime that those present in that first meeting at Waupun hospital so frantically wanted to pin on Macek. And they sat on the admission, acted as though it never happened. When my work was completed and I had logged over four hundred hours face-to-face with Richard Macek, I never received one acknowledgment for the information I'd gotten, not from Cowlin, not from Tomaselli, not from anyone. Once given the Kandel confession, they all darted away like cockroaches scattering when the light is flicked on. After years of thought upon the subject, I can conclude only that the real reason was pure ego, which pervaded everything from the prison system to the court system, ego that let an innocent man languish in a trap. It all seemed so iron-fisted to me. Milone was found guilty. Cowlin would not believe that what he had done with Milone's case was wrong. So that was it. End of case, even if prosecutor, judge, and jury were wrong.

Fortunately, Milone had other methods with which to prove his innocence. Dental evidence presented in 1994 to the Seventh Circuit United States Court of Appeals suggested that it was Macek, not Milone, who had bitten Sally Kandel's thigh and killed her. The evidence served up at Milone's trial linking Milone's dentition to the bite mark found on Sally's thigh was sorely incorrect. The brand-new practice of forensic ondontology, what I view as the real basis of the original case against Milone, was not well refined in 1973, the date Milone first went to court. As Milone made his appeals, reliable, expert testimony in advanced forensic ondontology proved the mark on Sally's thigh matched the teeth of Richard Macek (which Dr. Walsh, the dentist, had actually saved). Then there was nine-year-old Linda Sue Roseboom who "reaffirmed her trial testimony" that Milone's Dodge Polara was not the car that she spied in her driveway the evening Sally Kandel was killed. In his confession, Macek wrote, "At the time, I was driving a 1964 Chevy Impala a cream color. It was a beated up on the right side. And the door outer panels were caved or pushed in." This was the car that Linda Sue Roseboom saw. On the basis of this forensic evidence, Milone was eventually freed—after having served twenty years in jail for a crime he did not commit. He would try to reenter a life that was so mistakenly and unnecessarily interrupted and placed on hold. And though he would go on because there was nothing else to do, he would look upon that time long ago with occasional sadness . . . and much bitterness.

As wonderful as it was to hear that Milone was no longer stuck behind bars, it still bothers me that none of the courts ever saw Macek's confession. Thinking back on the crimes of Richard Macek, I have come to the conclusion that his acts of homicide were not externally precipitated. No one had done anything to him to make him lash out. No one had abused him sexually as a child, nor had they taken away his house, nor had he been fired from his job. Nor had a small thing set him off—like a tax bill or the way someone looked askance at him. Nothing you might consider as having any meaning to him had gone particularly awry. As far as I could see, there was never a distinct motive to any of his crimes. Sure, there were manufactured motives. Lawyers and police speculated that Macek was a victim of severe parental abuse and that he was a sexual deviant or that he couldn't deal with the idea of his father's death, though these ideas were never proven.

But I have never discovered in Richard Macek a true motive, one that made sense, one that stood up to both legal and psychiatric scrutiny. I am still confounded by this killer's chilling disregard for people, which provided me with so many occasions of uneasiness and discomfort during my examinations. A human was not human to him. In dreams and in stories, he would continue to debate whether someone was dead or alive. He really did not know the difference. Macek's necrophilia, in fact, was not sexual, but appeared to be denial, an effort to resolve his confusion about the line between life and death. By treating the body as if it were alive, he could try, as he said, "to bring it back" by putting life into it. And even though Macek often protested that he didn't recall his victims, it was never true amnesia or blanking out. It was an absolutely overwhelming erosion of whatever delicate psychological balance he had—from memory to thought to feelings to perception to the very muscles that controlled his portly physique.

As I went on to profile Ed Gein and John Wayne Gacy, I heard less frequently from Richard Macek. His lengthy handwritten letters had slowed to a trickle of notes that eventually ceased altogether in 1980. Because serial killers respond well when institutions hold rein over them, it wasn't surprising that the structure of incarceration was beneficial to Richard, who had become a model prisoner and was for the most part well liked by those around him. He was serving a life sentence for two murders and two attempted murders. In the middle of 1987, however, I received word by phone that Richard Macek had died. Only later when I called the prison for more information did I hear that Macek committed suicide in his jail cell. While I wondered what had precipitated the event, since Macek was comfortable in prison, I didn't really react to his death. I had truly learned a lot. The patterns that Macek displayed, from his way of speaking to the way he killed to his thought processes, would show up in other serial killers I would encounter. Primarily, there was a pervasive hollowness to his character, one that I would see constantly in other serial murderers, one that regarded humans as worthless annoyances to be dealt with and to be forgotten. Perhaps it is best expressed in his own words:

It was death. Beating on somebody, smacked right in face, Person screamed, got hit, started to hit back. Got hit, got more infuriated. Picked up the person, slammed them into the wall, beating until death, lifeless or unconscious. Had no controllable power over me. Until seen no response, until weren't fighting back. Person seems to change all the time. Small person, large person, huge and bulky-type person. Heads all cut up from teeth or buckle hitting person.

He wasn't talking about himself, but he could have been when he said, "Person seems to change all the time." That's one of the primary things I learned about serial killers from my time with Richard Macek. They will be whatever you think they should be. So when they become violent and kill, it seems to come out of nowhere. That's what intrigued me; that's what made me want to learn much more. I hadn't attached Macek to crimes other than the Kandel murder, but my original goal was really in the area of science, not in the police work of nailing a conviction. During my year with Macek, I had discovered scientific methods that I would use over and over again in speaking to a serial murderer. I had learned how to profile and interview a serial killer. I now knew how to break down his defenses to get to the heart of the matter. But where did the need to kill originate, exactly where deep inside? That's where I knew I had to go next. Deeper and deeper inside is quite literally where my long journey would lead.

FOUR

ED GEIN AND THE HISTORY OF SERIAL KILLERS

I t was not what I expected for such a notorious man. After all, he was the killer that Alfred Hitchcock's *Psycho* was based upon, and our nation's first true celebrity serial killer. But when I finally did meet him, he sat hunched, old, and alone.

The room was like this. There was the harsh glare of the black-and-white television. A few feet away, there was the chatter and occasional jarring hoots of deranged laughter. Away from the haze of cigarette smoke around some coffee-drinking card players, Ed Gein sat. No one in the common room full of patients and nurses really knew about him, about who he was and what he once did. He never gazed out the mesh wire-covered windows either, at the blue-gray lake nearby or at the people strolling along the path toward it or into the flourishing greenhouse directly underneath his window. He merely sat.

He was a shadow of the man who the little children in Wisconsin feared like some boogyman. "Don't go across the street," mothers would warn. "Don't go down to the river or play on the railroad tracks or down in the basement. Ed Gein will get you." And the children listened, and later in life they too would warn their offspring. As flames crackled around campsites, ghost stories were told about him. There were dolls bearing his likeness. An amateur humorist crafted lyrics about the mild-mannered serial killer (which are on the Internet to this day), to be sung to the tune of the old 1960s sitcom *The Beverly Hillbillies*. He was no longer the crazed killer portrayed in badly written true-crime books, no longer the sociopathic figure used as the basis for Alfred Hitchcock's interpretation of Robert Bloch's tale *Psycho*. He was certainly not larger than life. As a patient at the Mendota Mental Health Institute, Ed Gein was just an old man all used up and getting ready to die.

I was a staff psychiatrist at Mendota, where my duties included everything from admitting disturbed patients to being called upon to appear in court to testify about patients' mental states. To me, Mendota was an idyllic place with a soulful history, a place to work hard, yes, but also a place in which I could meditate, forget about murder and psychiatry, and just enjoy the beauty of the outdoors.

About a month after I began working at Mendota, I approached Ed Gein and told him I would like to ask him some questions, adding that I was a doctor and I wasn't going to further sensationalize his already sensationalized life. I bent over to look him in the eye and said, "I just want to understand a little more about you."

"All already been said."

"Just a little talk, Ed?"

"Well, sit down then," he said, gesturing to a nearby chair. Ed Gein was suffering from dementia, and his short-term memory was impaired and nearly nonexistent, but the dementia did not affect what he recalled in the past. Gein very clearly remembered the details of what had transpired long ago. Like Richard Macek, Gein lived calmly in the controlled setting, and his attitude was good-natured and easygoing. Like Macek, he seemed to be a genuinely kind man—when he wasn't killing.

"I heard that you did some things, Ed, some things that were not so good."

"I did some things. I did 'em," he snapped with a "so what?" kind of attitude. I had immediately touched a sore spot. It wasn't that he didn't like being reminded of his past crimes. Like a sideshow freak,

Gein had been poked and prodded ever since his arrest in 1957. During that week of November 17, when his acts banished the cold war and the space race from the front pages of many midwestern newspapers, Gein himself was the most significant story. Wisconsin police had been searching for a handful of missing people dating back to the late 1940s, and they suspected Gein as the murderer. While the number of suspected killings wasn't big, the manner in which Gein killed was highly unusual. He was convicted of the murder of Bernice Worden, whom he skinned, hung, and butchered, as if she were an animal whose carcass was being readied for market. Since the moment of that arrest, a parade of police, lawyers, and psychiatrists had repeatedly asked him the same questions. Sleazy journalists and Hollywood producers had promised him money and possible freedom for his story, and when he told them all he could, they never returned. At this point in his life, he just wanted to be left alone.

But I plodded on, speaking to him over the course of a casual ten-hour interview, spread over the period of two months. At that point, I had not formulated many of my theories about serial killers. I was still searching for more data and still putting together the general profile in which most serial killers could fit. Though I really didn't think that my research on these murderers would add up to a life's worth of data, I found I had an intense curiosity for more study.

Even though he lived in a town that was generally full of reserved, conservative people, young Ed Gein was the prototypical midwestern nice guy whose backwoods shyness made him the butt of jokes long before he stooped to murder. In the 1940s (and to some extent even today), Plainfield, Wisconsin, in Waushara County really was a "plain" town of several hundred residents. Gein inherited a sprawling 195-acre farm that had fallen into disrepair after his father, brother, and mother died. It has been widely but inaccurately reported that Gein began to kill because his father was abusive to the son he thought was a sissy. Augusta, his crabby, impatient mother, was a Bible-obsessed religious zealot who created a willing religious captive in Gein, who was said to have been unusually attached to his mother. When she died, as the inexact theory goes, Gein was supposedly absorbed into a world of mourning, which never really ended. He lived a life of constant sorrow, it's said, which partially centered on making his vast and broken-down farmhouse a shrine to his deceased mom. But there was nothing I'd found in my research that indicated his controlling mother had led him to kill. Certainly, nothing that Gein said led me to believe that he harbored any unusual love or hate for his mother.

At Mendota, I asked, "Ed, they said you never got over your mother's death. What do you think of that?"

"I cared about her. Cared about her a lot. But it wasn't like I didn't get over it. Everyone cares when their mother dies."

"But they said you sealed off a lot of your house and made it a shrine to her, and that you kept your mother in that room after embalming her."

"Those were just experiments. And the house was big. I left her room alone. But I closed off some of the house because it was just too darn big to heat, too darn big for one person."

But it *was* true that he killed, as if it were a craft at which he would be an unparalleled master. Inside the house, sawed and hacked and roughly hewn, was a bowl made from half of a woman's skull. Stretched taut, thin, and sewn tightly were lamp shades made of female skin. There was an unwieldy belt decorated not with studs or metal stars or knotted leather, but with a human head, nipples, noses, and a heart. Hung on doors were human heads, which were happened upon by boys for whom he babysat, souvenirs he said were shrunken heads from the South Seas. When the startled boys told their parents what they had seen, they simply weren't believed. Gein was eccentric, said the townspeople, but he would never do anything bad.

Gein wasn't just eccentric. He would literally prey on the dead. At the Plainfield cemetery a mile or two from his home, he dug up the grub-filled earth, prying open the coffins of the deceased, making off with their body parts: limbs, heads, and breasts.

Under the Wisconsin moon, which was his only witness, Gein would slip into a patchwork outfit made of skin and body parts, including breasts and a vagina, and he would dance. He would dance and sing and two-step and croon, parading around to songs only he could hear.

"Yeah, I did that" is all that he said to me.

I wished I had gotten more information directly from the mouth of Ed Gein, but he was drained and disinterested. With more questions than I had before I met Ed Gein and determined to discover more about serial murderers throughout history, I took to spending many long weekend days and evenings in the Madison university library, poring over as much information about the phenomenon as I could uncover.

I had thought that serial killers were a phenomenon of the last one hundred years of our history. And then I found someone the *New York Times* called "one of the most bizarre figures in European history." Gilles de Rais was a handsome, wealthy baron and war hero who fought side by side with Joan of Arc in the 1400s. When Thomas Mann wrote about him, de Rais was said to personify "the religious greatness of the damned; genius as disease, disease as genius, the type of the afflicted and possessed, where saint and criminal become one." But de Rais was no saint, by any definition of the word. From his three magnificent castles, especially one outside the French village of Machecoul, de Rais sent his servants to fetch unwitting peasant children. Lured, kidnapped, and sometimes boldly taken in broad daylight to de Rais's palace, innocent children were subject to horrors rarely seen since the dawn of recorded history.

How wealthy was de Rais? The security provided by privilege in fifteenth-century France was even more magnificent and coveted than it is today due to the constant eruption of bubonic plague and the bloody Hundred Years War, which pitted the French against the emboldened, brutal English. It was a time of suspicion, of conjurers, of belief in the dark power of demons, of the Catholic Church's omnipotence, of hope in alchemy and geomancy, of overriding terror about death and desperate attempts to overcome its clutches. It was into this milieu that Gilles de Rais was born.

After victory with Joan of Arc at the Battle of Orleans, Gilles became a marshal of France, a hero. When he rode into town, he rode a horse bedecked with jewels and ornaments at the head of a royal parade of two hundred soldiers he employed. Children, the most beautiful preteens with angelic voices from his own music school, sang his praises as they too rode on horseback. When he wasn't strutting around, he wrote plays in which he was the star center stage, backed by lavish theatrical backgrounds, and he offered gifts and feasts to those who came to take it all in. De Rais wasn't grandiose, he just did these things to meet certain cultural expectations. For de Rais, such parades were part of the trappings of his life and times. Other French nobles had huge entourages when they traveled from place to place. And as we'll see later, the infamous John Wayne Gacy did similar things within his modern-day community. He arranged backyard barbecues where hundreds of people communed, and he put together a big Polish parade in the Chicago area where luminaries gathered.

George Bataille, the author of *The Trial of Gilles de Rais,* points out that some of de Rais's life was not unlike the lives of other feudal lords of the time, "with whom he shares the pleasures of egoism, laziness and disorder. He lives in the same way, in those heavy and luxurious fortresses, among the men-at-arms in his service, and in contempt of the rest of the world." He existed in a "contradictory chaos of calculation, violence, good humor, bloody disorder, mortal anguish." So it was also for his relations, mighty feudal lords with vast authority over peasants and servants. De Rais's parents died in 1415, leaving the eleven-year-old Gilles in the care of his rich thug of a maternal grandfather, Jean de Craon. Instead of educating the child with books and Latin (as he had promised Gilles's parents) and passing on to him a grandfather's wisdom and care, Jean left de Rais with only the most minimal schooling or supervision. In doing so, says Bataille, he created a wild young pit bull of a child, free to explore any path, criminal or not, to which he was inclined.

I don't believe it was de Rais's upbringing that led him to kill, but that's how even the writers of the time rationalized his crimes. In fact, de Rais spoke of his wayward childhood with a scribe who wrote, "On account of the bad management he had received in his childhood, when, unbridled, he applied himself to whatever pleased him, and pleased himself with every illicit act. . . . He perpetrated many high and enormous crimes . . . , since the beginning of his youth, against God and His commandments."

De Rais became a warrior under the tutelage of two men: Guilliaume de La Jumelliere, an Angevin lord and military adviser, and Georges de La Tremoille, a politician so close to King Charles VII that he was considered to be the prime minister. With Joan of Arc in the Battle of Orleans, de Rais proved as unstoppable and almost as driven as the future saint and returned home a war hero . . . and somehow changed for the worse.

By 1432, de Rais was killing in earnest. De Rais sent his servants to town to search out the prettiest children, mostly boys (although a few girls were gathered up as well). His lackeys lied to parents, sometimes saying the great, heroic baron was going to send their sons or daughters away for a proper education or that they were being sent out of the country to escape the ever-threatening English. To the starving, they would simply offer a loaf of bread. If parents weren't around, the accomplices simply snatched up the children as they played in the street, put them on the backs of their horses, cleaned them up, and brought them to de Rais's castle.

De Rais reveled in children's panic as they were brought to him, led down the long, clammy halls. Invariably he was drinking, but I don't believe it made him kill. Alcohol might have decreased the ability he had to keep himself together, but it didn't cause his crimes. When a person is really drunk, he can't do much of anything, so my guess was that de Rais wasn't completely out of it. What happens with many normal people is that they lose inhibition when under the influence, but this doesn't occur with the serial murderer, and it can't be seen as a trigger. Most serial killers don't have any one thing I can point to that leads them to kill. So it was with de Rais and drinking.

Alcohol or not, imagine the child's fear as he was escorted into a room where de Rais stood. Beside him were mechanical implements used to raise the child by the neck and hang him with cords so that his terrified cries would be muffled. Just before the child passed out from choking, he would be lowered and freed. De Rais would hug him and dote on him, comforting the boy by saying he was merely playing a joke. As the child calmed down, de Rais would raise a *braquemard,* a large horseman's sword with a wide flat blade, pointed and sharp at both edges. Carefully lowering the sword, he cut a vein on the neck of the child. At that point, he began to masturbate as the blood spurted wildly with every waning heartbeat. De Rais enjoyed slicing open the belly of a child and masturbating until he climaxed into it. His valet, Poitou, a boy he had raped but kept alive for what de Rais saw as his unparalleled physical beauty, said the killing involved "sometimes beheading or decapitating them, sometimes cutting their throats, sometimes dismembering them, and sometimes breaking their necks with a cudgel."

De Rais's was indicted on October 11, 1442, by the French Catholic church for the murder of 140 children over the course of fourteen years. Two weeks later on October 26, he was hanged before a large crowd and then burned. Though the church's indictment states that he began to murder children in 1426, the first victim's parents said the killings started in 1432. De Rais himself affirmed that later date in his confession. It is a crucial date, since it also coincides with the death of the elder de Craon on November 15, 1432. De Rais began to kill once his closest relative had passed on. It was similar to Ed Gein in that Gein began killing after his mother died. And Richard Macek began his rampage after his father died. As with de Rais and Macek, even when they didn't like their parents, something about a parent's death was one of the triggers that led them to murder. But were there other triggers? They may never be known, since the trail of these killings has long grown cold. Still, there were triggers. Something made de Rais dispatch his servants to retrieve children for him. Bataille notes that it may have been the site of barbarism during war that triggered de Rais's fetish for blood. But there's no real proof of this, only Bataille's conjecture. Certainly thousands of others went forth in combat and later they never sought to murder scores of children. There must have been something else that plagued de Rais. He wasn't simply a madman because he gravitated toward a certain type of victim, children. A madman would just kill anyone willy-nilly from all strata in society. Like other serial killers after him, de Rais chose to kill the marginal in society, those that were easily attainable. But as with Ed Gein and Richard Macek, what could that something else have been? I knew it wasn't simply madness and it wasn't sociopathy. But what was it? I didn't yet know.

Not long after the terrible reign of Gilles de Rais, about eight hundred miles to the east, came the vicious fifteenth-century rule of Vlad Tepes, often nicknamed Vlad the Impaler. In most books, Vlad is considered to be a serial killer or mass murderer bar none. Wherever you search on the Web, you'll find Vlad called by these names. But this is a myth as unreal as the vampire tale, since Tepes was not a serial killer at all. Nor was he actually a mass murderer. It's important to say why this is true because the crimes of Tepes are so often misrepresented. That's not to say he wasn't a vicious murderer, but the labels are dead wrong.

Though he is widely considered to be the real-life template for Bram Stoker's gothic 1807 novel *Dracula,* Vlad himself was no fang-baring ghoul of the undead. He did not morph into a flying bat who lived to prey on the necks and genitals of young women as they slept. Nor did vengeful townspeople seek to end the fiend's immortal existence with a stake to the heart as he lay resting in his coffin.

However, sharpened stakes were to play an important role in the real-life story of Vlad the Impaler, the proud, darkly attractive ruler of the southern Romanian kingdom of Wallachia, south of Transylvania on the Arges River. Vlad was born in 1431 to a nobleman called Basarab. As a young boy, he was educated by monks and taught to fight with chain mail and sword, imagining the branches of trees were the limbs of Turkish sultans. Basarab ordered Vlad's warrior training early, as Basarab saw not only Turks but also Hungarians, Germans, and Poles battling for control of the rugged Carpathian mountains. And he wanted his children to be ready—even though they were young. Romania had been fought over and divided for centuries— since the Roman Empire laid claim to the pagan territory in A.D. 106. By the time Vlad was born, the Turks ruled much of the edges of Western Europe, hoping to spread to the Far East and farther west.

A fifteenth-century royal weaned on the ways of warriors, Vlad was one of the more passionate crusaders, a particularly sadistic Romanian who saw violence as the path not only to religious freedom and power but also to the religious superiority of a Roman Catholic world. In many battles against the Muslim Ottoman, Vlad Dracula proved his savvy . . . and his devious nature.

He sent his troops to kill with focus and purpose. Vlad the Impaler's seemingly insatiable appetite for blood was not driven by some mad, unknowable inner lust. It had much more to do with his need for what today we call homeland security, the protection of Romania from outside invaders. Vlad's imperious crusade to achieve rule over Romania was the work of a paranoid ruler full of religious fervor. If you were near Vlad, you wouldn't give him a sideways glance for fear of retribution. If he didn't like you, he'd kill you, in much the same way Saddam Hussein's servants and soldiers lived in fear of Hussein and his retribution in Iraq. Again, this is not the work of a serial killer, who is triggered to kill, or a mass murderer, who kills out of anger against a society he feels has oppressed him.

In many history books, it is assumed that Vlad went mad after being taken prisoner by the Turks. Not only was he tortured in a dungeon in Adrianpole, but from his window he saw daily executions— beheadings, killings of prisoners by wild animals and impalements on sharpened poles, often through the genitals. He vowed that should he live through his imprisonment, he would do the same to the Turks. That pledge became a life's mission when he discovered that the Turks had massacred his family, burying alive one of Vlad's brothers. When the Turkish sultan freed Vlad in the late 1440s, the seventeen-year-old joined the Turkish Army, inwardly vowing revenge. After returning to Hungary to become prince, he began to kill. During a six-year reign of terror between 1556 and 1562, it's said that he executed between 30,000 and 100,000 people. On one particular St. Bartholomew's Day in the Romanian town of Sibiu, Vlad is said to have impaled 20,000 citizens on sharp, oiled stakes that were inserted slowly so the peasants would suffer more before they died. When Court TV's crimelibrary.com and other Web sites list Vlad as a serial killer, he doesn't fit the bill. He had major motives based in politics: to conquer, organize, and eliminate. Once these goals were met, he stopped his rampage.

A century later, a distant relative of Vlad Tepes began a series of murders that even today is difficult to comprehend. Hungarian Countess Elizabeth Bathory was a vain beauty not only obsessed with her looks but also in constant search of a way to keep her body and face young for as long as she lived. Bathory, who ruled over a small portion of Hungary in the mid-1500s, utilized torture to discipline her servants—everything from making a young, suspected thief grip a sizzling coin until it burned and scarred her hand to taking an iron to the face of a servant whose work on a dress produced wrinkles instead of smooth cloth. Yet torture of peasants and servants was not uncommon during the Middle Ages. In fact, not long before the rule of Bathory, a peasant uprising was quashed by the Hungarian king. Their young leader was kidnapped; hours later he was grilled alive on a fiery throne. His followers were made to eat part of him. Then they themselves were hanged. Certain members of the ruling class devoted so much time to creative methods of torture that it was almost a kind of entertainment, pastime, or sport. Unfortunately, the lower classes were generally treated by royalty as though they were mere animals and severe force had to be used to discipline them. What led Bathory to be remembered by historians was the reason she killed over 650 virgin girls in the course of thirty years of despotic rule. In order to preserve her youth, which she believed was leaving her after giving birth to two children, the forty-year-old woman felt the need to bathe in the fresh blood of virgins. She was said to have taken a spike-filled cylindrical cage and then inserted a victim inside. She had the cage lifted up by a servant, then jabbed young girls with a burning poker. As they would jump back, they'd impale themselves. Bathory then sat herself beneath the cage, showering in the blood that spewed onto her.

The spurting blood of these teens (who were still alive as she bathed) was believed by Bathory to be the fountain of youth. It was only when the countess began to prey on females who were of minor nobility that the judicial system became concerned. Countess Bathory had also become slipshod in her disposal of the bodies, occasionally having the corpses thrown out of her carriage onto the road when she was done with them. And when she ran out of virgins in her own town, she sent her henchmen far and wide to procure more—which became extraordinarily costly, even for a woman of Bathory's immense means. Finally, Bathory began calling on old loans that her deceased husband made to the king, who was as wily as he was wrathful. Realizing that local law held that prisoners had no right to monies a freeman had right to, he called for Elizabeth's immediate capture and arrest. She was ultimately kept sealed in her castle chamber—for women of nobility were rarely placed in prisons in the Middle Ages. For the rest of her life, Bathory was kept safely away from the virgins she yearned for.

But Bathory was not a serial killer according to my definition. Like Vlad, she may have been unduly suspicious. She may have punished her servants severely. And she may have been ruthless in her quest for blood in the *bain*. But she had a focus and a reason for each killing. She wanted to remain beautiful. While the acts were far more atrocious than those of our current upper classes, who stick themselves with needles filled with poisonous Botox to remove their wrinkles or suck fat from their thighs or tie up their intestines to eat less and reduce their weight, the hoped-for effect of Bathory's bloody lotion was the same. I don't believe her killings had anything to do with strange sexual preferences. Nor were they combined with a deep aggression. Her horrible actions were just something she believed she had to do to remain pretty. Killing those virgins was the only way she felt she could make her belief reality.

In Chicago near the turn of the twentieth century, a strange man built something he called a castle. A pharmacy and other stores were on the first floor, but above the first floor it was like one of those old funhouses, a chaotic maze of a place with seemingly no rhyme or reason. The second floor, for instance, had thirty-five rooms when the building opened for business in May 1890. As the public flocked to his drugstore, above which was his castle full of Romanesque columns and frescoes, the strange man grew wealthy.

H. H. Mudgett, a pharmacist who also called himself Dr. Holmes, was like a mad scientist out of a B movie. He liked to inspect his place, opening and closing fifty-one creaky doors on the second floor, firing up a kiln with a cast-iron hatch, inspecting tubs of acid and quicklime, testing chutes that led to the basement. To sealed rooms he added gas jets, stairways that went up but ended at a wall, and trap doors. He also built an instrument like a modern-day rack that was said to be able to stretch a person to twice his height. Dr. Holmes, not a doctor at all, was later thought to be insane. He created a pharmacy that was more like a paeon to ugly architecture with its signs and gaudy paintings than it was a dispensary of medicine. In his identity of Dr. Holmes, Mudgett was an operator, a smooth conniver, a bigamist who thrived on swindling and schemed to fraud insurance companies from Chicago to Philadelphia.

Mudgett had a penchant for killing some of those with whom he had relationships and collecting their money—either their life savings or life insurance policies. In addition, during the high times of the Chicago World's Fair of 1893, Dr. Holmes attacked and murdered many wide-eyed fairgoers who used his castle as a kind of rooming house. The stealthy, fast-talking Mudgett often employed an accomplice to wash, clean, and articulate the bones, paid him about $30, then smirkingly sold the skeleton to local colleges for well over $250. He was indicted for murdering his most loyal assistant, Benjamin Pitezel, in late summer 1895, and that fall was sentenced to death by hanging. In a posttrial confession, he said he murdered twenty-seven people, though some estimate he killed as many as two hundred. But what put Dr. Holmes's deeds into the serial killer category is the way he ruthlessly experimented upon the persons whom he murdered. Dr. Holmes cut his victims, skinned them, removed chunks of flesh, burnt them, prodded them, and placed them in acid baths. He left one wife in a sealed chamber to hear her scream for days as she gradually died of starvation.

If Dr. Holmes was thought to be an eclectic mad scientist who experimented and conspired to extort money to make his crimes complete, Captain Carl Panzram thrilled to kill. An accomplished sailor, he traveled the world over between 1918 and 1926, killing everywhere from Oregon to New York City to South Africa. He seemed to prefer terrifying young boys, and he had a nasty racist streak to boot. In the 20,000-word life story/confession he gave to his only friend, a prison guard, Panzram says he coaxed a twelve-year-old boy to his place of employment, the deserted Sinclair Oil Company grounds. There he assaulted and murdered him with a large rock which he bashed again and again into his head. Wrote Panzram, "I left him there, but first I committed sodomy on him and then I killed him. His brains were coming out of his ears when I left him and he will never be any deader."

"His brains were coming out of his ears." It was this kind of bragging that Panzram used to describe his crimes more than once. The sight of crushed brains seeping from the head not only proved his victim had expired, but also pointed to his pride in the creation of death. After all, it wasn't that he killed by cutting the belly, which would be sloppy. Nor was it stabbing and shooting through the heart, the organ from which poets say romantic feelings emanate. Attacking the brain made sure that the center of intellect and thought and all things human, all things that we know and all things that we do not know, would be destroyed.

Traveling to what was then called the Dark Continent, he hired a group of natives from Lobito Bay to take him to hunt for crocodiles, which he said he would sell to merchants from Europe who were based in the Congo. When the men suggested that they were due a percentage of the profits, Panzram shot them—repeatedly—then tossed them overboard into the muddy river where the thick-snouted reptiles swarmed. The evidence of the crimes would soon be digested in their bellies. Then he quietly rowed the canoe back to Lobito Bay, without his reptilian booty, hurrying to leave the small town before being caught.

For Captain Panzram, killing was easy, and he often fancied himself not only as a dauntless mercenary but also as the world's greatest hit man for hire. He daydreamed of blowing up bridges, of killing massive numbers of people, of raping some and of robbing others. While there was no remorse for what he did, Panzram admitted, "I preyed upon the weak, the harmless, and the unsuspecting." Some might say this is an unusual degree of self-awareness for a serial killer. But they all know they're going after people who aren't going to fight back. Some, like Richard Macek, may not recall the actual details of a murder. But they certainly know that their victims aren't strong and tough.

Like other serial killers, Panzram spoke to law enforcement officials of a spotty recollection. "I have killed a number of people in different places and some of the facts escape my memory," he confessed. Despite his confession, he tried to defend himself in the courtroom, which must have been quite a sight to see. Panzram failed at his efforts miserably, threatening witnesses whose testimony he disliked by taking the index finger of his right hand and dragging it across his throat, as if to slit it. But when Panzram was eventually charged with murder, he admitted to twenty-two homicides and said he wished he had killed twenty-two more. Detectives asked him why he killed a child who was the picture of innocence. The angry, overly tattooed captain lashed out, "I hate all the fucking human race. I get a kick out of murdering people."

In the Roaring Twenties came Albert Fish. The elderly, balding father of six with a thick gray mustache was based in New York City, and in photos he somehow resembled the actor Wilford Brimley, but with a fixed, cold glare. When I read his letters, I felt chilled. It's one thing to use clinical terms in a medical conversation about someone being a cannibal. But the letter I read from Albert Fish to the parent of one of his victims was particularly gruesome and manipulative. Early in his letter, Fish talked of an acquaintance, Captain John Davis, who in a trip to the Far East had sampled the cooked flesh of children after spanking them "to make the meat tender." Fish was intrigued. Imagining himself a kind of connoisseur, Fish wrote he "made up my mind to taste it."

Six years after killing ten-year-old Gracie Budd and just ten days after Walter Winchell talked about her on his widely listened to radio program, Fish wrote about Davis to Delia Budd, Gracie's mother.

On Sunday June the 3—1928 I called on you at 406 W 15 St. Brought you pot cheese—strawberries. We had lunch. Grace sat in my lap and kissed me. I made up my mind to eat her.

On the pretense of taking her to a party. You said Yes she could go. I took her to an empty house in Westchester I had already picked out. When we got there, I told her to remain outside. She picked wildflowers. I went upstairs and stripped all my clothes off. I knew if I did not I would get her blood on them.

When all was ready I went to the window and Called her. Then I hid in a closet until she was in the room. When she saw me all naked she began to cry and tried to run down the stairs. I grabbed her and she said she would tell her mamma.

First I stripped her naked. How she did kick—bite and scratch. I choked her to death, then cut her in small pieces so I could take my meat to my rooms. Cook and eat it. How sweet and tender her little ass was roasted in the oven. It took me 9 days to eat her entire body. I did not fuck her tho I could of had I wished. She died a virgin.

Fish was said to be an emotionless prisoner who, when interviewed by detectives, explained that he had "a thirst for blood." Outwardly, he was meek and polite. Prior to his capture, he had already been arrested for everything from sending obscene notes to grand larceny—but none of the charges stuck. Fish, who claimed he was constantly whipped at St. John's Orphanage in Washington, D.C., also murdered young Billy Gafney, explaining that

I took tools, a good heavy cat-of-nine tails. Home made. Short handle. Cut one of my belts in half, slit these halves in six strips about 8 inches long. I whipped his bare behind till the blood ran from his legs. I cut off his ears—nose—slit his mouth from ear to ear. Gouged out his eyes. He was dead then. I stuck the knife in his belly and held my mouth to his body and drank his blood.

I picked up four old potato sacks and gathered a pile of stones. Then I cut him up. I had a grip with me. I put his nose, ears and a few slices of his belly in the grip. Then I cut him through the middle of his body. Just below the belly button. Then through his legs about 2 inches below his behind. I put this in my grip with a lot of paper. I cut off the head—feet—arms—hands and the legs below the knee.

This I put in sacks weighed with stones, tied the ends and threw them into the pools of slimy water you will see all along the road going to North Beach.

I came home with my meat. I had the front of his body I liked best. His monkey and pee wees [penis and testicles] and a nice little fat behind to roast in the oven and eat. I made a stew out of his ears—nose—pieces of his face and belly. I put onions, carrots, turnips, celery, salt and pepper. It was good.

Then I split the cheeks of his behind open, cut off his monkey and pee wees and washed them first. I put strips of bacon on each cheek of his behind and put them in the oven. Then I picked 4 onions and when the meat had roasted about ¼ hour, I poured about a pint of water over it for gravy and put in the onions. At frequent intervals I basted his behind with a wooden spoon. So the meat would be nice and juicy.

Much as detectives found him emotionless, psychiatrists who interviewed Albert Fish claimed he was detached, that he didn't care whether he lived or died. When examined by doctors, it was discovered that Fish had been inserting needles between his scrotum and rectum. X-rays, rushed to be developed, revealed twenty-nine needles in that area. Serial killers don't usually abuse themselves in this way. I knew that what Albert Fish did wasn't like someone who was a borderline personality disorder and is always cutting himself to let out the pain or to remember that he can still feel something. It may be that Fish needed to know what the pain he administered felt like. What I do know is what we'll see over and over again in this book: serial killers like to experiment simply for the sake of experimentation. That's what Albert Fish did, and it had no greater psychological meaning.

At the trial for the murder of Gracie Budd, it became clear that Fish's children were privy to the old man's odd nature, as they said they saw him drive nails into a board and then flagellate himself with it. The masochist even asked his children to hit him, and they occasionally agreed. Even when Fish sat strapped in the electric chair and was about to die, he told the guards that he couldn't wait for the thrill of electricity to surge through his body. Electrocution, he said blandly, was one of the few thrills he'd never experienced. And then, his life was over.

After reviewing these historical cases, I thought about the similarities these serial killers may have shared. The first thing I noticed is that they weren't considered by their peers to be odd, different, or dangerous. Their crimes were done carefully, and they were able to remain undetected for long periods of time. There was one fallacy I noted after researching de Rais's trial. Serial killing was not a phenomenon only of the United States, one that, critics said, occurred because the societal values in America had declined. It was a worldwide phenomenon. And if serial murders happened as far back as de Rais, they have probably been going on since the dawn of the very first communities in the time of the caveman. I also realized that with Gein, it wasn't necessary to be highly mobile to be a serial killer. You didn't need access to highways and thruways and the interstate system to get away and cover your trail. All you needed to do was to blend in.

But I still needed to find out more. I needed to talk to serial killers more, understand them more fully, if that was at all possible. I had begun with a null hypothesis that held "there's no difference among murderers." But as I collected the data from history, I began to see that there was a distinction between the average murderer and the serial murderer: there was no great rage or any jealousy or any deep emotion at all that prompted serial killers to murder again and again.

I was obsessed with gathering more and more information, reams of it, in the hopes that I would someday yell "Eureka!" and find an answer to the question, Why do these killers kill? I thought, This is going to be a long, long process, one that will take years, one that could nearly exhaust me because it means profiling dozens and dozens of serial murderers. But I'm hooked; I'm really hooked.

FIVE

JOHN WAYNE GACY

The phone kept ringing, and even though I was far too busy, I answered it. "Dr. Morrison, this is Sam Amirante. I'm the attorney for John Wayne Gacy."

The media was already in the process of making John Wayne Gacy the world's most notorious serial killer, but I wasn't in serial killer mode at all. In fact, I was deeply involved in the plans for my wedding. Sam Amirante had seen the paper that morning; an article about me and my work called "Tracking Down Our Mr. Hydes" had appeared in the *Chicago Tribune*. Within the story, I was quoted as saying that most serial killers are never caught. I said that serial killers shouldn't be "written off as psychopaths or sociopaths," that the reason they kill is much more complex. "It's not someone whom we would call crazy, not someone who's actively hearing voices. It's not that clear-cut. Someone like that could murder, but they're not as organized as people who do it across time. Multiple murderers have a much deeper inner disorganization that is not really seen until they're in the middle of a crime or just as the crime is beginning. At that point, they're like Dr. Jekyll and Mr. Hyde. They fall apart and then they come back together again."

The article itself pointed out that serial killing had become more rampant throughout the United States, and the FBI estimated that at least thirty-five killers were on the loose.

On that chilly mid-November morning when all I wanted to think about was the brilliant neurosurgeon I was about to wed, the very animated Sam Amirante said he was so intrigued by the story, he had tried to read the article while in the shower. He had his work cut out for him as the defense lawyer for Gacy, the thirty-seven-year-old contractor who was alleged to have murdered thirty-three young men and teen boys in and around Des Plaines, a suburb about seventeen miles from the center of Chicago. It was hard even for the police to believe he was guilty: Gacy was involved in local politics and even had barbecues in his yard for the community, and that included members of the police force. But the phone call wasn't about specifics of the crimes. Amirante was using his considerable charm with me for a reason.

"How did you know?" asked Amirante.

"What do you mean?"

"You described John Gacy's personality perfectly. Are you sure you've never met him?"

"Of course not." Sam and his staff didn't know that anyone had ever studied serial killers over a lengthy period of time, and he was thrilled to hear that I had.

"Dr. Morrison, I'd like you to be a witness for the defense on the Gacy case," said Amirante. "We're going to go for an insanity plea."

"Hold on, Sam. That all depends on what I find after I examine him." I couldn't simply sign on to be part of any old team, defense or prosecution. Too many people were already "doctors for hire" by lawyers, professionals who would agree to say what they were told to say for the money and the media exposure. That wasn't at all what I wanted, since it had nothing to do with science or the oath I had taken when I became a doctor.

Amirante was persistent, just as he would be persistent in front of Judge Louis B. Garippo during Gacy's trial. "Can you examine him this week? I can arrange it right now."

The young lawyer had seen Gacy go from acting casually and admitting nothing about the murders to acting frantic and panicky and admitting everything after Chicago police dug up the earth under the thirty-inch crawl space under his house north of Chicago. There they uncovered dozens of bodies.

And what a gruesome discovery it was. Almost overcome by a sickly sweet smell, Cook County evidence technician Daniel Genty went at the stinking mud with a shovel. After just a few shovelfuls, he hit bone, human bone. Meanwhile, Officer Michael Albrecht found a dark purple puddle, dug a bit, and encountered loose, rotting flesh. What he thought to be a leg covered by blue jeans was actually blackened, decaying human matter. Soon the police found dozens of severely decomposed bodies. Then the crowds came. Curiosity seekers constantly milled about the site, even though it was cold, even through Chicago snowstorms, as though the site were a tourist attraction.

Ten-year-old Kelly Pucca was one of Gacy's neighbors. What he told the *Chicago Tribune* was representative of the fear that gripped children and adults alike who continued to live on Summerdale Avenue. Kelly admitted, "I get scared. I'm afraid in the shower that someone will get me and I'm afraid spirits are going to come into our house."

The fear and the tourist draw, combined with the fact that December was a slow time for news, all congealed into one epic national horror story. John Wayne Gacy was on his way toward becoming America's most notorious serial killer.

While I was extremely interested in talking to Gacy at length, I told Amirante that I couldn't do anything that week but briefly meet Gacy until I returned from a short three-day honeymoon to Key Biscayne. I certainly didn't tell Amirante, but I was deeply in love. I didn't feel I'd ever find the right person . . . until I met my husband practically right under my nose. I found him in the parking garage of a nearby apartment building during Christmastime 1978. He is a well-respected brain surgeon and the son of generations of Chicago doctors, and his family was very Northern European proper; I wore white gloves when I first met his grandmother.

My husband was always thoughtful about romance, and I remember that it rained horribly during a trip we took to Manhattan. The winds pushed the rain sideways, but he had hired a horse-drawn carriage to take us around Central Park. After the summer rain stopped, and as the smell of greenery and flowers from the park wafted, he proposed to me. I know it sounds a little corny, but the romance of it all was just perfect. So I didn't want to think about lawyers, serial killers, or law enforcement until well after the wedding.

During that New Year's trip, I didn't once think of my work. It was, however, the only time that I was ever able to totally separate my work and my personal life. In the future, on every trip to every country from Brazil to Bali, I was compelled to spend part of my time on serial killers and mass murderers.

Upon returning from my brief honeymoon, I was refreshed and ready to talk to Gacy. They kept John Gacy in Cermak Hospital in the southwest part of Chicago. The concrete structure housed thousands of patients, but Gacy was in an area called 3 North, kept away from much of the prison population, who would have killed him in a minute given the chance. Child molesters were, and still are, considered the lowest of the low within the prison pecking order. And because of the constant media attention Gacy received, there were probably some guards who wanted to get Gacy as well. So Cermak was one tough, ugly place, a no-holds-barred asylum where inmates sometimes tried to commit suicide. Those unfortunates were called "swingers" because they had tried to hang themselves. In this facility I would spend hundreds of hours with Gacy.

The door slammed shut and was locked from the outside. I can still hear the singular sound of that lock echo in my mind. One sound, one moment, and there I was with Gacy in his room, no one but him and me—except for the guard posted outside the door. The bland yellow room held a bed and a tray table, a small table near the door, and a private bathroom. Gacy was writing in an oversize red ledger book when I came in, and he placed it on top of a stack of other such ledgers, diaries of his days of incarceration and an attempt at writing his own life story. Gacy loved to do jigsaw puzzles, and there were five completed puzzles glued onto the walls. He directed me to sit at the small table, an area without direct access to the door. It was a very subtle move, but an unmistakable power play.

On the surface, Gacy was a pleasant man of five feet eight inches, and he wore a white T-shirt with khaki pants and sneakers. Stocky yet fastidious, Gacy kept his living space neat and clean, with everything in its place. Gacy was portly, with an oval face and a double chin. It was almost as if he had no muscles there to give him expression when he talked. And talk he did, about watching TV or playing dominoes with the other inmates or about NFL football.

Still, immediately I felt threatened by him. I could see that Gacy felt he was better than anything or anyone around him. He was condescending about everything I said or asked, while at the same time he was trying to be ingratiating.

The phrase "dumb and stupid" was used often by Gacy, a term that was constantly used by John's father to demean his son. Always, I had the sense that he was thinking, Oh, you dumb, stupid person. Or, Why did you ask something so stupid? While he wouldn't dare say it to me, he constantly seemed contemptuous and smug. Gacy displayed a trait called grandiosity, something far beyond the arrogance found in some successful people, because a terrible aggression lies beneath everything he says or does. I could just feel that Gacy felt he was too good to explain his actions, that he was above explaining himself, not just to me, but also to anyone. Yet it was his seeming thoughtfulness that relatives, friends, acquaintances, and victims first saw and chose to believe. He was able to con most everyone. But to use the word *con* isn't really strong enough to convey the hold Gacy had over people. Compared to Gacy, con artists were babes in the woods. Often in magazine articles and books, Gacy is labeled a psychopath. But Gacy's pathology went far beyond that of the stereotypical psychopath skulking around the world without a conscience. First, the serial murderer is never as organized as a psychopath in his methodology. A psychopath can plot and carry out complex schemes. Secondly, psychopaths have a structured personality that doctors can pinpoint, utilize, and work with. That structured personality is like most everyone else's, with an ego, an id, and a superego. The psychopath has problems with the superego, where guilt and conscience reside; he has no conscience, and he's not scattered the way a serial killer is. With intervention, the psychopath's personality can be modified and contained by a psychiatrist, whereas the serial killer's is all bits and pieces. Since his self is scattered, all his day-to-day social activity is modeled on the way he has seen people act. In medical terms, Gacy was far worse than a psychopath, for he cannot be cured.

Gacy had already confessed to murdering teen boys and men, but he then changed his mind, recanting his confession. And even though our initial conversation didn't dwell on the details of any of his crimes at all, Gacy made it clear that he was innocent of the murders of which he was accused. To put it simply, Gacy felt he had been framed. Since I was just there to listen on that first occasion, I didn't push and ask how he had been set up.

"I didn't do any of those things they say I did," Gacy complained. Then he flashed a smile. It was not the kind of smile that made me feel closer to the man who offered it. It didn't make me feel that Gacy was being open and candid either. It was the kind of smile that was both leering and arrogant, and it stayed with me as though the smile could, at any moment, grow feral, almost as if he could sprout fangs. It inspired fear and made me want to keep my distance. I would remember it when I was alone at night and my husband was away. It was my job, however, to try to get inside Gacy. And I began to make my way inside, even on that first day, simply by listening and egging him on.

"I don't know if I actually killed anybody," said Gacy.

I'd heard this kind of thing before, and it's a very standard defense for the common criminal up against the legal system. The murderer could be lying or he could have the same memory problems Richard Macek had. But I did believe it was manipulative for John to bring his killings up so early in our meetings. I don't think twenty minutes had passed before he began his rants. Gacy said he was taking massive amounts of Valium at the time of the killings—"between thirty milligrams and fifty milligrams a day." He admitted he got the Valium illegally from pharmacists by having his successful construction company do work on their drugstores. Then, from a file folder, he brought out articles supporting the idea that Valium and poor memory are related.

He said, "I sleep four to five hours a night, and I think about it a lot. It bothers me. And it's a hell of thing to be charged with, thirty-three murders, and not know what the hell really transpired. [Especially] For a guy who is as organized as I am about things."

Organized? That was really an understatement. I looked around the place. "I've got to say this is one of the nicest places I've ever been to talk to anybody." It was obsessively clean. Gacy was able to organize small things in his environment, but he wasn't able to organize the big things, like what went on inside his head.

Gacy was pleased that I noticed, and he preened a bit. "What, roomwise? You'll find that cockroaches still crawl around here, but I can't stand that. So I wash the floor. I scrub the floor on my hands and knees. I wipe the floor. I washed all the walls; they just don't come clean."

"Uh-huh. Too many years. How long have you been here as of today?"

"Eleven months of being here and being secluded like this. I have not had no nightmares. I have no remorse. I don't feel sorry for anybody. I'm here and I don't understand it."

Changing the subject to his family, I asked Gacy about his relationship with his father. I knew he was an abusive man, a man who was never satisfied with his son, and he had died while Gacy was in prison in Iowa for sodomy.

"They waited four days to tell you that he had . . ."

"Died. Of course, you know, I took it hard. Cause, you know, all along, throughout my life, I've let my dad down. So here, once again, I did it again to him. My dad always thought I was dumb and stupid. That I would never amount to anything. Just dumb and stupid."

It was as if Gacy knew the kinds of things that would interest a psychiatrist, as if he were trying to do my own work for me. But it came too quickly, I thought. I left Gacy after three hours of casual, introductory conversation and returned to my office at the Evaluation Center, a psychiatric and neurologic diagnostic and intervention facility. Starting the Evaluation Center from scratch wasn't just a milestone for me; it was a dream come true. I had always wanted to bring a multidisciplinary group of professionals together to provide the best possible consultations. With as many as fifty consultants available for a case, we are able to utilize the best of academic medicine, clinical practice, and research. The goal is to have everyone do a top-notch job without the constraints of a quota or of having to deal with intradepartmental hospital politics. I had opened the center in 1980 to assess brain functions from a medical and psychiatric perspective. For instance, if someone is having memory loss, I always assess the person for blood-flow problems to the brain. If there is a positive finding, we have the person looked at by a neurosurgeon who is capable of doing bypass surgery in the brain. If the person is psychotic, we will continue with the evaluation, often done by me. We can provide a very comprehensive diagnosis using these two perspectives, and it's one I use with serial killers as well.

As I reviewed my notes, it just staggered me that Gacy was so like Richard Macek. Physically, they looked alike, thick-bodied, with slumped postures and puffy faces like the Pillsbury Dough Boy. To top it off, Gacy's manner—his ingratiating words and the anger I saw boil beneath—was just like Macek's. I was beginning to think these men were somehow cut from the same cloth. And I wondered if they had some kind of genetic mutation that made them appear human. But inside they were not like us. They do not have the same feelings you or I possess. It is as if someone took a cookie cutter from a kitchen drawer labeled "serial murderer." The baker stamps out the dough and puts them in the oven to bake. When they're done, they come out . . . ready to kill.

While the flagrant crimes of John Gacy may have appeared sexual in nature, they were really about anger and aggression. Gacy was described as a sickly boy who had various spells of fainting throughout his early years. When he was fifteen, Gacy had a huge fight with his father about use of the family car. Later that night while he was playing cards with friends, Gacy's eyes rolled back in his head, he listed for a moment, and then passed out. After three weeks in the hospital, where the doctors found nothing consequential, he passed out again when he returned. When he came to, he flailed about frighteningly in his own bedroom, where a doctor diagnosed him as having an epileptic fit. John Sr. despised his son for what he saw as the boy's hypersensitive, girlish, sickly ways and continued to label him "dumb and stupid." He occasionally beat him, as he even did his wife, who was once punched in the face and left bleeding. By the age of twenty, Gacy left his father and family life and migrated to Las Vegas, where he worked as an attendant at the Palm Mortuary. Gacy later admitted to getting into a coffin, holding a stiff, lifeless body close, and arousing himself by pulling it on top of himself. It's important not to read too much into this act, because Gacy was not a necrophiliac who commonly had sex with dead bodies. What he did was a combination of experimentation with a body and something he saw as comfortable. He wanted to lie down, and the coffin seemed to be the handiest thing available. The definition of *necrophilia* is basically receiving pleasure from sex with a dead person. It's not a completely uncommon act with serial killers, but it's certainly not a constant. What Gacy did with the body had nothing to do with the power and control that is said to fuel the need for necrophilia. And unlike necrophiles, who avoid relating to living people, Gacy had a full social life. For Gacy, what he did in the coffin was more about answering the question, What is this like? Like Albert Fish with his pins or like Kansas City's Robert Berdella, whom we'll deal with soon, Gacy was simply experimenting, trying to see what would happen if he did something.

When Gacy was twenty-six, near Christmas 1967, he began to lure boys to his suburban home. Long before he began to kill them, he would concoct elaborate plans to get sex from them. For instance, he invited fifteen-year-old Donald Voorhees to his home to watch stag films, saying that the movies were useful education for sex. He lied well and vigorously, telling Voorhees that the Kinsey Report (the landmark human sexual behavior study of white middle Americans under the age of thirty-five first published in 1948) said that many young people his age start their sexual experiences via oral sex with a man. When Voorhees said that semen might taste bad, Gacy claimed it had no taste, that oral sex wasn't dirty, that it was just like sucking on your thumb. Since Gacy was the chaplain of the local Jaycees at the time, he also made it clear that the act between the two of them wouldn't be immoral. He even gave Voorhees money to help the boy buy an amplifier for his rock band—and then coaxed him into having sex.

He eventually would coerce a teenage boy to pummel young Voorhees brutally in an effort to stop Voorhees from testifying against him in court. But the law caught up with Gacy, and he was jailed. While Gacy was awaiting trial on the Voorhees charges, which included malicious threats to extort and sodomy, police found that Gacy had had sex with other underage boys. One of these teens was Edward Lynch, a cook at the Kentucky Fried Chicken restaurant that Gacy managed for his wife Marlynn's father. In addition to being raped, Lynch was chained and choked to the point of unconsciousness until he lost control and urinated in his pants. Gacy would shackle other boys with their hands behind their back before he raped them. While Gacy claimed that the sex was always consensual, Judge Peter Van Metre of the Tenth Judicial District Court sentenced the twenty-six-year-old Gacy to ten years in the Iowa State Reformatory for Men in Anamosa for sodomy, which included tying Voorhees up and raping him. The jail sentence was the beginning of the end for Gacy's marriage to Marlynn and for any contact with his young son and daughter.

In Anamosa as in Cermak hospital, Gacy was an ideal prisoner, fastidious, orderly, often reading the *Wall Street Journal* in the library. Always scheming, he rose up the prison ladder to become one of the prison's top chefs, where he awarded gourmet meals to prisoners in return for favors like cigars or to guards in return for extra time on the telephone. He even started a prison chapter of the Jaycees and persuaded an elderly couple to donate their miniature golf course to the prisoners. He was convincing, charming, and ingratiating, a politician, really. Nonetheless, the prison wouldn't permit Gacy to visit his father, who died during Christmas 1969. Within seventeen months, John Gacy was released from prison because of his exemplary behavior. Psychiatrist Richard Lee's report to the parole committee read "The likelihood of his again being charged and convicted of antisocial conduct appears to be small." Unfortunately, Dr. Lee couldn't have been more wrong. Gacy became morose because he hadn't been given leave to go to his dying father, and that pall remained with him when he left the jail. When he visited his father's grave on Christmas 1971, John broke down and couldn't stop crying.

After my initial meeting with Gacy, I asked one of his surviving victims, Jeff Rignall, to visit me in my office at the Evaluation Center. Rignall was a man of medium height, thin but not skinny, with a mustache, long sideburns, and brown hair. He had been one of Gacy's more vocal victims, one who survived Gacy's cruelty, and he felt he was scarred for life.

In late March 1978, Rignall, a gay man who also dated women, argued with his girlfriend, left her apartment in the New Town area of Chicago, and decided to go to a bar. While Rignall was strolling down the sidewalk, a fancy black car pulled up next to him. Slowly, Gacy rolled down the window and affably struck up a conversation. Within seconds, Rignall judged Gacy to be a nice guy, probably a closeted gay man with a wife in the suburbs. He even felt somewhat sorry for him. When Gacy offered some marijuana, Rignall got in the car, and they began driving.

It didn't take long for Gacy to pounce. Just as Rignall inhaled for the second, possibly the third, time, Gacy slapped a reeking wet cloth over his face, and the chloroform went to work. Rignall tasted its sweetness, which doctors know to be forty times sweeter than sugar. And there was the intense burn on his face, a feeling of unbearable pain, before he passed out. When he awoke, he was in Gacy's house on a couch near a bar over which hung a painting of a clown. It seemed to leer at Rignall, mocking him, laughing at him. Gacy restrained Jeff in a kind of pillory he had fashioned. Then he forced Rignall to give him oral sex. While Jeff's face felt afire and swollen from the chloroform, Gacy shoved various dildos, even a sharp fireplace poker, into him. After beginning to bleed from the rectum, Jeff Rignall was in very bad shape. When he was done with Jeff, Gacy dumped him in Chicago's Lincoln Park, in an area full of weeds, litter, and scurrying rats. When he woke, he was able to make his way back to his girlfriend's apartment. There, his injuries got worse. Rignall spent weeks recovering in a hospital. He sustained permanent liver damage from the chloroform, which is also known to trigger heart attacks.

I thought meeting with Rignall would help me gain more insight into Gacy. Gently, I began to ask questions.

"Can you tell me what happened to you?"

Rignall became emotional as he recounted the story. "I didn't think I'd get out alive. I continued to bleed from the rectum in the hospital. And the police didn't believe me." It wasn't easy for Rignall to set aside what had happened. When he had bad memories of the experience, he said he'd get in a car, "drive a hundred and fifty miles and just cry."

"How do you feel about John Gacy now?"

"In a way, I'd really like to see him burn. See, I thought I knew horror. But I never realized that that kind of horror ever existed. And that has a tendency to come back sometimes."

"How so?"

"I've aged a lot in the last two years. I used to look a lot younger than I do now."

I felt that no matter what he said at the time, Jeff would gradually recover some semblance of a routine in his life. He may have thought he aged, but he was still only twenty-eight. Before him, he likely had a long and promising life.

"Why do you think you survived?" I asked.

"Any time that he did anything to me or when he started to do something to me, I never resisted because I was totally restrained and there's nothing I could do about it. He would wait until he would see the pain on my face and then he would put the chloroform rag over my face and I would be out. And I'd wake back up, and I'd be in a different position, then he would tell me what he was going to do and say, 'I just want to hear you say' . . . just real, I mean real vulgar things. And at no time did I resist. That's why I really kind of think I'm alive, because I think that kind of turned him off." That may well have been the case. Rignall may have played a role of submission that allowed him to live. That's not to say that submission would've worked for any victim of a serial crime or any of Gacy's other victims. But at that moment in time, perhaps because Gacy was tired, perhaps because Rignall didn't fight back, Rignall survived. I didn't gain a huge amount of insight into Gacy by interviewing Jeff, but it was important for me to speak to one of these young victims, if only to get a handle on the body type Gacy gravitated toward: thinnish light-haired or brown-haired young men. It was just one more piece of the Gacy puzzle.

It was not the angry, occasionally hysterical Rignall but Robert Piest who proved to be Gacy's downfall. Sadly, before Piest, the authorities didn't seem to care that much about the men and boys Gacy was alleged to have killed, and they wouldn't arrest him. Rignall told me that when he suggested that police go to Gacy's house, they hemmed and hawed, saying it was too out of the way. Those unfortunates like Rignall were the marginal in society—the poor, the runaways, the prostitutes, the depressed, the immigrant workers—people authorities must have believed were not high on their priority list. The authorities seemed to neglect and even eschew the tenet that no person should be considered disposable.

But Robert Piest, just fifteen years old when he was murdered, was different. Consistently, he made the honor roll at Maine West High School, where he was a gymnast and an avid amateur photographer. The slim but athletic Robert was considered handsome and wore his brown hair in a shag cut that was popular at the time. He was just about to become an Eagle Scout when he encountered John Gacy at the Nisson Pharmacy in Des Plaines, Illinois. Piest was a hard worker at the drugstore. But on the night of December 11, 1978, he wanted a job that paid him more money—perhaps because it was near Christmas, perhaps because he wanted to buy a Jeep, perhaps because it was his mother's birthday. Maybe Robert wanted to show her he could do even better than he was doing. Whatever the case, Gacy, who by now ran his own contracting business, was in the store to give the owner some advice on upgrading the place. While stacking the shelves with merchandise, Piest overheard Gacy mention what he was paying his employees, which was twice what Piest was making at the drugstore. Robert said nothing to Gacy, who eyed him occasionally while speaking to the drugstore's owner. Gacy left the pharmacy, then returned to pick up his forgotten appointment book.

Outside, snow had begun to fall, and the Chicago weather was icy cold. Piest asked a colleague if he could leave just a few minutes early to speak to Gacy about getting some extra work. Donning his blue parka, Robert went over to his mother, who was waiting to pick him up in her car.

Excitedly, he said, "I just want to talk to this guy for a minute or so. He might have work for me."

Proud of her son's work ethic, Elizabeth Piest agreed, then left her car to pass the time by browsing the aisles of the pharmacy.

Robert ambled over to Gacy's truck. He looked in to see Gacy rustling some papers. For a moment, he hesitated. Then he rapped on the window.

"Sir, are there any jobs available with you? Because I heard you talking in the store."

Piest flashed a smile at Gacy, who asked the boy to get inside the truck. With the snow and wind whipping around, Robert obliged.

"Can you tell me more about the jobs you have?" asked Robert once again.

According to Gacy, Piest was too aggressive about asking for a job. He suggested that if Robert really wanted money, he might think about selling his body for sex. Maybe Robert thought Gacy was joking. Maybe he was stunned by the suggestion. Whatever his true feelings were, Robert didn't say. He remained silent, and Gacy began driving toward his house on Summerdale in the Norwood township near Des Plaines. Once there, he wasted no time. Roughly, he handcuffed Piest. Robert begged him not to do anything more.

By morning, Piest was dead, raped then killed by Gacy's choking rope, and stuck like a rag doll between Gacy's bed and the bedroom wall. He slept with the body for a while, then Gacy placed Piest in the attic and went to work. Later, he drove forty-five miles to Interstate 55 and threw the body into the Des Plaines River. After months passed, Robert's decomposed remains were found near the Morris Dresden Dam in Grundy County, dozens of miles away. Gacy was charged with murder, aggravated kidnapping, deviant sexual assault, and taking indecent liberties with a child.

In my office, I looked at the photographs of all of the murdered kids, pictures that obviously were taken in high school. They all looked alike in a way. Yes, they were slim, attractive, and generally light haired, the kind of person Gacy always stalked. But more, under the mops of their longish hair they bore a look of hope and trust on their faces. None mugged for the camera. None made faces or appeared too shy to offer up anything but a face full of light. (Only one, nineteen-year-old Matthew Bowman, seemed somewhat suspicious of the camera.) As a psychiatrist I needed to remain objective, but sometimes emotions did creep through, despite all my training. These young people deserved to be alive . . . and free. I kept thinking, What a damnable waste of human potential, of precious life. But a key tenet of being a research investigator is to follow a protocol and to deal with the emotional impact later.

His family, of course, found it impossible to believe that John had done anything wrong. I asked Gacy's youngest sister, Karen, to come to the office so that we could talk about her brother. Karen was a small, nondescript, quiet woman with dark, shoulder-length hair that was done neatly. For hours, she spoke about Gacy in glowing terms, about his giving nature, about how he went out of his way to help people in the community, about how he was protective of the family, especially his mother, after his father, John Stanley Gacy, died. Like many family members of serial killers, she was suffering from a deep kind of denial.

"I can't believe this could have happened. He was always such a good brother. How could this have happened?"

"We're all trying to find out."

"Well, can't people find out without it being in the papers and on TV every day? It's like we're to blame, his family."

The media was indeed making the Gacy case a spectacle, and she was angry about what the family was being put through. Misinformation flew about like sand flies in summer, and in a battle to get the story first, some reporters wrote and broadcast rumors as facts without checking them. Because I had heard it before from Richard Macek's family (among others), I understood what Karen was going through and said as much. As the minutes passed, Karen began to open up.

"We were always together, even though there was some sibling rivalry. What I did notice was he got hit in the head with a swing lots of times, had lots of blackout spells; he had some at school." I understood what Karen was doing. A person who's had something bad happen within their family constantly searches for a reason. No one wants to think it's just the family member's fault. It's just natural to want to blame it on something. But in all the diagnostic work that had been done throughout Gacy's life, there was absolutely no indication that there had been any physiological damage that could have led to the future killings. Even the mildest head trauma would usually result in errors in schoolwork or perhaps as vision problems, and that was simply not seen.

"Did he have any other kinds of spells?"

"I remember that once he passed out at the top of the stairs and didn't remember who he was when he came to. He was like someone who was drunk, but he wasn't drunk. Something in his voice was different. It was not his voice."

Karen also recounted another alarming instance in which John keeled over. Taken to the hospital, John railed against being restrained. He had a "fit," tearing at and destroying the straps "like he had the strength of ten men."

"I hear that John and his father had problems."

Karen took a deep breath. "Sometimes they were small things. I remember he didn't want John to take a bath because he said it cost too much for the pilot light to heat the water. He'd shout at John, daring him to take a punch. But John never did." John Stanley maintained a Depression Era mentality that never waned, and in reality had grown obsessive over the years.

"Anything else?"

"When John was away in Iowa [serving time for the sodomy conviction] and our father died, John felt he died because he was embarrassed about the crime that was committed. He somehow felt he was responsible for his father's death."

I got Karen a glass of water, and when she finished, I said it would be of real importance to speak to her mother. Karen blanched.

"My mother doesn't talk to anyone," she said. Karen took another sip of water. Then there was a prolonged silence. She held the glass in her hand and looked into it. Then she looked at me, saying, "But I'll try."

It took weeks, but after Sam Amirante, Karen, and even Gacy himself asked her to cooperate, I talked to Gacy's mother, Marion, on the phone at length. Marion had been employed by a pharmacy and had worked her way up through the ranks so that she was a kind of pharmacist herself, albeit without a degree, ranking slightly above a pharmacist's assistant. Though Gacy's father continually berated young John by calling him "dumb and stupid," John and Marion were very close.

Marion believed her son was being persecuted unjustly, and she went on about that. But early in the conversation, she began talking about John as an infant.

"John was late as a child, and when he came out, he was blue."

"That must have been hard on you, Marion."

"I did everything I could to help him. For months, I even gave him daily enemas."

"Pardon me?"

"I gave him enemas and suppositories because he had problems before birth. He defecated inside the womb and that caused respiratory problems."

She deduced that John suffered meconium aspiration, in which a baby inhales his own feces while in the womb and has difficulty breathing because of it. At its worst, such a condition can cause pneumonia or even a collapsed lung. Several days after his birth, she said, he had what she described as breathing problems once again and became allergic to all kinds of milk. Rectal suppositories, she said, were inserted to decrease the breathing problems.

"Who prescribed this?" It certainly didn't seem like the proper prescription to me.

"I did. I am a trained pharmacist."

"How long did you continue this treatment?"

"All the time for about his first three months." Some might have jumped to the conclusion that John's mother was crazy herself and that her particular kind of mothering hurt John. The early psychoanalytic thinkers may have said that the enemas and suppositories made an older Gacy think the world in general was threatening and that what she did to John kept John from developing a full personality. I myself was surprised at her comments, but it was my feeling that while she saw things in her own, sometimes curious, way, she wasn't deranged at all.

Yet I thought it wise to travel to see Marion Gacy face-to-face. When she opened the door to her home, the seventy-five-year-old woman I saw was outrageously overweight, so much so that she found it difficult to move around. We sat at the kitchen table, drinking coffee, my notebook out as I wrote down what she said.

"What was John's father like?"

"He was like my own father. He was a great fisherman, a man, not a mollycoddle. He was a strict guy, though, perfection personified."

"Strict how?"

"Well, when the kids went out, they had to write out where they were going, the address and the phone number and when they'd be back. Things like that. John really didn't trust anyone much."

"Were there any medical problems?"

"He had some. Some from war injuries. He had a brain tumor, but doctors said they couldn't operate. That's why his behavior changed all the time. He could be verbally and physically abusive. Doctors said that's the way it was and I would have to live with it." Marion seemed resigned. She'd had a life that was sometimes difficult, and now with John's dire circumstances, it had gotten much worse. She revealed that the elder Gacy was hospitalized in the first years of their marriage for symptoms that included everything from total paralysis to headaches. "Something in our son bothered my husband a lot, though."

Once she finished speaking about her child and her husband, I again brought up the fact that she said she'd given him suppositories and enemas as a baby.

"I never said that. Never said that at all." Her face reddened, and she was having trouble breathing.

Marion must have been overcome by guilt, because she did indeed say it to me on the phone. More than likely, she had thought about what she said and felt it might be interpreted that somehow she was at fault regarding the murders her son John had committed. Mrs. Gacy also described some very remarkable happenings. Young John would sleepwalk and become completely unaware of his surroundings or actions during these spells. She said that one evening, she put her son down and the next morning noticed he had acquired a birthmark. The mark had disappeared from her arm and reappeared on John's, and she described it as though it was a kind of supernatural, religious experience. She also outlined another circumstance in which she had discovered that a tooth disappeared from her mouth. She looked at John when he brushed his teeth; the tooth, she said, reappeared in John's mouth. Again she spoke of this as if it were a miracle of sorts.

"It just shows how close we were. He was just like me. He couldn't sleep for more than four hours at a time. He didn't like to be alone, like me. And, well, he was overweight."

But unlike his helpless, aging mother who felt an overriding, unspoken responsibility for her son's crimes, Gacy was accused of murdering almost three dozen people.

I then spoke with Carol Hoff, Gacy's second wife, about whether or not she felt something was awry when she lived with the murderer.

"Carol, were there things that weren't normal going on at the house?"

"Not that I could tell."

"Did you ever smell anything that was different or unusual?"

"Yes, a bad stink, and I asked John about it."

"What did he say?"

"He said, 'We have a lot of mice and we're putting down lime to stop the smell.'"

"Was there anything suspicious that you had seen?"

"No, not at all."

"Why did the marriage end?"

"He was never around anymore, too busy with his contracting business and with doing things for the neighbors. He just wasn't available. He was always working."

"There was a young man he brought into the house to live, John Butkovich. John later killed him."

"I had no idea that there was anything going on there. Little John was a kid who needed somewhere to stay. John said we were doing a good thing by letting him live with us. And I thought, Gee, what could possibly be wrong with that? It was a shock to hear that John did those things, a real shock."

It's generally true that family and neighbors are often stunned when someone they think they know very well becomes involved in a crime like murder. Because Gacy was so involved with his community, the news was especially jarring. Gacy not only ran a flourishing contracting company, but also fixed things like faucets for neighbors without charging them. Carol was a nice, quiet person who had two affable daughters from a previous marriage. Outwardly, they seemed like the perfect suburban family. When he wasn't with his wife and stepdaughters, he was doing charity work. Gacy designed an outfit and dressed up as a character he called Pogo the Clown to entertain sick children in local hospitals, and he gave huge yearly backyard parties where hundreds of people—including well-known local politicians—were entertained and fed. He organized Chicago's mammoth Polish Day Parade. First Lady Rosalynn Carter came and posed for a photograph with Gacy. Lillian Grexa, who lived near the murderer and even prepared Polish sausage for Gacy's 1972 wedding reception, told me that John was "better than a neighbor. He was a good friend." Gacy wasn't merely well liked. He was admired.

But Lillian Grexa didn't know the nighttime John Gacy. It was during the wee hours of the night that Gacy haunted a then-sketchy area of Chicago. Called Bughouse Square because of its proximity to flophouses of the 1800s, the three-acre park was popular with local bohemians and radicals in the early 1900s. They gathered there from their cold-water flats and cheap hotels to argue and rant and face the occasional rotten tomato. Legendary Scopes monkey trial lawyer Clarence Darrow and political activist Emma Goldman even debated there. Today, the tree-filled park is surrounded by an upscale neighborhood of high-rises, and a yearly park festival commemorates those long-gone original bohemians with food, entertainment, and debating contests. In Gacy's time, however, Bughouse Square was a run-down, seedy place where male prostitutes plied their trade.

Though word had spread quickly about how Gacy engaged in rough sex and circled the park in his black Oldsmobile outfitted with a police spotlight and scanner, many male prostitutes in dire need of money paid no heed. Sometimes Gacy appeared as a gruff-voiced police officer, complete with fake ID. At other times, he was his affable, outgoing self. Gacy acknowledged frequenting these prostitutes many times without killing or threatening to attack them. He bragged to one police investigator that he had 1,500 bisexual relationships in seven years (150 of which were homosexual encounters). Because that meant almost one per day, it was probably, as far as I can tell, inaccurate. The comment reminded me of Richard Macek when he was asked how many days in a year there were. Macek said "Two hundred and five." Gacy wasn't exaggerating so much as pulling a number out of thin air.

But if a boy tried to hike the price for services rendered or if Gacy he felt threatened by him in any way, Gacy would get riled up and, by the night's end, end his life. After bringing a boy to his home, the way an animal brings its prey to its lair, Gacy would begin toying with him. To avoid the prospect of a swift getaway, Gacy would show handcuffs to the victim, then manipulate him into trying them on by saying it was a trick. Once his victim was incapacitated, he'd say, "There's no key to let you go. That's the trick." Like a magician in a bad B movie, he'd then say, "I have one more trick to show you. The rope trick." He would tie a rope around the neck of the still-handcuffed youth, knot it, place a board between the knots, and twist it with a stick, creating a kind of primitive garrote.

After the boy at his feet was nude and unconscious, Gacy might take photographs of the tortured victim. When a boy regained consciousness, he'd twist the rope again, taking away his precious air, repeating the process until the boy expired. Any thinking individual would have thought the authorities would have been so astonished by reports of the crimes, they would have arrested Gacy directly. But they repeatedly looked the other way.

One of the first examples of law enforcement's blunders regarding the Gacy case occurred with nineteen-year-old college student Robert Donnelly. While Donnelly walked to a bus stop, Gacy turned on the Oldsmobile's blinding spotlight and aimed it at him. After informing the frightened Donnelly that he was a policeman, Gacy shouted, ordering Robert into his car. Then he handcuffed Donnelly and drove to his house. He forced him inside, where he tormented the boy mentally, physically, and sexually.

"My, aren't we having fun tonight?" Gacy asked.

Taking a pistol, Gacy pointed it at Donnelly's head.

"Why are you doing this?" asked the boy, quavering, stuttering. He often stuttered, but now it was more noticeable. He thought he was going to die.

Ignoring Donnelly's plea, Gacy proclaimed, "There's one bullet in here."

After waving the gun around, Gacy decided to play a game of Russian roulette. Each time he took his finger to spin the cylinder of the gun, each time it clicked as the cylinder turned, Donnelly felt he would die. Gacy then pulled the trigger, once, twice, many times. Donnelly wanted it all to be over; he had already been raped, humiliated, and injured, and now he just wanted it to end. When the gun finally fired, Donnelly squinted, shutting his eyes as tight as he could. In a moment, he realized the bullet was merely a blank. It was another of Gacy's cruel pranks. Gacy laughed.

Gacy then led a dazed and wounded Robert to his bathroom, took his head, and pushed it under a bathtub full of tap water. Quickly, Robert's larynx tightened and closed. He felt a stifling, panicky suffocation. Gasping and coughing, Donnelly passed out. When Donnelly regained consciousness, Gacy forced his head underwater again. Gacy did this again and again until Donnelly was confused and began to turn blue.

"Please. Just kill me," begged Robert. Dazed, he felt he had been drowned four times. He had been tortured all night long and said he couldn't take it anymore. As the morning broke and Gacy felt the need to ready for work at his contracting business, he released Donnelly, telling him to shower. Then he drove him to work.

When police investigated the case, they strongly suggested to assistant state attorney Jerry Latherow that Gacy be brought up on charges of kidnapping and deviant sexual assault. Startlingly, Latherow didn't believe Donnelly. Perhaps because Donnelly was in therapy and appeared to Latherow as possibly mentally unstable, Latherow didn't think the charges would hold up in court. And because Donnelly stuttered and spoke slowly, Latherow didn't believe a jury would convict Gacy.

Though Gacy dumped a few of the bodies into the Des Plaines River and the Illinois River, he dragged twenty-nine of them into his crawl space, shoving them into shallow graves that he, along with his unwitting workers, had dug beneath the house. Arranged in a kind of circle, the dead were placed like spokes on a bicycle wheel. As he'd told his wife, Gacy did sometimes toss lime in the crawl space, but it was really to help speed up the decomposition of the bodies and to cover the smell of death, not mice.

When the police dug under the house, they found ten bodies that were so miserably rotted, skeletized, and putrefied that the cause of death could never be determined. Bodies were found with ropes tied about the neck. And those that weren't yet so decomposed were discovered to have wads of material placed far back past the throat and into the esophagus, probably to stop massive bleeding onto the floors of neat freak Gacy's home. Cook Country Medical Examiner Dr. Robert Stein theorized that some of the victims may well have been buried alive and that they tried desperately to dig themselves out. Gacy, who transported bodies into the crawl space late at night, assumed that each person was a cadaver. But they may have been merely battered and unconscious and, according to Stein, would have lived had they been given the chance.

Police had tailed Gacy for some time, watching him constantly after screwing up some earlier half-baked attempts at undercover work. Gacy even found them observing him, sought them out, and went to a restaurant with them, nervously trying to impel them to come over to his way of thinking: that they were following him for no good reason. But once they searched Gacy's suburban ranch home at 8213

Summerdale Avenue, Gacy did make his confession. Later, in retracting what he had said, he claimed he was hung over and on drugs when he confessed. He said he was overtired when the statements were made, and indeed he was exhausted. The murderer was so worried about being caught that he hadn't slept for days.

Gacy was no more manipulative than any other serial killer. That's not to say he didn't manipulate with vigor. Because he murdered at least thirty-three young men and teens, he cajoled and coerced more than most modern-day killers, and the story was told around the world by the news media . . . on a daily basis. In fact, with the advent of mogul Ted Turner's Cable News Network, headlines and one-minute summaries about Gacy were beamed out to the world hourly. And the newspapers! They had field days as gory headlines boosted circulation. There were stereotyped stories about serial-killing monsters, stories that seemed to want to make people not only fear Gacy but also be wary beyond vigilance: again and again they cautioned that a serial killer could be lurking in anyone's backyard.

On a one-to-one basis, Gacy himself was one scary guy, smugly smiling through many of his early conversations with me. And each time I received a typewritten letter from him as addendum to our conversations, I was reminded of his twisted point of view from headline-like Gacy-isms he had placed atop his letterhead: "Execute Justice . . . Not People!!!" or "Execution . . . Revenge for a sick society!!!" It was into all of this that I would be thrust if I decided to agree to work with Gacy for Sam Amirante.

SIX

THE GACY INTERVIEWS

On one cold winter night, while being driven through Cabrini in a cab, I barely avoided a thug who skulked up to the cab at a stoplight and tried to force open the door to rob me with a long knife. The cab pulled away just before the man could force his way inside.

In the late 1970s, it was not the safest place to be at night, not for me, not for anyone—especially since it served as the opening scene to many of John Gacy's murders during his four-year crime rampage. About five blocks away from the crime-plagued Cabrini Green, that sprawling low-income housing project known nationally for its gangs, drugs, and violence, was the notorious Bughouse Square.

On that freezing winter night, I felt it was important to retrace some of Gacy's steps as he picked up local hustlers. There is, even though I am a doctor, a fair amount of investigative work in my research. Bughouse Square was full of leafless trees whose scraggly branches reached over muddy footpaths that snaked through the rundown park. As I walked, occasionally a shadowy figure would emerge from behind one of the trees, stare at me until I was frightened, and then pass silently into the night. As a frigid wind blew through the park, I was thankful for my black earmuffs. I rubbed my hands together for warmth and continued my search.

It was not hard to find one. Half lit by a streetlight, he stood on a corner in jeans and a black jacket, waiting.

"Excuse me. How are you?"

"All right. . . . What do you want?" He appeared a little startled.

"I just want to talk. Have you heard about John Wayne Gacy?"

"Are you with the police?"

"No, I just want to talk."

Streetwise and fidgety, he spoke with a slightly feminine voice. "Yeah. I certainly know about him. Everybody knows about him."

After saying he'd read about Gacy in the papers, he admitted he'd even met Gacy. "Sure, I knew John Gacy. I had sex with him. He wanted to give it rough. He didn't hurt me . . . much."

"Weren't you warned about him?"

"Everyone around here said to be careful. We knew he could be violent. That's what we heard." He spoke with a kind of bravado, like he'd been on the front lines of a war.

"Then why did you go with him?"

He shifted his weight and looked at the ground for a moment. "Person's got to make a living, honey." With that he walked away into the darkness of the park. The brief encounter and the trip gave me some insights into how people picked up the prostitutes at Bughouse Square as well as the culture that existed there. Familiarity with the Bughouse scene would help me not only as a researcher but also as someone who had to speak to Gacy about his crimes.

Not long after this, I was called to the hospital in an emergency situation. I was told that Gacy was contemplating suicide. After I arrived, he calmed somewhat. When I asked him about it, the way Gacy explained his nature was certainly scarier than the person I met in the park, and it chilled me more than the freezing temperature that winter night.

"I think there are two distinct characters," mused Gacy from a chair in his guarded room at Cermak. As he talked, the tiny eight-by-fifteen-foot room seemed to grow smaller, and I felt a bit claustrophobic. Gacy continued. "One body, two persons. The active person, John Gacy, has fifteen characters, not personalities, see? Fifteen different characters evolved in one man. The sex drive, when it breaks in, it's two people. John Gacy and Jack Hanley."

"Okay." I quickly regained my composure and thought to myself, Is this a crock?

"This guy Jack controls me. Eighteen hours of the day. Sometimes twenty-four. But apparently when he's been drawn down and, not only by alcohol or drugs, and that, but evidently right at the crest, when I got angered, he picked them up. He comes out. He comes out! He's got loose morals. He's got loose ideas. And you know, anything goes . . . How the hell do I get him out? I don't know how to talk to him. I don't know how to bring him out."

"I see." It was just not possible that John had any kind of split personalities, since he didn't display the classic symptoms, symptoms that are seen very rarely in clinical practice. Dr. Morton Prince introduced the concept of split personalities in 1898 when he reported the case of Miss Christine Beauchamp, a Radcliffe student who showed three distinct personalities: saint, devil, and woman. With split personalities, there are situations in which a person can become stressed, and that stress leads him to go into another personality. Gacy often killed when he was under no pressure whatsoever. Still, I wanted to hear what he had to say.

"The only logical conclusion is one's gotta kill the other. If you can't separate the two, then you gotta kill both of them. I don't think I'm suicidal, but I'm afraid."

"You think you're out of control when you're doing, or not doing, something."

"The fear. Scared of what? There's nobody here except me, but I'm afraid of myself. And afraid I'm going to hell." But Gacy really had no concept of hell, at least as opposed to heaven. When he later talked about Jesus Christ and Satan, it was clear to me that he had developed no clear distinction between the two in his mind. To him, they were the same being. Gacy couldn't differentiate among people, nor could he differentiate among concepts that were more far more complex, abstract, and philosophical.

He even asked me to hypnotize him so we could find out what

caused his crimes. I remembered what had happened with Richard Macek and said, "The problem with hypnotizing is this. We could get you into a state and might not be able to bring you out again. That's why I won't do it." (In fact, *no one* would do it.) Since the turmoil within Gacy was exponentially worse than what was within Macek, I did not know what would occur. In addition, there was the chance that under hypnosis, Gacy might have displayed the same kinds of injuries he suffered while torturing his victims. Gacy could have hurt himself far more than Macek did with those blisters that spontaneously and mysteriously arose on his hand.

Undaunted, Gacy continued. "If that state would be where you'd uncover what really happened, and if I'm that way, I really don't want to live, anyway." Outwardly, he seemed to feel trapped, that he wanted to do something, anything, to change his circumstance. And he said he had methods of suicide that would work. "I could jump off in the courtroom and jump the judge. I could kill myself."

"How would you kill yourself?"

"In here? I could do the rope trick to myself. Secondly, I could hang myself with a rope. If I was really bent on suicide, any time they took me on a trip, I'd bust away from them. They have orders that if I escape, don't even bother coming back. Them goddamn mothers up there—they're gun happy and they probably would blow me away in a second if they had they a chance.

"Yet, you know something, if I was really bent on escape, I've had at least five opportunities to disarm an officer. They trust me. While I was at County Hospital [a few weeks ago], they're all there with their guns, sleeping in the chairs. . . . Then again, I could suffocate myself. I could take blankets. I could burn the mattresses, start a fire, rip open the matches and start a fire in this gas stuff [he meant the old oxygen tank connectors] here near the door. These plastic bags, put your head right in the bag. Tie it. You can suffocate. At one time I had a razor blade, but that's such a sloppy mess, and there's no guarantee."

"That's right."

Gacy was never a person of a few words. A self-proclaimed "motormouth," every time he spoke, he ran on and on, often writing what he said or what I said in his ledger book as we spoke. The clinical name for such a condition is logorrhea, one of the symptoms seen in persons who are in a manic state. They talk on and on, even if they're not hyperactive, and they can't seem to stop. Gacy was somewhat like a radio talk show host in that he seemed to love to hear himself speak. He was everywhere when he spoke, all over the map, ranting, explaining, cajoling, imparting what he believed were truths. The surprising undercurrent to many of his verbalizations was his belief that he was the victim. No matter that he raped. No matter that he tortured. No matter that he killed mercilessly. He was the one who was being persecuted by everyone else, and he reveled in voicing his rationalizations to all who would lend an ear.

On another gray afternoon in January 1980, Gacy began to tell stories about his childhood. He recalled being eight or nine years old, about having a young friend who had polio, and playing with him when other kids wouldn't. Then he mentioned dreaming of the wheelchair-bound child's father, "of looking at his father in a swimsuit or something, the muscular build." So did that statement indicate that John was gay early on? Absolutely not. Again, Gacy did not distinguish between men and women sexually or otherwise. It was as though people were one sex to him.

Then, knowing what I knew about Gacy's history, he mentioned two things that were a bit frightening and momentarily gave me the shivers. "I can remember when us kids were small, we used to play about the Black Hand. The Black Hand will get you. Scared the shit out of them every time.

"Then we used to go over to the Jewish cemetery and take the flowers. I used to collect the papier-mâché buckets and separate the Styrofoam and all the ribbons and all the artificial flowers. We'd have a wedding and we'd use all the funeral flowers. Once we found a dead dog. We'd get all these flowers and get like the casket and spread it over the whole wagon with this dead dog with the flowers on it. Had to bury the poor dog."

I asked Gacy if there was a time during his youth in which he became frightened of things like monsters and ghosts. He shrugged and said that he hadn't. "But you wanna know something? When I was a kid, I was afraid of firemen. Whenever I heard a fire truck, I would run like hell for home. Because they used to go by so fast and they were blurry on their faces, they looked like monsters. You couldn't see no face on those trucks. You just seen a blur."

I was at a momentary loss. I had no idea from where his fear came, especially since most children like fire engines and firemen. As Gacy indicated, it may actually have been the unpredictable noise of the sirens that frightened him, but most boys want to be firemen. I took the statement at face value, and certainly Gacy couldn't figure out precisely why he was scared. Gacy equated firefighters and blurry faces with monsters. That was all.

Gacy then mentioned his compulsion to steal panties, which first began with stealing his mother's silky underwear off the line and hiding it in a paper bag under his porch. He also pilfered underwear from various clotheslines as the mood struck him, often when he worked at a local store delivering groceries to neighbors' houses. It continued through his teens. "I used to masturbate with them. When I was fourteen or fifteen, I just took 'em all at once and I was burning garbage out in the alley, so I burned all of them. But they wouldn't burn. They actually melted, because of the acetate in them. Some of the guys I went out with would be wearing girls' underwear and I would take it from them."

"It wasn't the smell or anything like that?"

"The feeling of it. I'd keep it and never use it for nothing. Just liked the silky feeling when I was a kid." It was the same with Gacy's masturbating with the panties. It wasn't that the panties had sexual meaning to him. He just liked the feeling of them in his hand and on his body. To him, it was about simple comfort and quick release and not about fantasies or dreams.

During the time we spent at Cermak Hospital, Gacy's perception of me would vary, to say the least. Sometimes I was a friend. Sometimes he would lash out at me. Sometimes he saw me as a doctor. Sometimes he saw me as "dumb and stupid." Sometimes he saw me simply as someone who would bring him magazines or cut through the red tape at the hospital.

On the surface, of course, Gacy liked to portray himself as powerful and influential. And he seemed to be smooth, and occasionally suave. But there was always something ambivalent about Gacy, even when he spoke of those closest to him. Even when his mother, the person closest to him in the world, was ill, he couldn't express anything but the facts of her situation. Of these inconstant emotions, he was always unaware. There were periods when, even though he was incarcerated, he felt he could rule the world. These then alternated with feelings of being down. Gacy would say he was lonely and lost and confused. He even said he had lost all will to live. But I believe that's what he thought people expected him to say. Both his elation and his despondency were extreme. He never tried to hurt himself, but he sure talked a blue streak about how up or down he was. For a while, he would become suspicious, his face seeming to change subtly. Then he would flash that creepy smile of his and start gabbing again.

During one of our meetings, I gave Gacy a language test and asked him to characterize what was happening in these sentences: "Arthur threw the ball into the woods. Barbara was very angry."

Gacy made his answer into an elaborate story, beginning:

It seemed to me that Arthur and Barbara were playing ball and that Arthur threw the ball into the woods. She may have thought he did it on purpose. The [*sic*] again it may be that she was his mother, and thought that he was being disobedient. She may have told him not to throw it in the woods and he was showing that he was going to do what he wanted. There is a lot of things a person could take from the two sentences. Maybe is Arthur was too young to understand, that it was an accident. I can't see why she became very angry, unless she was drinking or not feeling well. Everyone is not perfact and can make mistakes. Barbara was very angry, maybe she missed the ball herself, and thats why she was mad. The question doesn't tell if Barbara was angry at Arthur, it just assumption. Maybe they are both older and the ball came into there backyard and instead of throwing it back he through it into the woods out of spite, and his wife got angry at his action, because he took such action.

Although Gacy had an above-average intellect, he lapsed into a very primitive mode of thought. His sentence structure disintegrated into thoughts propelled by such sheer impulse that they were disjointed. There was no focus, just a series of unconnected thoughts. A normal person would come up with a structured beginning, a middle, and an end to the story, maybe like this: Arthur threw the ball into the woods because he wanted to see Barbara's reaction. Barbara was very angry because Arthur had done this before. So Arthur went and got the ball and Barbara was happy again.

As I've mentioned, he did not know how to restrain himself verbally. Throughout much of his life, his impulses and his wishes were most likely experienced as stimuli coming from outside himself. It was almost as if he felt he were drowning when subjected to emotional complexity of any sort. He couldn't sit back, think, and come to a logical conclusion. When confronted with the complexity of others, he fell apart. He didn't think; he acted. He didn't pause; he pounced. For instance, if he thought a person to be "dumb and stupid" and the person didn't act that way, that same person might well become a victim.

One evening, I received a short note from Gacy saying, "Just thought I would drop this short note, and enclose my latest fan mail, as you can see he used the words dumb and stupid, just like I do." The note was anonymous and carefully written by hand. After expressing the hope that Gacy would be given the electric chair, the writer began to rant:

> You are dumb, you really are, you are real super-stupid and dumb since you were caught in all of those crimes you committed, no matter what you had before or what you were like before, you are real stupid, stupid, dumb. . . . You are, right now, royally, and always be dumb, you are really super, extra stupid, extra dumb. . . . You don't have enough sense or intelligence to be insane, you're too dumb to be that. You're too stupid to be crazy.

It was a haunting note, as though his abusive father were writing him, chastising him from the grave. But if it gave Gacy any pause, he didn't mention it. It was not in him to feel grieved by so complex an idea. It simply was something to add to a bland letter that mentioned trite facts about his lawyer, his sister, and his mother. (He never once mentioned Carol in letters, since they were divorced and he never saw her anymore.)

But there was nothing trite about what was about to come—the media circus of the Gacy trial itself. In a way, I dreaded the idea of it. The publicity, the newspaper and TV reporters, could very well distract me from my work. The press constantly indicated that Gacy's murders were homosexual crimes, and some even called Gacy an "avowed homosexual." It was a truly antigay tactic that was perpetuated throughout the trial and before, one that almost seemed to glory in leading readers to believe that murder was a punishment for homosexuality. At the same time, I was curious to see how it all played out. How would Gacy fare before the court? Would he sit quietly or break under the pressure? And how would the court and the jury react to what I had to say about the man who had become the world's most notorious serial murderer?

SEVEN

TAKING THE STAND AT THE GACY TRIAL

I t would be a first for me, my first experience as an expert witness in a high-profile criminal trial. As the trial date approached, it became clear that this would be a pivotal moment in my career as a forensic psychiatrist who researches serial murderers. Because of the surrounding publicity, I already guessed I'd gain access to many more serial murderers in the future. Gacy's attorneys had given me all the information they had. I had spoken at length to Gacy, and I felt I had seen enough and read enough information to testify that he was a disturbed person who could not have been considered normal. Furthermore, by studying him during this particular case I had learned a lot not only about Gacy but also about serial killers. What struck me most was that there was more than one person who was so similar to Richard Macek. Every time I saw Gacy, I thought to myself, This is like seeing Macek in a different body.

All these thoughts swirled around in my head as I was about to take the stand for the defense of John Wayne Gacy, in an effort not to free him, but to get him a life sentence as opposed to death by the electric chair.

Gacy's attorneys Sam Amirante and Robert Motta would do their best to convince the jury that Gacy's life should be spared because he was legally insane. A coterie of well-known psychiatrists for both the defense and the prosecution, each armed with at least slightly different points of view, was called to the stand to comment upon Gacy's state of mind prior to and during his crimes. But the quality of some of the psychiatric testimony at Gacy's trial made me wonder whether some psychologists and psychiatrists are simply hired guns. While I had gotten used to the boys clubs in law enforcement and accepted them as people who didn't really understand the medical community, the Gacy case brought up another barrier. I saw how petty men in the psychiatric community could be. If you didn't agree with them, the insults would fly and you'd become an instant enemy not only inside the courtroom but outside as well. It wasn't professional and I didn't like it, but that's the way it was.

As the trial began, the jury tried valiantly to make sense of the complicated individual that was Gacy, and the complex case that all the attorneys had concocted. But as the facts behind the murders became known to the jury, so did the finite aspects of the insanity defense. The state penal code held that "a person is not criminally responsible for conduct if at the time of such conduct, as a result of mental disease or defect, he lacks substantial capacity to appreciate the criminality of his conduct or to conform to the requirement of law." The law seemed fairly ambiguous to me, but after sixty hours with Gacy, it became evident to me that he was medically insane at the time of the killings. During this time, I was studying for a health law degree, so I was immersed in definitions and the philosophy of law. It not only led me to be privy to the way the law works, but it led me to understand the language of the law and how to use it when speaking to lawyers and law enforcement types. For the purpose of the Gacy case, the law defined mental disease or mental defect as something that didn't include "abnormality manifested only by repeated criminal or otherwise antisocial conduct." This means that simply because Gacy committed a series of murders didn't mean his lawyers had a basis for the insanity defense. Beyond this, the Illinois Supreme Court at the time said that evidence of a sociopathic personality, mental disease, or defect was not sufficient to establish the insanity defense. Furthermore, according to state law, the young lawyers had to prove that John Gacy was so overwhelmed by his mental disease that he didn't comprehend that what he was doing was criminal. It would be no easy task. (The insanity defense *does* work, but it works only occasionally. It worked for Ed Gein, for instance, who spent ten years in an mental institution before he was competent enough to stand trial. Gein was judged to be guilty of murder, but criminally insane. That's how he ended up in Mendota, where I met him, and not in jail.)

The Gacy courtroom itself was full of drama early on: the prosecuting lawyers postured; witnesses broke down; and in the gallery, parents of the victims grew woozy and sometimes fainted. Gacy himself sat there at the defense table, blank faced and rigid, his lawyers somewhat concerned about his heart, as he had been taken to the hospital earlier during his incarceration, feeling faint, his nose dripping blood. Some time later, when the defense began to call witnesses, the jury listened as victim and defense witness Jeff Rignall stated that Gacy could not have understood the law "because of the beastly ways he attacked me." Rignall, queasy in a recollection so detailed he must have reexperienced the attack in his mind, then lay his head on the witness stand and vomited. Rignall wept so incessantly that he had to be helped from the courtroom. Nonetheless, Amirante felt that Rignall had helped him begin to prove that Gacy was legally insane.

Amirante continued his efforts to bolster the insanity defense. He called clinical psychologist Thomas Eliseo as a witness for the defense. The expert on schizophrenia shocked the jury somewhat when he leaned forward and explained that Gacy was extraordinarily intelligent, in the top 10 percent of the population. After a minutely detailed look at various psychological tests he performed on John, Eliseo testified that Gacy should be "classified as a schizophrenic, classified as a paranoid." He went on to say that Gacy "is a borderline personality, a person who on the surface looks normal but has all kinds of neurotic, antisocial, psychotic illnesses." Certainly one of the more sympathetic witnesses, he explained that Gacy was a paranoid schizophrenic, someone who believes there are "constant dangers out there." People, at any time, could try to get you, wound you, even kill you, said Eliseo about Gacy's state of mind.

Big and brash, prosecutor William Kunkle dismissed the idea of insanity, bashing away at Eliseo, saying that if Gacy seemed normal, he must have *been* normal, not schizophrenic.

Psychiatrist Lawrence Freedman, then chairperson of the Institution of Social and Behavioral Pathology, was an accomplished professional whose vita itself was long, detailed, and impressive. He said that Gacy was primarily psychotic but also was neurotic, which he defined as a compulsion that bothered or saddened him, but one that didn't impair him from doing his day-to-day work. He said Gacy had no feeling for any of the people he killed and that he was obsessive and compulsive. While he admitted that he diagnosed Gacy as a paranoid schizophrenic, he would not go so far as to say Gacy was legally insane. Furthermore, under questioning from Kunkle, he said he had never seen John in a dissociated condition, a state in which two or more personalities are found to live within someone, personalities that reveal themselves at various times. While John often claimed he had different personalities that he assumed when engaged in killing, including that of a gruff police officer, Freedman seemed to be saying he never was witness to any of these personalities in the fifty hours that he spent diagnosing Gacy's condition.

Dr. Robert Traisman spoke to Gacy for only three and a half hours. Still, after administering a draw-the-person test (in which the patient is given a pad and pen and asked to sketch), he diagnosed Gacy as not feeling strongly about his masculine identity. He called Gacy an ambulatory schizophrenic, someone who, as Dr. Traisman theorized, would appear ordinary to most people who spoke to Gacy casually. But, in Traisman's opinion, Gacy was anything but normal.

Richard Rappaport, a forensic psychiatrist, spent sixty-five hours studying Gacy. Once on the stand, he told the court that there were no physiological problems with Gacy that would have led to mental illness. He *did* comment that Gacy had what's called an XXY chromosome arrangement. Also called Klinefelter's syndrome, this genetic mutation, discovered in the early 1970s, meant that Gacy was born with a supposed predisposition for acting badly and violently. It's a curious aberration said to occur anywhere between one in five hundred and one in one thousand births, and today, this theory of genetic anomaly has its critics. Otherwise, Dr. Rappaport called Gacy a borderline personality and agreed with Dr. Freedman's diagnosis. He also thought that John had great difficulty in forming a strong opinion; he would present all sides of an issue and would rarely come down firmly on one.

When Amirante questioned Dr. Rappaport, he said that John was a paranoid schizophrenic who was unable "to control his behavior at the time of each of those crimes." Dr. Rappaport was positive Gacy was powerless to "conform his conduct to the requirements of law." Dr. Rappaport was talking about the crime of murder. But you might ask, How could this be true if Gacy *could* conform to the rules and regulations of imprisonment? If he could function in prison, did that mean he wasn't insane? Not at all. Insanity doesn't mean the patient is running down the street, wild-eyed and naked, in utter chaos. Insanity doesn't mean the patient can't follow the rules. Imagine the most paranoid person in the world, for example, a person who swears all his neighbors are after him, a person who may kill somebody on the basis of a paranoid delusion. That same person is usually the consummate rule observer, an absolute stickler. He can still abide by the rules of a structured environment, and so could a serial killer like Gacy.

When it was his turn to ask questions, William Kunkle tried to rile Rappaport. But he couldn't. Rappaport stuck to his guns about Gacy's psychosis, even when Kunkle brought up the fact that Gacy conducted his contracting business on the phone while the dead body of Robert Piest was still in the room.

The time for my testimony came at 10 A.M. on Saturday, March 8. During the week prior to my appearance in court, I pored over my notes about John and immersed myself in the transcripts of our conversations. While Amirante and Motta met with me about the case, they did not coach me and they did not rehearse the questions that they would pose while I was a witness. (I certainly wouldn't have stood for any sort of instructions on what to say.) They did, however, ask me generally about my diagnosis.

We talked in the law office for a while about Gacy's mood, and finally Amirante asked, "Do you feel that, after examining him fully, that he is insane?"

"Yes, Sam, I do." And that was all he needed to hear.

Though I was mildly anxious about appearing in a trial with so much publicity attached, I was not a stranger to the process of testifying in a courtroom. I had spoken as a witness over 250 times in civil trials where my focus was to diagnose whether or not a person was mentally ill and required hospitalization. But there are two major differences between a civil trial and a criminal case. In interviews before a criminal trial, I tell the patient that whatever he says is not going to be held in confidence. And in a criminal trial the law is more complicated; I have to deal with the legal definition of insanity in addition to the medical definition.

Whether it's baking a pie or speaking before a group of people, once you've done it 250 times, you really don't worry about the process too much. Nevertheless, the whole world was looking at the goings-on at the trial, and that kind of attention is a little unsettling.

Since it was a Saturday, my husband accompanied me to the courtroom. For some reason, he was escorted to the defense table, where John flashed him a big, creepy smile. He was far more uneasy than I was; Gacy's murderous smile stayed with him for some time.

Walking to the stand, I felt a bit nervous. After the clerk swore me in, Motta, Amirante's quieter, mustached partner, began his queries. Once I sat down, the microphone at the stand was badly placed, so initially, those in the courtroom had some trouble hearing me. But once they adjusted the mike, I settled down.

"Doctor, what is your diagnosis of Mr. Gacy in psychiatric terms?" Motta put his hands in his pockets.

"In psychiatric terms, the diagnosis is mixed psychosis."

I began to explain that John Gacy exhibited portions of different mental diseases and symptoms. What was in Gacy's brain was a very complex network of mental disease, the various criteria of which I tried to detail for the court and for the jury.

"Now, with relation to Mr. Gacy, can you explain, firstly, what you mean by primitive psychotic defense mechanisms?"

"There is a defense called splitting, and that's where the ego detaches from reality. For example, in Mr. Gacy, this is shown by his lack of memory for certain things." By "certain things" I meant the killings themselves along with the recollection of portions of his own life. I added the idea that he had a grandiose view of himself, but his puffed-up nature was combined with significant feelings of inferiority, the same kind of cross some say a nerd would bear. So while he felt he could do anything well, he also felt he would never measure up because his father always called him "dumb and stupid." In addition, Gacy had a penchant for the psychological defense of projection. Painful ideas or rage that welled up from inside him were placed upon another person. That person, usually a victim, was then viewed as a terrible enemy. I then tried to explain the difficult concept of projective identification, where the person to whom Gacy was speaking became part of the killer, taking on his characteristics. Projective identification refers to a defense mechanism where one places blame for one's difficulties on others or attributes one's own unacceptable impulses and actions to others. First described by Freud in the Schreber case and later in Judge Daniel Schreber's autobiography *Memoirs of My Nervous Illness,* projective identification can arouse feelings of hostilities, persecutory delusions, suspiciousness, and hallucinations.

I also brought up John's perpetual hypochondriasis. Most everyone knows someone who constantly complains of illnesses that aren't really there. Lonely old Aunt Nellie might even magnify her pains to make them severe enough to garner some sympathy. Gacy constantly complainted that something was wrong with his body. In 1978, for instance, he was convinced he had leukemia. At other times, he was hospitalized and then said he had strokes and heart attacks—palpable delusions. It wasn't real at all, but he felt it was real. In reality, these were probably only fainting spells, certainly nothing that would keep him from working or from appearing in court. Such swooning often followed complaints of temperature changes. Gacy could walk from a warm room into a cold room and faint dead away.

Motta wanted more clarity. "Did he actually manifest symptoms of an illness that did not exist?"

"Yes, he did. There are symptoms that are called autonomic. It means that they are not under your physical control, like when you are nervous and your palms start to sweat. You are not telling your palms to sweat, but they do. And when you are really nervous, your heart starts pounding. You are not telling your heart to do this, but it is doing that because part of your nervous system is not under your control. It shows how anxiety can be manifested in your body."

Motta stroked his mustache. Then, he said, "Now as far as the second criteria that you have listed, aggression, expressed in polar attributes. Can you please explain that?"

"Such a person has within himself simultaneously a hateful and a powerful destructiveness but at the same time, an impotent or helpless or very vulnerable or weak kind of way of expressing aggression." It's the type of aggression that moves like lightning, rapidly and very dramatically. Gacy could be sweet as Ronald McDonald in his clown outfit, treating kids to Hershey's kisses. And within a fraction of a second, he could become like an inflamed, incensed animal, thoroughly out of control. Gacy never learned how to modulate his aggression as a child, and he never found a usable way, a way that was accepted by family and friends, to release his anger as an adult. For him, it was expelled as an explosion of no small proportion. It was an all-body aggression—he felt it everywhere, from his pumping heart to his joints to his very pores, which made the hair on his arms stand up. To understand this, take a look at Gacy's unrelenting torture of Jeff Rignall.

John learned from his father how to release aggression. His father was sometimes a silent if overly wary man who became the drunk who hid away in his basement and then without reason or warning lashed out, beating John physically. From this John learned that he could walk into a room like Dr. Jekyll and transform into Mr. Hyde, which is the way the father was described by his own family.

Motta wondered, "Is this something conscious that he did, or was it unconscious?"

"These are all unconscious, not under his control. It's like that autonomic nervous system. We can't tell it to do it. It's just there."

"You mean behavioral pattern can be just as uncontrolled as your palm sweating?"

"Yes, it can."

"You also think he has difficulty in maintaining object constancy. Explain that, please."

"I mean, it's like he doesn't see you as a separate individual. You are just part of him." More generally, it's a psychiatrist's term for the foundation of psychological structure.

In an effort to describe this more fully, I said to the court that Gacy had a problem with "maintaining intercohesiveness." Intercohesiveness is the ability to recognize the separateness of other people: your father, your mother, your friends, and what they are doing for you. If you recognize them as separate people, you have enough self-awareness to see that they love you or have a personality that likes thoughtful people, or gives you presents out of fondness, or makes you laugh when you're down. Since Gacy was not able to develop a separate and independent identity from others, he identified with parts of them. Outside, he was male. Inside, he was female, at least far more than he was a man.

"So is this also called confused sexual identity or—"

"Yes, and it can be a basis for what would be called bisexuality or various forms of homosexuality."

Motta asked me if I thought Gacy developed emotionally.

"He did not develop emotionally. He carried and has carried into his adult life the emotional life of an infant."

"His entire emotional makeup is that of . . ."

"An infant."

Even though John Gacy progressed intellectually and had an above-average IQ, these infantlike characteristics were, as an adult, expressed as cringes of doubt, quakes of total helplessness, falling apart, and, really, complete annihilation. His universe was rife with dark, shadowy persecutors. It was a world full of constant danger, a deep, endless world from which flowed paranoia. Overwhelming the murderer, paranoia was everywhere, as if it were a liquid pumped through Gacy's veins. Gacy had these prodigious, tangible fears, and he needed someone to protect him. Gacy identified with his own kind of powerful hero who could defend him from most kinds of persecution. Jack Hanley, his alter ego who was a police officer, took care of all sorts of things for John, protecting against his inner chaos and anxiety.

I said to the court that Hanley was Gacy's "safety mechanism."

"He wasn't using it to establish a multiple personality, was he?"

"That's too advanced. He was not using it for that purpose."

"He needed some need for protection."

"Safety, yes."

It was safety against the rest of the world.

But more, part of Jack Hanley, the Jack that Gacy called Bad Jack, was an asylum from Gacy's terrible explosiveness. It was he who held the key to explosive and murderous behavior. It was Bad Jack, not Gacy, who killed. Gacy was absolutely certain he knew a Jack Hanley well. When investigators finally tracked down James Hanley, the cop from a hit-and-run unit who worked out of 54 West Hubbard Street, Hanley said he merely was a patron at a restaurant where Gacy was a cook in 1971. To Hanley, they were not friends at all. To Gacy, Hanley was one of the most important people he'd every met. He fantasized about him. He made him part of himself. He *was* Hanley, a warrior-like Hanley he created from somewhere deep inside of his being.

When Gacy's feelings overwhelmed him, his psychological state wasn't stable. The minimal controls he had were shaky, and the violent acts took over. And all of this could take place within moments. Emotions and feelings changed rapidly for Gacy, and he didn't have enough internal structure to keep track of what was happening, let alone prevent it. He became disorganized, unable to perceive what transpired in even the most familiar of environments. His perception of others became grossly inconsistent and extremely variable. When I examined Gacy, he was often unaware that he contradicted himself from one sentence to the next.

Motta asked, "You mean there's consistency to his inconsistency?"

"Yes, because of the way he sees the world . . . there is an incapacity to really relate to other people."

John Gacy did not see people with any sense of reality. They were not well-rounded or complex and they had no variety of traits and qualities. To Gacy, all people were dumb and stupid.

I said to the court, "[For Gacy] there is no way of viewing another person in their complexity. I mean, people to him are inanimate objects. They have no life to them."

Finally, Motta tried to ask me whether or not all of these conditions made John Gacy kill.

"Objection!" cried Kunkle for the prosecution, and Judge Garippo sustained the objection. Motta was annoyed but tried again, and Kunkle still had a problem with the sentence's construction. Then, in a long and detailed but careful question that went on for seventy-eight words, Motta rephrased his wording, and the court permitted me to speak.

"My opinion is that Mr. Gacy has been suffering from a mental disease over a period of time . . . from at least 1958 to the present time and continually with his mental disease called mixed psychosis."

To end the questioning, Motta asked me whether Gacy lacked "substantial capacity to appreciate the criminality of his conduct at the time of each of the alleged acts."

"Because of the mental disease that Mr. Gacy had, he was unable to appreciate and conform his conduct during each of the acts." In other words, I believed he was medically insane when he committed each and all thirty-three of his grisly murders.

On cross-examination, prosecution team member Robert Egan, dressed in a new three-piece suit with a thick-knotted striped tie, forcefully made clear to the court that he believed a person who could plan and kill thirty-three times was aware of what he was doing.

"The fact that he drove Robert Piest to his home would not change your opinion as to the psychosis at that time, correct?"

"No, it would not."

"The fact that he coerced Robert Piest into being handcuffed would not change your opinion, correct?"

"That's correct."

"And the fact that he answered the telephone and spoke with a business associate immediately after murdering Robert Piest would not change your opinion. Is that right?"

"It would not."

"By the way, do you think that under the circumstances, John Gacy would have killed Robert Piest if there was a uniformed police officer in the home with him at the time?"

"Yes, I do." I made it as clear as I could that I felt Gacy could not control his actions. Gacy would have done what he did if the president of the United States were there with him at the time.

After two tense and fairly exhausting hours, it was over. After a brief recess, my husband and I left the court building through a side exit, avoiding the swarms of TV cameras and reporters.

While the defense had concluded their case, the prosecution had just begun. Donald Voorhees took the stand, but he was so plagued by his encounter with Gacy, that he took a long time to answer each question and more than once broke down on the witness stand. Dr. Leonard Heston, a professor of psychiatry who spoke to Gacy in 1968, said that Gacy suffered from no mental problems whatsoever. Instead, according to Heston, he was merely antisocial and possessed a character flaw that made him want to kill.

Robert Donnelly testified that Gacy had plied him with drinks, shackled him, jumped on top of him, and took off his pants. "He went and he got on top of me and I could tell that he didn't have any pants on because I could feel his knees, and he, he put his knees between my legs and grabbed my shoulders." Donnelly couldn't take it. He stuttered painfully and collapsed amid a torrent of tears.

Gacy suddenly stirred in his chair. He gripped the table and sat up as straight as his corpulent body would permit. In a move that surprised everyone, he rolled his eyes and laughed out loud so the jury could hear him. It was not the first inappropriate comment he would make when a witness was on the stand. Was there something deep down within him that told him that these actions would help his insanity case? Or was he so steamed by Robert's testimony that he felt he had to defend himself by verbally mocking the witness? Whatever John's feelings, his outburst certainly could not help his cause.

The court took a break, and when Donnelly returned, somewhat composed, he described the rape. He testified that Gacy banged his head against the wall and intermittently put his head into the bathtub full of water until he could not breathe. He kept Donnelly's head under until Donnelly became unconscious.

Then it happened again. Gacy snickered aloud. While John told his lawyers that he thought that his outburst would counter what he saw as the outrageously overblown nature of Donnelly's testimony, some in the jury must have taken it as laughter at the boy himself, as though a demon were gloating over his handiwork. The reason for Gacy's shenanigans was simpler, in my opinion. In the courtroom, he was experiencing a lack of the familiar structure he'd become so accustomed to in prison. Gacy couldn't hold back and erupted in a way that he shouldn't have.

Longtime chief psychologist for the circuit court of Cook County A. Arthur Harmon indicated that Gacy was merely antisocial, who, like other antisocial personalities, lied his way through life. When called to the stand, Harmon's colleague Dr. Robert Reifman made no bones about it. He said that Gacy was lying, making up things to lead the jury to think he was insane. There was one succinct comment that the jury would remember in particular. In terms plain and certain, Reifman stated, "I don't believe you can have thirty-three cases of temporary insanity."

Dr. James Cavanaugh from St. Luke's Medical Hospital in Chicago really uttered something to the jury that I thought was highly inappropriate and outside his purview as a forensic clinician. Fully anticipating the bombshell to come, Kunkle asked if Gacy were to be confined to a mental hospital, would he stay there for all of his life?

"Absolutely impossible," said Cavanaugh flatly. Cavanaugh apparently believed that John could be somehow cured and readmitted to society. That *never* would have happened. I thought it was unprofessional for Cavanaugh even to make such a prediction. It was highly prejudicial, more like a comment that a lawyer for the prosecution would make than something that would come from the mouth of a supposedly unbiased expert in psychiatry. But don't forget, he was hired by the prosecution, and he became the prosecution. Cavanaugh had seriously overstepped his boundaries, and the judge ordered the jury to disregard this testimony.

Was Gacy a cold-blooded criminal who plotted his crimes and knew precisely what he was doing or was he legally insane, driven by urges that he would never be able to control?

I don't think any of the defense lawyers or even John Gacy himself believed that the jury would return a verdict of insanity. Though I knew Gacy suffered from mixed psychosis and was medically insane at the time of the murders, I was certainly a realist. The gravity of his crimes, the rampant media attention, and the work of the prosecuting attorneys all combined to make an impression on the jury. In addition, I felt in my heart that there were too many psychologists and psychiatrists on the case. It was a matter of "too many cooks who spoiled the broth." Even though many tried their best to speak in layman's terms, some were full of scientific terms and theories that would bore, frighten, or annoy the average person on the jury.

Summing up the case, prosecutor Terry Sullivan called Gacy "an evil, vile and diabolical man, a sadistic animal." Further, he called Gacy, "a rat, mean, vile, base, and diabolical . . . the personification of evil . . . insanely evil." And then there was this exaggeration: "John Gacy has accounted for more human devastation than many earthly catastrophes." It was one heck of a sideshow.

Dramatic in his own way, the five-foot-two Sam Amirante read passages from Robert Louis Stevenson's *Dr. Jekyll and Mr. Hyde* to support his views. He stood straight and read clearly, "If I am the chief of sinners, then I am the chief of sufferers." Then he pled with the jury, saying, "John Gacy is a madman who has been reaching out, saying, 'Stop me before I kill again.'" Imploring the jury to see the defense's side of the case, he beseeched them to return the verdict of not guilty by reason of insanity. He said Gacy should be studied to discover scientific answers to the quandary that was his brain so that others might be prevented from committing such unfathomable violence.

On Wednesday, March 12, 1980, the jury moved behind closed doors to decide the case. Within 120 minutes and after 108 witnesses and testimony that lasted twenty-eight days, the twelve members met and agreed unanimously to convict John Wayne Gacy of thirty-three murders. In merely two hours, they emerged with their verdict written on a piece of paper. In the courtroom, resounding applause and cheers rang out from victims and their families. Gacy's reaction to the jury's decision was not unexpected; the convicted murderer began to blame others for his failure to win a life sentence because of insanity. He blamed his lawyers; he blamed the jury; he blamed the government; he blamed the whole judicial and political system.

It would do Gacy no good to blame, and his attempts at appeal would go nowhere. For me, if there was blame to be cast, it had nothing to do with what went on within the trial itself. Though I had heard it from Rignall and others before, after the trial it became clear: if the police had done their job properly, many of the murders would not have happened.

Jeff Rignall said the police were so uncooperative that he had to help track down the killer himself, carefully looking for clues to his identity, waiting interminably in a car with friends for Gacy's car to pass by. Police actually told Rignall to wait until Gacy was stopped for some other offense; then they might look into his complaints. And even when Gacy was finally apprehended for the brutal treatment of Rignall, the state's attorney decided against seeking a conviction. Rignall felt he was the victim of what was, at the time, an antihomosexual police department, and I'm not so sure he was totally mistaken. Robert Donnelly ran into a similar roadblock, and police preferred to believe Gacy's story that the torturous encounter was a sexual romp agreed upon by both. John Syzc's family was told their son, one of Gacy's early victims, was simply a runaway, and the case proceeded no further. When confronted with a victim's disappearance, police sometimes wouldn't even check to see if Gacy had any prior arrest record (like the conviction and imprisonment in Iowa). All of this prompted victim John Butkovich's father to exclaim, "If the police had only paid attention to us they might have saved many lives . . . they can't put two and two together." Young John Butkovich was one of Gacy's first victims, and he was killed back in late July of 1975.

And the police? Their excuse was that they were burdened by too many missing persons cases. Citing the statistic that in 1977 nearly seven thousand missing Chicagoans were under the age of seventeen, law enforcement seemed to say "Don't blame me." There was a continuing and distinct danger in Chicago in 1980: if Chicago police didn't improve their computers and information systems, more serial killers in the Chicago area would roam wild and unfettered. Those who ran law enforcement in Chicago also needed to be far more receptive to minorities and those with nonconventional lifestyles. Prejudice and racism have no place in a police precinct or in a courtroom.

As I thought about the police, I later reviewed my transcripts of conversations with Gacy. Strangely, Gacy had one more group he needed to blame, those who were the most innocent, the victims. "Look at Jeff Rignall's book," began Gacy, revving up. "He claims in July he came back to my house with a friend of his in a van. He came to the house and leaned against the railing. There is no railing. He claims he rang the doorbell and waited for my mother to come to answer the door. There is no doorbell at my house.

"He says he was tied, that somebody was poking his zozo up his ass while a blond-headed guy was giving him a blow job. I never got into three-way sex. He also claims that he can identify me because I have stretch marks. Why, I can show you right now. I don't have no stretch marks. Even when I was heavier, I didn't have any stretch marks."

His offer rankled me, and I quickly declined it.

But so it went, monotonously, illogically, as Gacy endlessly tried to make himself out to be the one who was abused. He even planned to write his own book, boldly called *The Thirty-fourth Victim*. John felt he had an answer for everything. Often they were explanations that didn't make sense.

The day the trial ended, my husband and I went home to relax. I put the world of lawyers and witnesses and the law itself out of my mind. I dismissed the unprofessional manner of some of the witnesses in the case, like Cavanaugh, who rudely had said I didn't know what I was talking about. That's the way some of these guys are, but I resolved never to be so undignified.

Depicted in this antiquated Romanian wall drawing is Vlad Tepes. "Vlad the Impaler" is often labeled a serial murderer because he was responsible for killing thousands in the 1400s. But I don't believe he was a serial killer at all, as you'll discover. (© BY REUTERS NEWMEDIA INC./CORBIS)

Albert Fish stunned Manhattan in the 1920s with the killing and cannibalism of young Gracie Budd (the remains of which police search for here). An X ray later revealed Fish had stuck pins and needles into his groin area. (© BY BETTMANN/CORBIS)

The affable-looking Ed Gein made an ashtray of a woman's skull and fashioned a suit of her skin, which he wore. But when I met with him at the Mendota Mental Health Institute, he was all used up and ready to die. (© BY BETTMANN/CORBIS)

(Left) Richard Macek was labeled "The Mad Biter" by the media. This photo of one of his deep bite marks on a victim shows why.

(Opposite) Richard Macek sent me many letters, but one of the most startling was this one, in which he suddenly confused me with his wife.

Dr. Morrison   Time 12:45 A.M.   6-9-77

I just received your letter. I hope and trust that your trip was pleasant and beneficial.

Somehow some way our wires are getting crossed. I do want to see you. I want to see you very badly. More than you can imagine!

I find letters are useless in my case. And I'm sure our visit will be just as useless if we can not have personal contact like we did at the Hospital and privately.

I'm becoming unstable! My headaches are increasing and more stronger than before. They are on the right side of my head. My temper blows sky high. And my head feels like it is or wants to burst. I get dizzy and break out into sweats. My strength seams to increase 3 to 4 times. Now I recall I had similar incidents long ago. But I don't recall what happened at those times. Puzzled-Confused!!

Remember me and my own ideas, and thoughts of tests experiments ect? An analysis of treatments what I need ect to help myself. This place this jail, this cage I'm living in is getting to me! These Klods and ect are getting to much for me. I need to be in a Hospital for a week or 10 days or so to collect myself. And I need you so very much! I trust and have faith in you. I need to see you as much as possible. But you see, I'm just Klodding myself. I can talk and tell you of what I feel, I don't know whatever. But who would listen or who cares? But with the exception of you, of course! But with the exception of you, of course! I mean the children. I need them so very much! I'm very

very lonely without you and the children. I guess there doesn't seem to be much for me to say for now. And then I guess it doesn't matter anyway. You never answer any of my letters anymore. You know it's been a year since I have seen you and the children. Why? Why are you doing this?

Be good. Remember daddy loves his little girl very very much! Give my love to the children for me. And my love to you always.

Love Your Husband
Richard

P.S. XOXOXO
     XOXOXO
     XOXOXO a Barrel of them.

On the surface, this landscape painting by John Gacy seems perfectly realistic and cheery. On closer examination, the perspective is off kilter, somewhat like Gacy's mind.

WEST VIRGINIA
LAW REVIEW

ARTICLES

THE CONSTITUTION OF THE BUREAUCRATIC STATE   Mark Tushnet

CUSTOMER, COERCION AND CONGRESSIONAL INTENT:
REGULATING SECONDARY CONSUMER BOYCOTTS UNDER   Larry S. Bush
THE NATIONAL LABOR RELATIONS ACT

PEOPLE OF THE STATE OF ILLINOIS VS. JOHN GACY: Donald H.J. Hermann
THE FUNCTIONING OF THE INSANITY DEFENSE AT THE   Helen L. Morrison
LIMITS OF THE CRIMINAL LAW   Yvonne Sor
                                                      Julie A. Norman
                                                      David M. Neff

NOTES

THE PERSONAL RESIDENCE: DISPOSITION ALTERNATIVES

THE FREELANCER'S TRAP: WORK FOR HIRE UNDER THE
COPYRIGHT ACT OF 1976

INDEX TO VOLUME 86

Volume 86   Summer 1984   Number 4

PEOPLE OF THE STATE OF ILLINOIS VS. JOHN GACY: THE FUNCTIONING OF THE INSANITY DEFENSE AT THE LIMITS OF THE CRIMINAL LAW

DONALD H.J. HERMANN*
HELEN L. MORRISON**
YVONNE SOR***
JULIE A. NORMAN****
DAVID M. NEFF*****

I. INTRODUCTION

The conviction of John Gacy in 1980 of 33 counts of murder demonstrates the limits of the criminal law in a number of significant ways. As one of the state's prosecuting attorneys put it: "John Gacy now had the singular notoriety of having been convicted of more murders than anyone in American history."[1] Mass murder itself involves crime at the outermost extreme of prohibited conduct. Homicide, the most serious criminal offense, is multiplied. At the same time, this case demonstrates the limits of the criminal justice system in providing protection for the citizen. For four years boys and young men literally disappeared from the streets of Chicago and its suburbs without any serious efforts by the police to determine their whereabouts.[2] Family members and friends of the missing persons were unable to induce effective investigation, and other victims were unable to persuade authorities to instigate prosecutorial action.[3] Even with the conviction of Gacy, the criminal law has been pushed to the limit in its efforts to fashion a proper disposition for this offender. Given the psychiatric evaluation of Gacy neither a final sentence nor a program of treatment for a mentally disordered offender may be adequate or appropriate. The case suggests the need to consider the possibility of permanent isolation and incapacitation of dangerous persons who are not treatable nor rehabilitable, nor properly subject to execution.

A case like John Gacy's is most often not the subject of study in a legal

* Judicial Fellow of United States Courts, 1983-1984. Professor of Law and Professor of [Philosoph]y, DePaul University. A.B., Stanford University, 1965; J.D., Columbia University, 1968; LL.M., [   ] University, 1974; M.A., Northwestern University, 1979; Ph.D., Northwestern University, 1981.
** M.D., Medical College of Pennsylvania at Philadelphia, 1972. Currently director of the [   ] Center in Chicago, Illinois. The Center assesses physical and emotional brain function. Cer[tified by th]e American Board of Psychiatry and Neurology in General Psychiatry and Child Psychiatry; [   ] Board of Forensic Psychiatry. Member, American Psychiatric Association; American [Psychoanal]ytic Association; American Academy of Psychiatry and Law; American Academy of Forensic [   ]
[   ]B.A., B.S., Mundeleine College, 1970; M.S., Northwestern University, 1982; J.D. DePaul [University, 1]983. Teaching Fellow DePaul University.
[   ]B.A., Northeast Missouri University, 1967; J.D. DePaul University, 1984.
***** B.S., Northwestern University, 1982; J.D. (candidate), DePaul University, 1985.

[1] T. SULLIVAN & P. MAIKEN, KILLER CLOWN: THE JOHN WAYNE GACY MURDERS 340-41 (1983).
[2] See, C. LINEDECKER, THE MAN WHO KILLED BOYS 216-17 (1980).
[3] See generally Behind Growing Worry Over Runaway Youths, 86 U.S. NEWS AND WORLD REPORT 63 (Jan. 15, 1979).

The lengthy article I cowrote in the *West Virginia Law Review* was a turning point in my research career. My profile of John Gacy began to change the way people think about serial murderers and the insanity defense.

Dear Dr. Morrison,

Just a short note to let you and your
Staff know that I received the 12 Magazines
Thanks much for sending them, always enjoy
reading them. Nothing new to tell you,
waiting to hear from my last letter to you.
Note, that Pam Lane, is not what I thought
she was, I asked Harlan, and he told me
that I had it wrong, she is a family
psychologist, lives in a suburb of Dallas,
called Grapevine. He gave me her full
address, in case I wanted to talk to her
myself. Talked with Karen, she is just out
of the hospital, with back surgery, will be
layed up 4 to 6 weeks. Mother is getting
forgetful again to the point of not taking
her medication, and who people are in the
house. I haven't heard from her since the
end of January. Well I will close again, Thanks, for Magazines.

Like the beacon of the lighthouse, Your love reaches me.

Arise, shine; for thy light is come, and the
glory of the Lord is risen upon thee.

Isaiah 60:1

Gacy was fond of sending greeting cards. In this one, painted by jewel thief Murph the Surf, Gacy's typewritten comments show no emotion, even when he talks about his sick mother. The card's inscription, "Your love reaches me," is ironic to say the least.

This wedding photo shows Gacy playing the role of devoted husband and loving son. No one in his family knew that John had a dark, murderous side.

Police involved in the Wayne Williams child murders pulled this unfortunate victim from the muddy Chattahoochee River at midnight on April 1, 1981. When I spoke out about the Williams case before he was apprehended, I was greeted by much anger and hostility.

Serial killers sometimes psychologically overpower their partners, as Alton Coleman did with girlfriend Debra Brown. The "partnership killers" went on a killing spree in 1984 and even used Vise-Grip pliers on the head and face of one victim. (© BY BETTMANN/CORBIS)

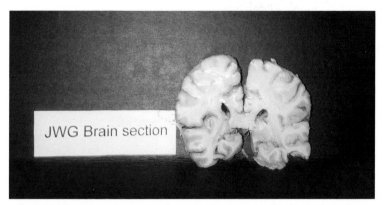

John Gacy's brain was given to me for scientific purposes after he died. I've kept pieces of it for many years in a plastic container.

DATES	DRUGS FOR SUBMISSION	TORTURE ACTS	SEX ACTS	TODD'S RESPONSE	BERDELLA'S COMMENTS; OBSERVATIONS; AND CARE
Tuesday 6-17-86 7:50 PM			Front fuck (C pg 449)	Some grunts from him and muscle contraction in his stomach area (C pg 449)	
8:00 PM	Ketamine 1cc neck (C pg 449)			Lying on his side sighing, some oral discharge. His eyes blank. (C pg 449)	"I don't know if it's classified as vomiting, but regurgitating something—regurgitating on a more passive level, bringing stuff up into the mouth and then just pouring out of the mouth." (C pg 449)
8:20 PM			Butt fuck (C pg 449)	Grunts, no muscle reaction (C pg 449)	
8:45 PM		EKG's to the legs (C pg 449)		No oral discharge, no oral vocalization (C pg 449)	
9:15 PM		Started to bend his fingers and hands (C pg 449)	Front Fuck (C pg 449)	No reaction (C pg 449)	
9:45 PM		Finger sodomy; EKG to the legs and back (C pg 450)		No reaction (C pg 450)	"I have a notation here Loose which I guess would just refer to anal wall. Referring to the eyes; at this point I was trying to blind him. As far as the EKG; his muscles would have tightened up but it was not a movement that he made; it was just the electricity" (C pg 450-1)
10:30 PM		EKG to the eye (C pg 450)	Front Fuck (C pg 451)		Blind him to disable him as far as any long-term captivity. "I might make a notation here, a footnote. At this time his body was not only dealing with chemicals that I was putting into it, but also the chemicals that he injected himself with. One of the most noticeable effects was that while in a position where he was totally tranquilized, he got an erection. I guess the excitement or energy had gone to his penis." (C pg 451)
11:00 PM		EKG to legs (C pg 452)	Cucumber fuck (C pg 452)	First movements were in his hands and back area (C pg 452)	"Just that he was either finding out that he was restricted or that there was some kind of movement into the hands and back area." (C pg 452)
11:15 PM				He was trying to lift his head (C pg 452)	
11:45 PM	Ketamine 1.5 cc neck (C pg 452)			Some grunts (C pg 452)	

-3-

In this page from Robert Berdella's crime diary, he chronicles his torture objectively, coldly.

Dreams.

3-29-85   5·Am

die never had a dream like this before it
involved me having some sort of pro
blem with my lower lip and chin
I was with a woman, Cindy I
think, living with her and one
day my lip and chin were so
swollen up and ...
lip. It was aw...
worse, I got to
talk, eat, or an...
hurt like hell.
    It terrified me
what was wrong
worse and worse
finally woke up
realistic I ...
make sure it ...
was real relieved

I havent had ...
Sometimes I ...
and can almost ...
not quite.
If things like ...
to remember the...

Bobby Joe Long wrote to me about his dreams, but the content of his letters was not so different from those I received from other serial killers. Even in his dreams he was overly concerned with being sick.

CINDY AND HOLLY ARE SUPPOSED TO COME
SEE ME NEXT WEEKEND. I HOPE SO.
AND I HOPE I CAN BE NICE TO THEM
    ITS VERY WIERD TO SEE OR TALK TO AN
ONE FROM THE REAL WORLD. ITS LIKE A
THAT WAS A DREAM OR A BOOK, AND
THAT IVE ALWAYS BEEN IN JAIL.
    ITS NOT A GOOD FEELING TO KNOW MY
LIFE IS OVER. TO KNOW THAT AT THE VER
BEST I'LL BE LOCKED UP LIKE AN ANI-
MAL THE REST OF MY LIFE. ALL BECAUSE
I KILLED A BUNCH OF SLUTS AND WHORE
AND I DON'T EVEN KNOW-WHY?
    VERY HARD TO COPE WITH, AND NOBODY
MAKES ANY EFFORT TO MAKE IT ANY
EASIER.
    MAYBE ONCE I GET ON D.R. AND SET-
TLED IN, I'LL BE BETTER. FEEL BET-
TER.
    I DON'T LIKE FEELING LIKE THIS,
AND IF I HAVE TO, I'LL STAY ON
AS MUCH MED. AS I CAN.
    WHEN THEY PROCESS ME 'IN', I'LL BE
SURE TO EMPHASIZE THAT I NEED
MEDICATION.
    MY BRAIN HURTS.
    I FEEL WEAKER THAN I CAN EVER
REMEMBER FEELING BEFORE. IF I
COULD GET ABOUT 24 HOURS SLEEP,
I'D BE FINE. I'M SURE.
    NOT HERE THOUGH. THESE CLOWN LIKE

Eventually, Bobby Joe Long began to write to me in capital letters in an odd combination of anger against his victims, desperation, self-pity, hypochondria, even hope.

Later that evening, we went out and enjoyed dinner and a movie. John Wayne Gacy, shackled yet defiant, turned to Illinois's death row as his new home, a not-so-welcoming place where he would exist, and sometimes endure physical attacks, for many years.

It was an ugly, barren place. At the points where State Road 150 and Kaskaskia Street intersect, the 125-year-old building was a combination of federal and Greek Revival–style architecture, and it sat not far from some railroad tracks, where weeds poked out from under the gravel. Under clouds and in the heavy Illinois rain, the brown brick facade with its forbidding four-pillar front looked something like the gaping mouth of a haunted mansion. A few blocks away ran a particularly dull stretch of the Mississippi River, a river that John Wayne Gacy could not see. Inside the grim structure, Gacy (along with about fifty others) waited for either an answer from the courts for his appeal or a quick death by injection, a change from the electric chair to which he was originally sentenced.

Most of the lawyers and psychiatrists ignored Gacy once there no longer was a paycheck to be cashed. One or two of the doctors tried to get more information from Gacy for their books, but they didn't get very far. Robert Egan, one of the prosecutors in the case, took a kind of sideshow on the road, with slides and a black-humor-filled speech, to titillate the cultlike fanatics who attended horror movie conventions.

For myself, I felt there was more to be gained medically and scientifically from a long-term study of Gacy, and I kept up a research relationship that lasted for more than a decade. I asked John to begin writing down his dreams, and his first note about his dreams read:

went to bed at 21:35. 01:53 woke up semi-wake urinated Dreaming about time schedule woke up for breakfast

Dreaming about a parade through a cemetary with big bands and colorful formation just so these two rich people would get married kinda like boy meets girl

The people at the wedding and the funeral were people I knew from garamar school and high school.

It seems that I was bringing them all together. The parade was through big beautiful garden all neet and shaped perfect. With alot of musical background.

Despite Gacy's ragtag note, the content of which really didn't mean anything when I didn't have other dreams to compare it with, I believed a diary of dreams might lead to more clues about his condition. I urged him to send more dream journals through the mail, but he never did. Maybe the things he did remember were too horrible to write down. Maybe he was just lazy. Over the years, he did, however, send volumes of letters, mostly carefully typewritten and often double spaced.

Perhaps to compensate for the rape and rope-filled horrors he forgot or could not remember, Gacy paid obsessive attention to detail in these notes. In June 1983, he wrote to me, saying,

> During the month of May, I received 143 pieces of mail, and sent out 59 pieces. During 1982, I received 1167 pieces . . . out of 8,760 hours in the year (1982) I was out of my cell 2,274 hours and 20 minutes. I sent out 568 pieces of mail, took 353 showers, blood pressure taken 16 times, and out of 1095 meals served, I ate 463 . . . Today marks the 39th month here.

Like Richard Macek, he took to the organization required by his jailers, and his work as a contractor came in handy.

> I have been busy with plastering and painting. They changed the visiting area, and I was going to do the remodeling, but after thinking about it, told them that they would have to do it by there other crew. See I don't mine doing work for them, but building security areas is not in keeping with the inmate code, and I would only have problems with it . . . After they built it I took over and did the taping and plastering, now all I got is the painting to do.

Gacy convinced the authorities to paint it sky blue.

Shortly after he was sentenced to death row, John Gacy began to paint on canvas. They generally were of clowns like Pogo, the scary entertainer with a frightening, distorted mouth Gacy became when, as a free man, he mugged and joked for children. Additionally, he drew the thorn-crowned head of Jesus Christ, the occasional landscape, and the Seven Dwarfs, which the Walt Disney company immediately asked him to cease doing. He did indeed listen and stopped painting versions of the artwork called *Hi-ho, Hi-ho*. He sent to me country and rural scenes, which I hung in my office. In two years, he had painted over 250 works and earned nearly $10,000 selling them. During this time, a government worker caused quite a stir by purchasing one of Gacy's works, especially when it was discovered that the employee who made the purchase was Mars Kennedy, the governor's photographer. Governor James Thompson tried to order John's drawings removed from the Illinois State Fair, where a 500-piece display of inmate art was featured, but his decree came too late: all of John's six paintings sold quickly.

I wasn't interested in whether they sold or not, nor was I interested in the reason Gacy painted them (which he said was out of boredom, not out of an artistic sensibility). When I looked closely at the amateur paintings Gacy sent to me, I was completely intrigued by what they seemed to say about his internal state. In a letter to John on January 18, 1984, I wrote, "Although you can see something in real life, what you paint seems to come from inside and some of the depression and despair as well as the anger [you feel] comes through in the painting." For me, the comment was like a move on a chessboard. I wanted to see if Gacy would object or even deny my suggestions of depression, despair, and anger. Instead, he just ignored the words in his reply.

Gacy's painting of a lake and mountain landscape looked like something between unschooled folk art and near photo-realism. In the forefront, the lake and evergreens first appeared primitive. And the snowcapped mountain in the background seemed somehow hyperreal. On closer examination, however, many evergreen trees were colored wrong in orange and yellows and reds, as though they were deciduous trees in the fall, and their branches pointed erectly upward, as though they were made of iron and the sky were magnetic. The painting showed that Gacy perceived the world much differently than most other painters, schooled or unschooled. Looking closer still, I noticed that the shadows are backward, opposite to where the sun would cast them. It was just like Gacy the person. On first glance, the person seemed fine, nice, almost cheery. But peering at the inside, into the grim underbelly, he was all off-kilter.

During his time on death row, Gacy became known as "Boss Hogg," after the moonshining, politically corrupt banker police commissioner on the *Dukes of Hazzard* comedy show. Outwardly, it was a perfect sobriquet for the jowly Gacy, who, like the TV show character, smoked as many as fifteen cigars a day and was exceedingly portly. Which is not to say his demeanor appealed to most of the prison population. Gacy wrote to me, saying,

> Last week I came on one guy in the library, who wanted me to go into the back room to talk with him, with four more backing him up. Now, I informed the captain ahead of him, that I had been threaten by this individual, but they just say to go in and kick his ass. . . . While I am not afraid of him, I am afraid of myself. I don't believe in fighting, never have, but if I have to set an example, then someone will get killed. I told [the guy] which side of me does he want to talk too, and which side of me does he want to fight with. He didn't answer, just walked away. But sooner or later that's not going to work. I am afraid I am going to hurt someone. Because once it starts, I will have no control over it.

There was no doubt in my mind that Gacy would never have started something. He was able to respond positively to externals in prison like the guards and the rules, and he was glad to sublimate his impulses, the thoughts or triggers that would induce him to anger and kill. In prison, he knew what his boundaries were, and he adhered to them without fail. Again, it's worth noting that his adherence to prison rules is not evidence that Gacy was sane. He simply had no access to potential victims, to his black Oldsmobile, to Bughouse Square, or to any of the familiar things that may have helped to trigger his attacks. And even if he did want to kill, he didn't have the tools—no rope, no way to drug his victims. He was prison-rule-bound, and that was a good thing.

Occasionally, Gacy was attacked by inmates during scuffles in which he'd be, say, stabbed by a prisoner wielding a sharpened pencil. Gacy wrote to me, complaining, "It got me in the left arm and went in about an inch and a half. I lost a lot of blood, but they replaced it in the hospital. . . . While I am not mad, which I don't understand, I think that he is an animal." Gacy also felt that the prisoner wanted publicity, saying, "I guess he thinks he can get it with me." He was probably right; anyone who attacked Gacy would be looked upon as a hero within the prison. And in this way with a combination of fear, hypochondria, and monotony, the years passed for John Gacy.

Outside, as the clock ticked toward midnight on May 9, 1994, a crowd of hundreds waited. Some prayed reverently while others drank and partied as though they were at a rock concert. Inside, a prison worker took six straps to secure the country's (and arguably the world's) most notorious serial killer to a gurney. Grumbling family members of the victims were forced into a basement room, not to view the execution but to watch the news carried live on a local TV station—as if they hadn't had enough of that. John Wayne Gacy had consumed a meal of fried chicken, shrimp, and strawberries that cost taxpayers about eighteen dollars. On the day before, he was surrounded by his family. Even the two children by his first wife, Marlynn, came to speak to him one last time. Having said his farewells, Gacy was a motormouth to the very end, chiding the warden in the death chamber. "Taking my life won't compensate for the lives of others. This is only a state murder." It was almost as if he hadn't been able to make the connection between his murders and his punishment.

Two needles were placed into his arm (an extra needle in case the first didn't work). A team of prison personnel (licensed doctors are not allowed to do this) monitored Gacy's heart. Just as a slow saline drip began to flow intravenously into his arm, a curtain rose and the witnesses were revealed in an adjoining room. Into his right arm, a double dose of the anesthetic sodium pentothal put John Wayne Gacy to sleep in a matter of moments. Briefly, he strained, moaned, gasped. His hands, tightened into pudgy fists, went limp. Pancuronium bromide made his muscles stiff, and as his breathing ceased, potassium chloride halted the murderer's heart. Death had long stalked Gacy and finally won, with some help from the anesthetic overdose and the respiratory and cardiac arrest, which occurred while Gacy was asleep. Almost three dozen witnesses began talking in hushed tones as they saw Gacy in his dead pallor.

Gacy was gone. No more would he torture, no more would he rape and kill, no more would he choke or drown his victims. And though I had known him for more than a dozen years, I had no remorse about his passing. As a doctor, if you carry around every individual you have ever worked with, you can't function. It's not easy to learn, but you begin to address learning objectivity early in medical school. You learn to work through it. Some doctors react by becoming very cold, thinking, This case is done and over and I don't have to deal with this case anymore. Others react by becoming so enmeshed that they lose all objectivity, all capacity to consider the problem before them. I certainly addressed those issues in great depth when I worked in pediatric oncology with children who were being treated for terminal cancer. I became objective enough to work caringly with families and to help them say good-bye. And then I was able to leave it. I did cry a lot at times, letting myself feel the emotions. But I could let it go. Gacy was no innocent child. I collected data for over fourteen years, yes. But I had no friendship with, or even fondness for, Gacy the person.

John Wayne Gacy, who'd lingered on death row for well over a decade, was pronounced dead at 12:58 A.M. I turned off the news on the television set at the Holiday Inn on Larkin Avenue in Joliet, Illinois, to which I had driven silently on back roads at night to avoid the media. As I flicked around to find some music on the radio, I thought what an almost fantastic experience this was; the fourteen-year journey of following Gacy had been almost otherworldly. (There had been one last chance that the governor would change Gacy's sentence to life in prison, but this was not to be the case.) Inside the hotel room, the minutes seemed to pass unnecessarily slowly as I waited alone. To pass the time, I tried to study for a tort law exam I would have in a few hours. At 3 A.M., the phone rang and I took the elevator downstairs, oblivious to the sappy music within, oblivious to the people in the lobby, except for the doors through which I walked. Outside, I waited briefly until a car picked me up. Nothing was said during the short trip to Silver Cross Hospital. All I could hear was the constant hum of the car engine in the soundless blandness of the middle of the night.

At 3:21 A.M., I found myself in the autopsy suite. It had been arranged through Gacy's family that I assist in the autopsy. The body had been moved after being lifted into a van. But the van was being tailed, perhaps by the media. The body then had to be surreptitiously loaded into another vehicle in order to ditch the ghouls who often give a bad name to their profession.

In addition to the pathologist (also called a prosector) who would perform the procedure, a policeman, big and burly, stood nearby, out of the way and silent. A police officer rarely attends the autopsy of a former prisoner, but because of Gacy's notoriety and the media attention it garnered, I realized that having him there was probably necessary—as long as he didn't disturb our work.

The blue-tinged body of Gacy was removed from the van and placed upon an aluminum table. The table itself was more than functional. Plumbed with faucets, spigots, and drains, it was designed with high edges and was slanted. All these prevented Gacy's blood from running onto the floor. First, the body's trunk was opened and the internal organs were removed, measured, and labeled. There was no talking during the procedure, and no music playing, as there sometimes is within an operating room. Flesh is sometimes said to have the odor of lamb, but we were so focused on what we were doing (and there was so much to do) that the only sense we had was one that commanded "Complete the work as carefully and as orderly as possible."

As I assisted, the pathologist carefully opened Gacy's cranium with an electric Stryker saw and removed the calvarium (top of the skull). There, then, was his gray matter, the 1,300-gram organ that caused such misery and grief for so many.

I was very excited to begin the search for what may have caused him to exist in his persecutory, murderous netherworld. After connections to the spinal cord and various membranes (dural reflections) were easily severed, the brain, soft, was removed with a kind of a "swoosh" sound. It was placed into a glass jar filled with formalyn, a mixture of formaldehyde gas and buffered water. The solution does two things: it prevents decay and also thickens the matter so that it can be handled without breaking up. Not unexpectedly, I observed no abnormalities in the brain after a cursory examination that night. And so, just as his body was readied for a funeral, John Gacy's brain would be readied for study—cut into sections and placed on microscopic slides. As the dark sky began to brighten over Joliet and the damp, misty halos left the streetlights, I got into my car and returned home with Gacy's brain in tow, hoping my next task wouldn't be as complicated as I imagined it would be.

I considered which neuropathologist could perform the appropriate tests on John Gacy's brain, but this was no easy task. Because of the media attention surrounding the case, most of which was more subjective than objective, most of the qualified doctors I knew wanted nothing to do with the serial murderer, even though he was now dead. Physicians often want to uphold an appearance of propriety, which is an adjunct of the oath we take, and no one wanted the label of "mad scientist," which would have been like branding them with a scarlet letter—even if the resultant research would discover something important. Beyond this, if the neuropathologist was connected with an academic institution, the danger of helping in the research could have a wider effect by entailing the risk of losing millions of dollars in endowments. After many phone calls, I was able to find the pathologist who would agree to do the tests, but only after the constantly reiterated promise of anonymity. There was one more stipulation. Gacy's name would never appear with the sections of the brain that were sent away for study. Instead, on the brown box and the glass jar inside was a simple number, a code that only we would know.

Weeks later, the Federal Express envelope arrived at my office, and I looked at it with real anticipation. Was there really something there, something that would begin to help me understand Gacy's actions? Was there a kind of tumor, or would some minor microscopic aberration be found? I ripped open the tab on the envelope and looked at the documents within.

Ultimately, the report I'd waited so anxiously for found nothing abnormal with Gacy's brain. But as the anonymous pathologist had agreed with me, "There's no replacement for the study of a person, one who is alive, in different situations with different stimuli." A dead organ is almost like a piece of steak that was once a cow; it doesn't allow you to penetrate the living functions of the organism. I'd hit a dead end.

In reality, there is no current body of scientific research or psychiatric literature that truly explains the exact nature of the serial murderer. I expected that nothing would change this, not any time soon. Unlike other diseases, no one, not the state or federal government, not a private national or international institution, would set aside the funds for serious discovery. Even if they did, the law would not allow anyone to examine a serial killer properly and extensively while he was still alive.

And yet through this quagmire, which grew deeper and deeper, I had hope, hope that things would change. In fact, it was even more than a hope; it was an expectation.

EIGHT

THE YORKSHIRE RIPPER AND WAYNE WILLIAMS

After ten years of research and investigation, I felt I'd barely scratched the surface of what goes on inside the head of a serial killer. I had collected volumes of data and had begun to theorize, but the theories led to more questions than answers. I knew a little, and while that was more than anyone else, I still needed to know a lot more. So when the British magazine *She* contacted me in May 1980 about my thoughts regarding the Yorkshire Ripper, I agreed to talk. The hunt for him was the biggest manhunt in the country's history, beginning in late 1975. From the serious to the silly, the public reaction to the Ripper ran the gamut. Concerned women by the hundreds took to the streets to protest movies that portrayed violence against women, believing that these portrayals led men to kill. Meanwhile, badges bearing the phrase LEEDS UNITED—MORE FEARED THAN THE YORKSHIRE RIPPER were hawked outside of Leeds United Stadium. The British writer from *She* was herself full of fear, having once been beaten during an attack near Bergdorf Goodman in midtown Manhattan. Instead of playing the fear factor to sell magazines (which is what many of the daily tabloids had done), the writer said *She* wanted something that told the populace how to better protect itself from serial killers.

While no one is ever safe from a determined serial murderer because his violent determination is anything but human, some believe there are ways to reduce the odds of attack and/or abduction. While no one knows exactly what makes a person become a victim, people can reduce their chances of capture. One might avoid a serial killer by being wary and watchful of his or her surroundings—by being alert but not alarmed. It sounds like common sense, but some don't know that it's more dangerous to take a shortcut through a deserted park at night than during the day. So the alert person wouldn't take that walk through the park at night alone. And a confident demeanor, including a brisk, confident stride, couldn't hurt either. As I told *She,* if you walk into a party, you can almost immediately tell who the life of the party is. Similarly, a serial murderer can tell who is or isn't vulnerable or approachable. If you are actually confronted by a serial murderer, some say hysterical resistance and screaming can help, if the murderer doesn't incapacitate you before you can fight back. But what happens when the serial killer, the one who has a dominant, aggressive personality, is actually encouraged by distress or screams? It's been said that in such a case, a polite, quiet approach might save the victim. If, however, the serial murderer is himself reserved and tentative in his approach, fighting back and yelling may indeed work. All this is a little bit like the advice given regarding rape prevention. They used to say, if you're going to get attacked, don't fight back. And now they tell you to fight back. That doesn't mean you're not going to get killed one way or the other. Whatever the rape victim does may or may not work. And the same applies to victims of serial murderers.

Although Jeff Rignall was passive with John Gacy, he was seriously injured. But he did escape with his life, a life that he would try to mend over time. Rignall guessed that he wasn't killed because he meekly went along with Gacy's torturous experiments; indeed, Rignall didn't know exactly why he was freed. More important, John Gacy didn't know either. My guess is that the sparing of Jeff's life had more to do with Gacy than it had to do with Rignall. Was there some kind of a distraction going on in Gacy's brain that prevented Jeff from being the major focus of what Gacy was doing? If Gacy was singularly involved with his victim, the serial murderer would just proceed, as if following steps 1, 2, 3, and 4 in a cookbook recipe. The distraction could have been something simple. Gacy could have gotten bored with his victim or he could have become tired physically. But it was not something Rignall did that made this occur. Rignall's passivity did not allow a distraction to occur; it couldn't have. It was purely something deep within Gacy himself. If we follow the cookbook analogy, Rignall was like food to Gacy. Sometimes a serial killer snacks; sometimes he feasts. With Rignall, Gacy snacked.

In these strange relationships between victim and serial killer, there's an underlying, preconscious clue that comes from the victim. To a serial killer, this clue is like a flashing sign saying he or she is available. That beacon may be something as innocent as the victim's willingness to talk to a serial killer. I'm not talking about small gestures or subtle movements or anything that has to do with body language. Ultimately, there's no personality type that's consistent in victims. The shy, the meek, the assertive, the brash, and everyone in between can be victims. The answer lies more in what the serial killer is looking for in a victim, and we can't yet identify or define what that is. Some researchers will say it must be something in the pheromones, the chemical that also inspires people to get acquainted in a love-at-first-sight kind of way. I believe that the initial interaction between serial murderer and victim is as unpredictable as, though similar to, the chemistry that occurs when people meet and become attracted to one another. One has to do with love at first sight and falling in love. The other has to do with something I call "falling in death." Serial murder at first sight exists and thrives much like love at first sight. No one knows exactly what it is and how it works, but it hits quickly and, as we've seen, usually with tragic results.

I explained all of this to the writer, but after the August 1980 issue of *She* appeared on the newsstands, I was disappointed with what I read. The story was a puff piece, a sensationalized take that seemed more scary than helpful. I should've known better.

Nevertheless, once the article was published, I was contacted by a member of the special British task force from Scotland Yard who was involved in the Yorkshire Ripper case. In essence, what he wanted was no different from what police search for here in the United States. Most law enforcement people want a definite answer to their problems immediately, and this official was no different.

"Can you tell me exactly the kind of person who did this, Dr. Morrison?" asked the person on the other end of the line.

"No, I'm sorry, I really can't give specific answers. You're there and I'm here."

"Are you sure you can't tell us anything more?"

"No. No, I can't unless I am there and I have done my work." I am not able to give detailed, specific answers until I'm close to the crime and the facts and have analyzed them. It is not professional to make such predictions, and I don't do it. But police don't want speculation. They don't want "It may be"; they want someone to say, "This is it and go get him." I'm sure they were happy when psychics they hired came in with "definitive answers," even though the psychics were eventually proven wrong. Still, I became intrigued by the Ripper case and studied it closely because most people believed at the time that serial murders could happen only in the United States.

In the late 1970s, the almost rural town of Bingley, England, was nothing much to brag about. Set in a valley about two hundred miles north of London and about seven miles from Leeds, the place has a history that dates back to the Druids. In the 1970s, the primary diversion for many men in the town was going to pubs for entertainment, sobering up, and then . . . going straight to the pubs for entertainment again. So it was for John Sutcliffe, a World War II veteran who never saw frontline action (or any battle at all) but entertained the troops with his talent for singing. While John enjoyed hanging out in the local pubs and playing cricket, he also struck fear into the minds of his children when he returned home and fell into frequent rages.

Peter Sutcliffe, John's first child, was dubbed a "weakling" by his father. It wasn't so much of an insult as something that smacked of absolute truth. The five-pound baby was thin-legged and runty, and he took longer than most babies do to begin to walk. As he grew to be a boy, he was still small, silent, almost like a hermit. When John bought

his young son a soccer ball and a new uniform, he had to coax and ca-
jole Peter into playing. While he surprisingly kicked the ball around
with aplomb like he was born for the sport, Peter played only that one
time with his father, relegating the ball and uniform to collect dust in
the closet. Once he was so bullied by young school thugs that when he
was supposed to be at school every day he hid instead in his family's at-
ticlike loft space, which he entered through a trapdoor. There he lolled
for two weeks, daydreaming and listening to the sounds of the outside
world, until the school authorities sent a letter to his parents, wondering why he had missed his classes.

In Bingley, the people that Peter knew best were those like his
brother Mick, hard-drinking toughs, macho boys and men who preferred their fists or brass knuckles over talking to settle a dispute and
preferred to berate women rather than come to their defense. The
close-knit but troubled Sutcliffe family wasn't immune to the culture
and the general tenor of the town, and Peter's rough-and-tumble
brothers Mick and Carl were always in and out of trouble. Mick was
once jailed for three months for punching a police sergeant. All three
boys in the family seemed to be happy to steal things now and then,
everything from jewelry to hubcaps. Carl, Peter's underemployed
younger brother, once decided to live in the woods in the winter, taking only his sleeping bag, his motorcycle, and a gun. To say the least,
these folks were not considered to be pillars of the community.

Peter adamantly fought against his weakling image, staying for
hours in his room, bulking himself up with a Bullworker isometric
muscle-building contraption, enough so that he could take the strenu-
ous job of gravedigger. But soon, the repressed, shy, and mysterious
young adult who never seemed to show much emotion began to rob
the dead bodies of any jewelry with which they were buried. It was at
work, around the age of eighteen in 1964, that Peter, for no apparent
reason, swung a mallet at a coworker, who was much older than he
was. The blow landed squarely on the old man's head, but the seasoned
tough pressed no charges. Like other serial murderers, Sutcliffe began
his experimentation with aggression while he was still in his teens.
When I heard of this first incident, one that is usually ignored in any-

thing written about him, I felt this was the first moment when Sutcliffe learned a unique behavioral mode: the thrill of hitting someone with a mallet. In my mind, it was the beginning of aggressive behavior that would escalate.

Whenever he drank too much, Peter would indeed open up, only to collapse in fits of hooting laughter, incessant giggling, that often went on for up to ten minutes. Once he got started, he couldn't stop. Often he appeared frightened for no reason, and his eyes darted about the room; he rarely looked anyone directly in the eye.

Peter tried hard to cultivate a look that was somewhere between a 1960s and a 1970s rock star. Dark and grim, he carefully trimmed his hair and beard for hours on end in the bathroom and wore a black leather jacket and black Cuban-heeled boots. To me, this was another small clue to his murderous future. Serial murderers are always extremely well put together, whether they have a lot of money or not. They're well groomed and are never dirty. They're highly presentable individuals who take care of themselves. When looked at together along with a number of other signs, the pieces of the puzzle begin to form a detailed picture of the serial killer.

Obsessed with engines and motorcycles, Peter liked to tinker with engines, doing tune-ups for hours on end, even when an engine was brand-new. When he looked in the mirror now, he was proud of what he saw. Beginning to like his body, he showed off his newly created muscles by walking up and down the stairs of the Sutcliffe family home—on his hands. But he seemed to hold emotions inside during stressful moments until he would sometimes explode with rage. He once punched one of the toughs that was teasing him with such force that the burly man literally went flying like something out of an Arnold Schwarzenegger movie, and Peter broke his wrist. Here was yet another possible clue. Serial killers rarely can control the intensity of their impulses. When they go to do something, they don't modulate their reactions. It's all or nothing, broken wrist or not.

Despite these outbursts and his silent manner, Peter was the favorite of the Sutcliffe progeny, and he often dropped whatever he was doing to help his family. Even his father came to like him. At a local pub called the Royal Standard, the Sutcliffe brothers' haunt, Peter fell for an odd Czech woman, who, like him, was the wallflower type. Unlike him, she was very demanding, and Peter's family found her difficult to get along with. Together in the bar, Peter and Sonia would sit away from their friends, talking and laughing for hours. Sonia was an eminently troubled woman who, not long after meeting Peter, had a breakdown. Sonia claimed to be the second coming of Christ and said she saw her hands bleed with stigmata, the wounds of the passion of Christ. Sonia was immediately diagnosed with schizophrenia, much to Peter's dismay. But Peter made it his mission to be there constantly for her (with the help of her parents) once she was out of the hospital. This is not to say that Peter cared desperately for Sonia the way Romeo cared for Juliet. Neither serial killers nor psychotics have strong attachments to their spouses. He was merely fulfilling a role he felt he was expected to play, one that he had seen others play. Eventually they would marry.

Through all this, Peter himself was changing, and the transformation went beyond feeling his oats. With a friend or two, he took to taking trips through the various nearby towns—to the local red-light districts. On one night, he gathered up enough courage to approach a woman. But it didn't go well. The first time he asked a woman if she was "doing business," he got ripped off, and the woman absconded with ten pounds. It was a lesson he would not forget. As he walked back to his friends, Peter felt mortified and completely embarrassed. He even felt vengeful.

Not long afterward, at a restaurant on St. Paul's Road near Manningham Park, an area populated by prostitutes, Peter unexpectedly stopped eating his dinner of fish and chips. With a suddenness that was unusual even to his pals, he got up from the table and quickly left the place. He searched the dark streets, and within minutes found what he wanted. He looked around and placed a shard of brick into a sock, and he approached a woman he called an "old cow." Wielding the rock-filled sock as a weapon, Peter hit her on the head. Though the police went after Sutcliffe within twenty-four hours, the woman decided against pressing charges.

Not only had Peter begun to rage against women, but he also began to have "company" during his work at the graveyard. Peter didn't tell anyone, but while digging graves, he heard a voice, a compelling, humbling voice that thundered in his head, echoing loudly. After looking around to find its source, he climbed from the grave he was digging. He felt haunted, saying that the ground rose up, creating a slope that was difficult to negotiate. The voice led him to walk near to, then over to, the slightly overgrown plot of a long-dead Polish man. Peter stared for a long time at the large crucifix on the headstone. And he heard the voice again. He looked slowly around to see who was nearby, but he saw no one. The voice emanated from the headstone, still echoing, the words somehow fused together as one. Yet Peter was able to understand perfectly. The words commanded Peter. For him, it was probably as profound as Moses' experience at the burning bush. But Peter Sutcliffe was no prophet.

"I felt it was very wonderful at the time," explained Sutcliffe later. "I heard what I believed then and believe now to be God's voice.

"It was starting to rain. I remember going to the top of a slope overlooking the valley and I felt as though I had just experienced something fantastic. I looked across the valley and all around and thought of heaven and earth and how insignificant we all were. But I felt so important at the moment." If you look at history, Peter Sutcliffe wasn't the only serial murder who said he heard religious voices. Jeffrey Dahmer, who had sex with his dead victims and who ate parts of their bodies, built a kind of altar to both God and Satan in his apartment. It was a gruesome sanctum that included skulls of his victims in which he would burn incense so that he might absorb "special powers and energies." Joseph Kallinger, who in addition to committing other murders also drowned his son Joey with the aid of another son, Mike, stated that he was also on a divine mission from God. When these killers hear voices from God, what they're really hearing is only their own inner voice, imagined permutations of what's in their own minds. They may want to have someone else to blame for their inhuman deeds or they may want to feel more important than they really are, as if they are angels of God sent to earth to scrub it clean from its immoral filth.

In the case of Sutcliffe, the comments that he saw "how insignificant we all were" and that "I felt so important at the moment" make me think once again that, like other serial killers, he was emotionally a very young child. Who, other than an infant, feels like he is controlling not just the world, but the universe around him? Who else but an infant feels so important that he thinks he is the center of the universe? And who else but a child would think in this way for no particular reason, not for wealth, not for power, not for human domination, but just to maintain and protect his own personal cosmos?

Sutcliffe indeed felt he had been chosen. As the months began to pass, the voice, which had been initially comforting, suggested to Peter that he become violent. After the encounter with the absconding prostitute, Peter believed the voice of God had said to him, "It was the prostitutes who were responsible for all of these problems."

"It kept saying that I had to go on a mission . . . to remove the prostitutes. To get rid of them."

Unbeknownst to his family and even his wife (who was by now on medication and feeling much healthier), Sutcliffe embarked upon his "mission" against women with a passionate zeal. His MO was somewhat unusual: he skulked up behind many of his victims and whacked them repeatedly with a common ball-peen hammer or a claw hammer, until their skulls were cracked. He also carefully sharpened a screwdriver to a point and used that to stab his victims, along with various kitchen knives. With these, he would rip and slash the bodies of his victims until they breathed no more. Sometimes he stabbed the women in an eye, sometimes he stabbed repeatedly, so much so that one woman suffered fifty-two stab wounds. Sometimes the five-foot-seven Sutcliffe kicked and stomped upon them so hard with his size 7 Dunlop Warwick Wellington boots that the imprint remained on the body of his victims. Primarily, though, he hit them with hammers.

When Sutcliffe was compelled to kill, it was indeed first to kill prostitutes. He prowled around the red-light districts, and when he had that urge, nothing would stop him, not even celebrations with the family. But it wasn't only prostitutes whom Peter approached. Something in his head told him that any woman he had a desire to attack or kill was a prostitute. With his hammer, he struck Dr. Upadhya Bandara, who was in from Singapore on a scholarship from the World Health Organization. He killed Barbara Leach, a young student who attended the University of Bradford at the time. And he also struck sixteen-year-old Jayne MacDonald, a Grandways grocery store clerk.

Through all this Sutcliffe played the role of caring son and doting husband. But he also liked to venture somewhere that had nothing to do with pubs or the red-light districts. Sutcliffe found he was fascinated by a waxworks. He would go to a run-down museum at the working-class Morecambe resort, an hour and a half west of Bingley on the pretty Lancashire coast. Once in the museum, he didn't care so much for the impressive figures of Princess Margaret, Joseph Stalin, or Johnny Ray. Instead he spent time in the Chamber of Horrors, which featured the likes of Jack the Ripper and other murderous criminals of English history. He didn't mind the moldy smell of the place or the rain that dripped from the ceiling. Peter didn't notice because he was mesmerized.

Sutcliffe was also enthralled by another exhibit called "The Museum of Anatomy"—especially "The Macabre Torso Room," which was dimly lit and constructed in gruesome detail. Here he carefully viewed cut-up, limbless, headless women. Further on was a display of the ravages of sexually transmitted diseases, sculptures of diseased genitalia. Did looking at the bodies in wax drive him to do anything? No. Was he able to say, these prostitutes make these people have venereal diseases, even if they're in wax? Did he then say, therefore, I'm going to cleanse the world? No. It was just a morbid fascination, an extension of his ever-broadening experiment into killing others.

As the days passed into months and years, the public demanded answers, and the murders he committed led to the largest manhunt Britain had ever witnessed. As British writer Gordon Burn wrote in *Somebody's Husband, Somebody's Son* (one of the very few good books written about serial killers), 150,000 people were talked to by the police by mid-1979. That included 27,000 searches of houses and 22,000 statements taken by the authorities. There were 17,000 possible suspects in the morass that was the case of the Yorkshire Ripper. Police had spoken to Sutcliffe himself eight times, but they never went further than asking a few questions. Sadly, the Brits were thrown off by a tape recording (sent to police) that claimed to be the Ripper. As the tape's sprockets turned and turned and the police listened and listened again, one of the heads of the investigation, assistant chief constable George Oldfield, felt he was right to eliminate any suspects who didn't have the Geordie accent. Geordie is common in the North East of England, sometimes mistaken for an Irish or even a Scottish accent. Some linguists estimate that accents in England change after just a distance of two or three miles. So Sutcliffe from Bingley sounded completely different, with his Yorkshire accent, which contained sounds much softer, like animator Nick Park's characters Wallace and Gromit. Because of the tape, some began to believe that there was more than one Ripper, a copycat killer.

That idea seems to be very common in serial murder cases. The cry is "only one person could not do something so horrible. There must be others." This concept is especially prevalent when people have in their minds the belief that murderers always kill in the same way. But one of the things we know about serial killers is they don't kill the same way every time. The victims indeed may be similar, but the way of killing varies somewhat, since serial murderers like to experiment. However, the horror of the killings does provide some interesting theories. In fact, there's one gentleman who lives in Ireland who thinks of it as his life's work to promote his theory of a second Yorkshire Ripper. The killings stopped when Sutcliffe was apprehended. That was the end of the story.

But it wasn't easy to get him. The authorities were so flummoxed by the Ripper's crimes that they resorted to just about anything, including the faulty psychics, to solve the case. Police had indeed come close. When Peter Sutcliffe got Jean Jordan to agree to sex for a five-pound note, he attacked her near a cemetery overgrown with weeds, debris, and hawthorn bushes. Jordan was hit with a hammer eleven times until her moaning led to the silence that comes with severe injury. When he saw the headlights of a nearby vehicle, Sutcliffe left hurriedly, fearing discovery. Later, he recalled forgetting the brand-new five-pound note, serial number AW51 121565, somewhere near Jordan's body. Returning to the secluded scene of the crime, he found nothing. In anger and frustration, he took a broken windowpane and began slashing at the body. When her stomach blew open with the odor of death, he vomited. Even more angered, he decided to remove her head with a hacksaw to throw the police, who were used to his Ripper methodology, off the trail. Exhausted, he could not complete the arduous task. Eventually the police found the five-pound note in Jean Jordan's purse and traced it to a bundle of cash that had been distributed to twenty-three companies. During their 8,000 interviews, police did indeed speak to Peter, but they determined that nothing was amiss.

If Peter had no guilt about his crimes, one of the pals who accompanied him to Yorkshire's red-light districts did. After thinking and worrying about it for some time, Trevor Birdsall, one of Peter's few friends, suspected that Sutcliffe was the Yorkshire Ripper; Birdsall went to the police in person to report his story. He said that after one of Peter's first encounters with a prostitute, Peter confessed to Trevor that he had hit a woman with a rock contained in a sock. Peter didn't say she was a prostitute, calling her an "old cow" instead. Birdsall admitted that he saw the rock along with the bloody sock. Authorities never followed up on the tip.

On January 2, 1981, two South Yorkshire policemen chanced upon a suspicious-looking car parked in a driveway off a seemingly private road. Sutcliffe was inside with a prostitute, about to have his murderous way with her. Sergeant Bob Ring and Probationary Constable Robert Hydes walked over to the car and talked to Sutcliffe. As they checked on his strange license plates, which were badly taped over the real plates, Sutcliffe said he had to pee. Off by himself, he tossed his killing tools onto a pile of leaves. When he returned, the police took him into custody, since the license plates that were attached by tape were stolen from another vehicle. It took Sutcliffe sixteen hours to spew a detailed confession, sixteen hours during which he was described as being relaxed and almost serene.

When his lawyer asked him to take the stand in his own defense,

Peter often used the "voices from God" excuse. There is no doubt that Peter Sutcliffe used the idea of commandments from God just to kill people.

At one point, Peter told the jury he once stopped himself from killing. But no serial killer I have known talks about summoning the strength to be able to halt his urges. He just stops, without thought or consideration. It's a very unusual statement that implies the person was in complete control of what he was doing. It goes completely against that statement that "God was telling me to do this." Why did he go against God during this one time? And why did God tell him to kill women who weren't prostitutes? Suffice to say that in May 1981, the jury convicted Peter Sutcliffe of thirteen counts of murder and he was placed in Parkhurst prison. But a new mental health law was written in England in 1983. Under it, Sutcliffe was considered medically insane and was moved to Broadmoor Hospital in the spring of 1984. He is held there to this day.

By the time Sutcliffe was convicted in 1981, a series of murders deep in the South began to receive a massive amount of attention here in the United States. Just as the murders in London caused an unmistakable national fear, furor, and confusion, the killing of black children in Atlanta, Georgia, spawned an unrelenting chaos that was covered almost daily on national television.

Atlanta has boomed magnificently since the late 1950s. People from all over the South flocked there, and those with artistic aspirations no longer moved north to make their way, since the city had become so cosmopolitan. By 1970, Atlanta became the big shot city of the South. In fact, visitors from up north came to Atlanta as tourists—and many stayed. From its place in history—it was, for example, the birthplace of Martin Luther King Jr. on "Sweet Auburn" Avenue and home to nearby Ebenezer Baptist Church—to Ted Turner's CNN, the region had proven itself to be truly diverse, a mighty force for economics and politics in the United States. Yet even today deeply ingrained racism rears its camouflaged head like a copperhead snake, especially when you look and listen closely in a local bar or in a restaurant. Tom Wolfe writes extensively about it in his fiction in *A Man in Full*. But when you see it in real life, it's so much more.

In the late 1970s and into the early 1980s, Atlanta bore the burden of one of the highest crime rates in the country. The crime problem was complicated by extreme poverty in the black community, which was devastating to its residents. In early 1979, a well-known white doctor and a legal secretary were murdered by black people. Then in July 1979, the lives of two black teen boys, Edward Hope Smith and Alfred Evans, were taken, marking the commencement of a troubling crime pattern that would dwarf the murders of the doctor and the legal secretary. Edward and Alfred loved playing sports and were fans of the Atlanta Falcons; these kids loved life. I looked at photos of the faces of the teens, fresh and round and full of hope despite their poverty. They were kids with smiling faces who in no way should have suffered injury, let alone murder (Edward, by gunshot; Alfred, probably by strangulation); they had so much more of life left to live. But twenty-seven more lives would be extinguished inexplicably over the course of the next two years in an almost surreal series of murders that would parallel the apprehension, mistrust, and near hysteria of the good people across the water who feared the Yorkshire Ripper.

Kids just kept dying. Fourteen-year-old Milton Harvey disappeared while riding a bike to the bank. Nine-year-old Yusef Bell, a smart, well-liked child, never returned from an errand to buy a neighbor a tin of snuff. Twelve-year-old Angel Lenair was found tied to a tree with electrical cord, panties that were not her own forced into her mouth. A day later, ten-year-old Jeffrey Mathis never returned from a trip to the store to purchase cigarettes for his mother. Fourteen-year-old Eric Middlebrooks was repairing his bicycle when he was killed with a bludgeon. Then twelve-year-old Christopher Richardson was murdered while on his way to the local municipal pool. The slayer became bolder as the seasons changed. Seven-year-old LaTonya Wilson was kidnapped from her home, never to be seen alive again.

The seven senseless crimes ushered in the dawn of a summer of hell for Atlantans. Yes, the police messed up investigations in England regarding the Ripper case. But that was nothing compared to the nearly laughable investigative activities of many of the authorities in Atlanta, who misidentified the victims' bodies and sometimes destroyed essential evidence at the scene of a crime. Some of the victims were thought to be missing runaways and their cases weren't pursued as possible murders. An eleven-year-old boy who called the task force created to deal with the murders, a boy who was in obvious fear when he phoned, was consequently ignored. Patrick Baltazar was later found strangled to death.

Atlanta's people of color were justifiably worried, angry, and at their wit's end. One frustrated group got together and walked through their community with baseball bats in hand. Even as they walked together in a show of force, the nightmare continued and a young member of their community disappeared and was himself murdered. Celebrities like Muhammad Ali and Atlanta-born Gladys Knight came to Atlanta's aid by donating money to help the victims' families. But many of the donations never got to the relatives. As the errors continued, some of the money was actually lost or misplaced.

At the height of the murders, I was asked to appear as a guest on a Washington, D.C., AM radio talk show. It was a less crazy time for radio talk shows back then, as hysterical hosts hadn't yet invaded the market with their constant tirades. Jeffrey St. John at WRC-AM wasn't a milquetoast kind of personality, but he wasn't Don Imus, either. After introducing me to his early-evening audience, the talk show host asked me about my work, just as many other journalists and interviewers had in the past. They were the typical questions: what do you do, what do you see, what do you find, how do you stomach it?

From a phone in my office, I explained my work for about a half hour. Then he asked the question "Who do you think has been killing the children in Atlanta?"

I took a deep breath. When you're about to put yourself on the line, you really have to ask yourself, Do you trust your own judgment? Do you trust what you've learned? Are you willing to be considered a complete idiot by your peers and by the people who are listening to you? Are you going to go out on a limb and expect someone to saw it off behind you? I felt I was ready, but I knew full well that what I was about to say would not be taken lightly.

"I feel it's someone in the community, someone who knows the community well."

"What do you mean by that?" asked St. John.

"Well, he's probably in his twenties or thirties. He's probably someone who has many acquaintances but no very close friends. He may be seen as a nice, quiet, and helpful man who doesn't annoy anyone. And my impression would be that the person who would do this is black."

And that's when the phone calls started coming in. The response was hostile, hostile, hostile. And most of the callers were people of color. They felt I was being racist.

Asked one caller, "What right do you have saying this about black people? Why are you trying to cause trouble?"

It was clear that the audience couldn't believe that a person of color could have committed these terrible crimes. Some angered callers mentioned the paucity of black serial killers in American history; others mentioned newspaper reports that quoted officials who were convinced that the eventual suspect would be a white man. It went on and on. The question had exposed something beyond the murders in Atlanta: the continual travails regarding race relations in America.

Sitting at my desk as the host signed off, still holding the receiver of the phone, I was stunned by the callers' comments. After I hung up, I turned off the lights to leave my office.

I just couldn't get it out of my mind. At home, while I chopped up romaine and butterhead lettuce for dinner and cooked up two steaks, it all weighed on me. When my husband asked what was wrong, I mentioned what had happened, but I didn't explain it with the real emotion and sadness I felt. At night, alone after he had gone to bed, I second-guessed myself.

This was the first time that the possibility that the serial killer in Atlanta could be black had been broached publicly. It might have been thought of behind closed doors at meetings of police and politicians, but no one had come out and said it. Yet I was still surprised at the level of hostility. I wasn't doing anything personal. I was imparting what I thought to be a sound theory that was based on what I had learned from and about other serial killers. It's true that there aren't that many black serial killers in America, but I felt that if the person was white, he would have been noticed by people in the black community. Someone would have seen something. However, someone who was a member of the community would have been able to move around freely without being noticed. To me, it was as simple as that.

I wondered too if I should deal at all with the media, and I came to the conclusion that, yes, they do help. To this day, I still trust the media to tell the story about serial killers, but I'm much more wary about what their motives might be. Initially, I think I expected that they just wanted to present information to people. I never thought about them in the context that they want to sell something. One of the things that people usually don't look at is the possibility of an ulterior motive for media bias or involvement, such as presentation of a specific viewpoint not only in editorials but also in news stories. It's not as much about the principles of journalism, not as much about who, what, when, where, and why—not anymore.

But had I gone overboard? Had I said something to the radio audience that was completely wrong? Was I making an assumption? I had no factual basis for what I said, but I had research and history behind me. Was I overstepping my bounds as a researcher to say that this is what I expect would happen, since I hadn't scientifically discovered facts that would support my idea? I went through that process for at least a couple of days. I came to the conclusion that what I said on the program was what I truly believed. Whether he was or he wasn't of color, it wasn't going to stop my research. I would have to go on and shrug off the feeling of doubt that had nagged at me for days.

I hadn't been involved with the police or the authorities in the Atlanta investigation. The whole thing had become increasingly political (much of which is well documented by James Baldwin in *The Evidence of Things Not Seen*), but I had begun to follow the awful events even more closely than I had before my comments on the radio show. And then I received a call from a high-level member of the Atlanta task force.

I made it clear immediately that I did not want to become a member of the task force. One of the things that's so hard in my line of work is trying to be separate and independent. What had been driven home in the last few weeks was the fact that more than ever, I didn't want to belong to anybody or be identified with any group. If I belonged to this task force, then I became like a policeman and my work would be compromised. It's like a forensic psychiatrist being so involved with the FBI that he goes to Quantico to learn to be a sharpshooter. Is he being a physician/researcher or does he want to be one of those guys? I didn't want to be one of them.

Additionally, I was very aware that the South is not the North. The ties there are those of blood and of extended family, and an outsider would not be welcomed. I couldn't break into that in a short period of time. I wasn't going to try.

I did what I could on the phone, however.

"Dr. Morrison, what did you make of the fact that this person down here has been throwing bodies into the river?"

"We have seen here in Chicago that John Wayne Gacy disposed of bodies in that way."

"Would a killer stick to that pattern?"

"Not necessarily. He might well vary it, and he could do that easily."

"Interesting. Because the pattern varies down here."

The patterns of killing were indeed assorted. The killer wanted by the task force went from killing boys to killing girls to killing young adult men. He dumped the dead off bridges and he placed them in a ravine and even in a school. In the darkness of early morning on May 22, 1981, police heard a splash off the Jackson Parkway Bridge that spanned the Chattahoochee River. Officers stopped twenty-three-year-old Wayne Bertram Williams, a self-described but unsuccessful music industry entrepreneur, after he traversed the same bridge from which the splash had been heard. Everyone felt they had a huge break in the case, especially after a body was found in the water shortly after Williams was interrogated. But Williams himself never confessed to any of the crimes. There were no fingerprints to match to Williams's, and the green fibers found on many of the victims and in the house in which Williams lived with his parents were fibers so common that many homes could have had that kind of carpeting. Still, two blood-stains discovered in cars Williams used were consistent with the blood types of two victims who were stabbed to death. But DNA tests, rare in the early 1980s, were never performed to link the blood to those who were murdered.

After a trial in which those in the Georgia courtroom were dizzied by the seemingly endless amount of fiber evidence, a jury composed of four whites and eight blacks convicted Williams to two life sentences, and today he sits at Valdosta State Prison. There are those who still firmly believe in the innocence of Wayne Williams, including some of the victims' mothers. No one will precisely know the true story about the killings for which he was condemned until the results of DNA testing become available for all to see. And I hope the Georgia courts allow that process to begin soon. Because if Wayne Williams is innocent, he is owed a new trial and perhaps an ardent apology and eventual freedom. If he is guilty, however, he deserves to continue his long life in prison.

As for me, these two cases made me somewhat more suspicious of some of the media with which I had to deal. In the future, I'd have to pick and choose more carefully, because the way some of them interpreted what I said did me no good. More important, they really didn't serve their readers, listeners, and viewers with objectivity or honesty.

NINE

BOBBY JOE LONG'S
LETTERS AND DREAMS

With the exception perhaps of California, Florida is a land of dreams, *our* land of dreams, affordable, warm, and within reach for young and old alike. People across the country flock to Florida, especially during the stormy winter months when snow falls by the foot for midwesterners like me. American artist Winslow Homer wintered in Florida, painting *Palms in the Storm* there. Ernest Hemingway lived and played in the Keys, and Tennessee Williams wrote his dramas and painted there. Even the mention of the Sunshine State gets our minds going, yearning for the placid beaches, the palm trees, and for sand warming the toes during oceanside strolls at sunset.

For me, I'd gone boating with my husband in Tampa Bay, and we were relaxing while fishing. It seemed I could forget all the troubles in the world as I watched him teach our oldest child how to fish. I was touched when he said, "When I was about your age, my uncle John taught me how to fish, and now I want to teach you what I have learned." Passing on knowledge to children: there's nothing better than that, I thought. Out there in Tampa Bay we were expectant because someone said we might catch huge tarpon or even a sailfish, but it didn't matter because we were spending time together away. For me, that meant some time away from serial killers, which I actually stopped thinking about when I reeled in an elusive ten-pound bonefish, much to everyone's surprise.

It was probably that dream for a better life in the sun that Louella Long sought for herself and her son when she packed her bags and boarded a Greyhound bus for Florida, leaving her husband, Joe, behind in dusty Kenova, West Virginia. For a while, that dream came closer to reality for Louella, or so Louella thought. But within her young son, there seethed an anger that began to grow as the boy reached school age. The two moved from place to place, often renting a room in someone else's home. Although Louella seemed to be oblivious to it, he began to harbor a dislike for his mother that eventually turned to hatred. For instance, he and his mother reportedly slept in the same bed until Bobby Joe was twelve. Part of this was the result of circumstances: they often lived in one room of someone else's home, so living space was a precious commodity. But part of it was the result of an overprotective, smothering nature that was ingrained into Louella's personality. This overmothering may have added to Long's inability to function without structure. In one of his first letters to me, Long wrote, "Mother is a strange one, she's always been so overdramatic, always been so negative about me in life . . . I NEVER once hit her. I wanted to. I wanted to twist her head off, but I *never* did."

Indeed, it wasn't Louella who was the recipient of his frequent rage. He got into brutal fistfights in school over his misshapen teeth and with his various relatives. Long said to me:

> I used to have terrible fights with my aunts and my cousins, that many times would end up with my hands around their throats. Over and over, they all used to tell me, "You're crazy," or "You're going to end up killing someone," or "You're going to end up in prison for killing someone." Most of this was between the age of ten to twelve years old, and I used to think—no way—*they* are the crazy ones, I could *never* kill anyone.
>
> There were these times when it was me against them and the dam would break, and I'd get ahold of one of them. It was awful. Then, they'd all start their "You're crazy" or "You're gonna kill someone"

garbage. Then my mother would end up beating my ass or some other type punishment, never considering or believing that about half the time the whole thing started because I was taking up for her while she was gone, and they started calling her a whore or slut.

Looking back now, it's too bad I didn't go ahead and kill one of them. I'd have gotten the help I needed.

By help, Long meant psychiatric and social intervention, probably some kind of juvenile detention and an eventual easing back into society. He knew that Florida and West Virginia wouldn't have jailed a minor, nor would they have considered the death penalty for a minor. Inside, in whatever speck of rectitude he had, Bobby Joe Long wished, like many of us do, that he could somehow undo the past. It was not so much to save the lives of the innocents he killed (he harbored no guilt), but to save his own skin. Though he didn't kill any of his relatives, Bobby was proud of his fistfighting ways, as he wrote in his letter of April 2, 1985. "[I] boxed in the Boys Club, Army, and Golden Gloves. Had more street fights than I can imagine having had. I used to like it, I was good at it. I grew up fighting, always the new kid. Always having to prove myself. I guess it carried over. I've ruined several guys faces, real good." As I read the words, I could almost see him bragging about bashing those faces during those old battles, his mustached lips curling into a self-satisfied grin. Then, as if he had told a chummy story with a heartwarming ending, he ended his letter, "Nighty night." It was so incongruous, but that's what makes a serial killer. You'll never know exactly how they'll appear next.

As a child, Long would neglect his schoolwork to the point of failing and had to repeat first grade. Even though he disliked the regimen of school, it wasn't the teachers that disturbed him so much. He felt his life was dark and lonely, writing:

I was always alone as a kid. . . . No brothers or sisters, no parents really. I hated most of the people (family or otherwise) who lived with (off) us. We were never stable anywhere for more than a year till I was 12, so no close childhood friends, till then. I always felt I was born a hundred years too late. I'd have been perfectly happy in the Frontier days, up on a mountain in a cabin, on my own, with nobody around to bother me. I'd have loved it. A dog or two, to hell with everyone else.

When I read this, I thought how the rest of the country and the people of Tampa would have loved it too if Long were in a faraway time in a place where he would have never taken a life.

Long continued to expound upon nature and his dreams that could never be, and about loves he had lost. It was just too sugary sweet and banal at that. Then, suddenly, he wrote, "I am . . . Darkness, I always have been." Using *darkness* with a capital *D* as he did, he must have pumped himself up to believe he was evil incarnate, like some ram-horned devil out of *The Exorcist,* as if some immortal power lived inside him. While he may have been trying to achieve some effect with his words, I had seen too many of these people already to be disturbed by what they write on a piece of paper. It would probably surprise him to hear it, but it was clear that Bobby Joe was the "overdramatic" one.

He did, however, contemplate what it meant to be bad early on. "When I was 12 or so, I started thinking how easy it would be for me to become one of the wild animals I knew. Kids who were always in trouble, mean, cruel, drugs, wild in every sense." Bobby Joe wrote that he felt he was strong enough to avoid that road, or at least outgrow it.

But by then it had already started, with his frequent beatings of his cousins. And there was something else, odd eyes his grandmother said Bobby Joe so frantically feared, feared so much he'd run into the closet to hide. Explained Bobby in a letter,

I've always had a thing about eyes. What's the saying—eyes are the window to a persons soul. OK, I don't believe in a soul, but Yes, I think they are a window to the person inside. Its hard to lie or fool someone when they're looking in your eyes. Too weird. Looking into those girls eyes while they died. None of them looked back into mine very long. Maybe they could see it, that they were going to die. Usually they looked over or past me. All but Simms. I kept her blindfolded and tried to knock her out first. I didn't want to look at her. I don't know why. Maybe I was afraid she would see it, and I didn't want her to. I didn't want her to know she was dying, I liked her. Maybe I was afraid I couldn't or wouldn't go through with it if I was looking in her eyes. Maybe both. I don't know.

Bobby Joe met his girlfriend Cindy at a young age, and in some ways they were inseparable, kindred spirits. At the very least, they shared a need for rebellion. Soon enough, though, Bobby began comparing her to someone he hated. Bobby wrote,

I saw Cindy turning into another Louella (Mother) in many many ways. Like always running around, bitching moaning and groaning if she didn't get her way, unreasonable, and either playing head games or the Silent treatment, without ANY real communication.

She started changing not too long after we were married. Personality wise, sexually, really about any way she could. I guess it's no new thing. She got what she wanted since we were 16.

After reading this, one thing became very clear. An arrogant Bobby Joe lived with the recognition that he was not in control of those closest to him, his mother and his wife, Cindy. Noted psychiatrist Melanie Klein believes that a baby, in the first six months of its life, feels a constant paranoia, a watchfulness, lying there on its back vulnerable and prone, unable to get anything for itself. An infant can do nothing but lie there and see and look. If a serial killer has the emotional level of a baby, as I believe he does, a killer like Bobby Joe has no real control over his family. Long wanted to "twist off" his mother's head. He wanted to kill Cindy. But emotionally, he couldn't get beyond that fantasy. It wasn't as if he projected this fantasy onto other women when he killed. With the emotional maturity of a baby, Bobby Joe couldn't even act upon a concept as complicated as projection.

As a criminal, Bobby Joe Long became a compulsive rapist first and moved into serial killing fairly quickly. Long raped over 50 women (though some believe it was closer to 150, because the assaults began as far back as the mid-1970s). In early 1984, after he and Cindy had divorced, Bobby Joe lavished jewelry upon a new girlfriend, gems and rings and necklaces he stole and sometimes tore from the bodies of the women he attacked. Although Long didn't have the money to purchase any of the rather expensive gifts, his girlfriend never questioned the origin of the presents. Long's methodology in these attacks often centered around the pretense of responding to an advertisement in the local newspaper, sometimes for the sale of bedroom furniture, sometimes for the sale of a house.

After buzzing the doorbell, he listened closely for the sounds of footsteps. He'd stand at the door, waiting in anticipation, shifting from foot to foot. Once the door was cracked open, Long was affable and almost handsome to some. If he saw a woman, he looked the woman straight in the eye and smiled. "I'm interested in buying. Can I come in and have a look around?" Much of the time he was permitted entry. If the woman at the door blanched, however, he'd simply force his way in. Then he'd tie her up and rape her viciously, sometimes over and over again, "usually two or three times," according to Long.

And then his violence escalated beyond rape.

The Hillsborough Country sheriff's department is located in the Ybor City section of Tampa, an area famous for its cigar-making factories where wonderful old craftsmen roll cigars by hand in huge spaces and tobacco covers the floor like sawdust. In a nearby nondescript building, the department (in tandem with the FBI) began investigating the murders of Tampa's women, and all those murders had similarities. At the peak, the murders occurred at a rate that staggered officials—one every other week. Often they were found in rural, almost bucolic settings—in an orange grove or near a cattle ranch. The first mutilated body that was found was discovered nude, that of a pretty Asian female with shoulder-length permed hair, a former exotic dancer at a Tampa club who was about to attend the University of South Florida. Coincidentally, her last name was also Long, Nguen Thi Long. Nguen Thi Long was found lying facedown by two teenagers playing with toy parachutes in a pasture. A parachute one boy threw came to rest on the Laotian woman's partially decomposed remains. She had been strangled, bound, and gagged, and the feet of her small body had been pulled so far apart that there was a five-foot distance between them, almost as if Long had tried to pull her legs off. The askew form of her body stunned longtime Detective Lee Baker, so much so that he believed her hips were broken from the strain.

Hillsborough County on Florida's west coast is an area of over a thousand square miles that includes Tampa. Beyond the quaintness of Ybor City, it's a vibrant area that some say rivals Miami in its metropolitan beauty. Before the case of Bobby Joe Long, this tourist destination had averaged fewer than three dozen murders each year and had never before dealt with a serial murderer of Bobby Joe Long's magnitude. But the authorities immediately believed that Nguen Thi Long's legs were pulled far apart and that she was bound for a sick and sadistic reason. They thought these might be the signatures of a murderer who might strike again. After police sent various items to the FBI lab in Washington, D.C., a single red nylon fiber was also discovered near the victim, probably torn from the floor of the car being driven. This particular break in the case was kept concealed, since officials feared the killer would change his way of murdering if the evidence was leaked to local media. Police hoped against hope that he wouldn't strike again.

Fourteen days later, while cruising in his red Dodge Magnum, Bobby Joe Long stopped near a pretty but world-weary young woman, a former California beauty contestant turned prostitute who had moved to Tampa that very day. He chatted her up, complimenting her until she stepped into his car. Still shooting the breeze, he drove her to Park Road, the local lovers' lane. But it wasn't love or even attraction that was on Long's mind. He bound twenty-two-year-old Michelle Denise Simms, tying her neck with thick, rough rope, fashioned that into a kind of hangman's noose, and tied her hands with clothesline, and placed her facedown in the back of his vehicle. He bashed her head with his fists until her beautiful face was almost unrecognizable. He raped her, then threw her from the car.

Michelle, however, was still alive. When he tried to strangle her,

Michelle decided to fight against Long. As retribution, he slashed her throat . . . again, again, and again. From a tree, he hung her blood-drenched clothes. When the authorities found her, her eyes were filled with blood. Even the peach nail polish on her toes was chipped.

Long proudly admitted to me, "That was the most violent killing I did. The most gruesome."

The same kind of lustrous red nylon fiber that was discovered on the Asian woman was found on young Simms. The broad rope used was the same as well. Then another woman, shy, bespectacled Elizabeth Loudenback, was found facedown, dead, in a rural area amid verdant orange trees, and the red nylon fiber was again discovered. Various microscopes and a microspectrophotometer confirmed that the dyes from all of the fibers were the same. Elizabeth had been bound, raped, and strangled to death with a length of rope.

Long's method of strangulation was not the same kind of thing one regularly sees on television or in the movies. In most entertainment, ten or fifteen seconds is all that it takes for someone to expire from being choked. Reality isn't so quick, nor is it so tidy. The victim struggles and screams. The eyes bulge, and blood vessels in the eye burst, so the eye appears blood-filled. It can take as long as ten *minutes* for a killing by stranglehold, and in Long's case, he sometimes broke the hyoid bone, a U-shaped bone in the upper neck, tucked just beneath the skull. He'd pull along a woman facedown on the ground with so much force that her features were sometimes no longer there, scraped away by pebbles, rocks, and sandy dirt. While he raped her, sometimes anally, he pulled on a collar made from a rope attached to her neck, yanking horribly hard, as if he were trying to tame some wild animal. Into one victim's vagina, Bobby Joe Long inserted scissors, perhaps because the woman tried to fight back with the scissors before his six-foot, two-hundred-pound bulk overpowered her. Later, Long would relate to a TV crew that he once put a TV dinner in the oven and discovered he had no milk to drink. During his shopping trip, he was compelled to kill a woman after he had bound her, but he returned to his apartment afterward, boasting that the TV dinner was still in the oven, albeit burned.

Binding his victims may have been Long's way of completely im-
mobilizing them. In addition, he placed them on their stomachs.
That's because people can't be good fighters when placed on the stomach. Also, they can't see what's going on. But Long didn't do this only
so the victims wouldn't see him and identify him. Making women lie
on their stomach is another way to exercise complete control, because
it makes them become completely passive. If they don't know what's
coming, they can't protect themselves. So Long disarmed as many of
their senses as he could. It's the ultimate terror in a way, because if they
don't know what's coming, they may begin to think something bad is
going to happen. Victims then recede into an illogical state where they
can't really process what's going on. They can't try to reason with the
murderer because there's no way to be prepared or to think clearly, no
way at all.

On November 3, 1984, Long skulked along in his car and spied a
seventeen-year-old girl slowly riding a bicycle equipped with a small
basket in front. She was returning from work at a fast-food restaurant.
After passing the teen and then parking the Magnum, he quietly got
out, softly shut the car door, and hid near a van. When the girl passed,
he grabbed her by her long hair, ripping her from her bike, which fell
in a heap onto the asphalt. Long shoved Lisa McVey into his car and
blindfolded her as the teen shivered with fear. It was the beginning of
a fierce kidnapping during which he repeatedly raped the girl, a kidnapping that would last for twenty-six hours. In an oddly surreal moment, the injured Lisa sat next to him on his couch, bound, gagged,
and blindfolded while he watched one of her favorite shows on television, *Airwolf.* As she wondered whether she'd ever again see the
double-amputee father she helped to care for, a news report detailing
her abduction came on the set.

"You don't need to hear that, do you?" asked Long, switching off
the television. He pushed her onto the bed. As he raped her again, his
mood moved from feelings of pure anger to caring, even fawning. "I
don't know why I did this," he said. "You're such a nice girl." Then he
showered her, dressed her, put on her shoes, tied the laces, drove her to
a parking lot . . . and freed her.

The surprising release of Lisa McVey was the beginning of the end for Bobby Joe—she was instrumental in giving police crucial details that led to his capture. She had peeked through her blindfold to see the area where she was driven, if not the precise address of Long's apartment. Lisa described Long's car to a T. Police caught up with Long at a movie theater and took him into custody after he watched a screening of the Chuck Norris action picture *Missing in Action*.

During the half-dozen times that I spoke face-to-face with Long, he told me of an eleventh murder that the police tried to pin on him.

"There was this one girl that vanished out of a bar room and O'Connor [his lawyer], he probably still thinks that I did it, but I didn't. Every time I would come upstairs in a little room like this one, he would be sitting in a corner and . . . O'Connor would throw a paper clip and it was a clip of this girl and then ask, Where is she? I don't know, I said, I told the guy it was about ten of them."

"So."

"So, why wouldn't I tell them about one more?"

"Why not tell them about five or six more?" I felt he had killed more than ten people and that this might be the time to confront him with that idea.

"There ain't no more." Then he laughed. It was the same kind of small but nefarious chuckle that Richard Macek would make. It threw me off for a second or two.

"So how many are there?"

"I hope you don't start there." Long was getting defensive.

I softened my tone. "So how many are there?"

"Ten."

"It's a small number."

"I stopped quick."

"Did you start quick or did you start slow?"

"Slow."

"Who was your first victim?"

"Murder?"

"Anyone."

"Some Cuban woman." She was just "some woman" to Long, not

a person, not someone who thinks or feels or someone who can be described as having virtues or faults. She was just something to be used. He didn't even remember her name.

"When was this?"

"Nineteen seventy-five or seventy-six, Miami."

"That was the first one? That's only been ten years." I felt there must be more much earlier, but Long wasn't going to confess to anything more.

"That's all," he reaffirmed.

"That's not very long, considering most of the people in your circumstances started a long time before that."

"Is that right?" He was getting cocky.

"John Gacy was one. Wayne Williams was another." Long laughed. It wasn't a maniacal laugh, but a kind of condescending low cackle. It was lacking in emotion and rang hollow. It was completely jarring. And again, it sounded just like Richard Macek's laugh. Long ignored the comment about Gacy and Williams, as though he didn't want to talk about anyone but himself.

"Did they run every test in the book on you?"

"These guys here? They did an EEG, they did a mag particle scan and neuropsychological testing." Long threw medical terms around as if he were well informed. In reality, he didn't really grasp their meanings.

"What did they come up with?"

"Nothing."

"Nothing. I'm not surprised."

"They say slight brain damage on both sides, but not enough to warrant any kind of uncontrollable behavior."

He continued to be brazen for the rest of the interview. Bobby Joe had trouble with those who he thought lorded power over him, yet he had joined the army. Then he often showed up late for formations. Also, he was put on probation for having sexual relations with the daughter of an officer even though he was still married to Cindy. In another of his many mistakes in the service, he was once put in a drug-rehab unit for abusing various illegal substances.

"You think they had it in for you, singling you out?"

"Everybody there had it in for me. I'm not paranoid. I'm realistic. I had four or five failure to reports. One was because I was hunting and decided to go for two weeks, rented an army camper and took Cindy and went out and stayed for a couple of weeks in the Glades and said to hell with them. I was getting pretty pissed off by this time. I had no business in the drug-rehab unit, painting buildings and cutting grass with swing blades and pick up cigarette butts all damn days and doing this and all their shit details. They were messing with the drug-rehab people because if they worked them to death they would sleep and not do drugs and stay out of trouble."

Not only did Bobby Joe fail to avoid trouble, but he also upped the ante in the coming years. When I saw him, Long was incarcerated and more suspicious than ever. It was up to his court-appointed public defenders to try to save him from death row. Around Thanksgiving 1984, I received a telephone message from Charles O'Connor, one of Long's attorneys. The message? "Need help on case." "Need help" was underlined three times by my assistant, Tinamarie. The lawyer seemed somewhat frantic.

And so I flew down to Tampa. When I spoke with O'Connor and his colleague Robert Norgard, it seemed to me that they did not yet have a clear plan of defense for the trial, which was looming. While that's not unusual for attorneys, who often wait until the last minute to pound out their plans of attack, their desperation seemed to indicate they weren't completely sure how best to defend their case. Continually during the many hours I spoke with them, they wondered out loud whether or not Long could be considered legally insane under Florida law.

Said Norgard, "I'm going to have to determine whether or not he is legally insane and then I don't want to use up a lot of credibility by four days of malarkey in front of a jury."

Norgard looked directly at me. "Somebody has to tell us how to approach, and this is a major decision. Do I say he is insane in the first phase or do I spot them that because he is possibly not, and then go into a second phase where I can get what they call aggravating and mitigating circumstances? What do you think I should do?"

Already I didn't exactly like where this was going. I was there to be the doctor, not to be the lawyer. "I can tell you what will work. Not what you should do. I think it would be wise to get to the guilt phase early and the mitigating circumstances, if you have them. No jury on God's little green earth, let alone in Florida, is going to say that this man is insane."

"But that's the question. Did he meaningfully know what he did was illegal?"

"There's no meaningful knowing with Long. There is not even knowing because knowing requires not only the mind to register, but it requires processing. Long has the emotional maturity of a child. From what I have seen when I talked to him, he didn't know and he still doesn't know."

O'Connor began to pace around the room. Both Norgard and O'-Connor were having some trouble understanding, yes, but they were desperately pondering how to present all of it in a court of law.

Norgard then said, "Excuse me if I try to interpret and stop me if I get it wrong. But are you saying that on some basic level of how people think and how they react that is fundamental, there is a whole bunch of holes for him? And as he courses around life and he happens to be over one of those holes, he doesn't know, in any sense of the word *know,* know what is going on."

Now he was getting it. "More or less right."

"How do you defend this guy then, which is a pure psychiatric case?"

"With a lot of guts."

"I'm talking about the simple mechanics."

"Pretty much in the same way that the defense dealt with John Gacy in Illinois. You've read that *West Virginia Law Review* article that I sent, haven't you?" I had coauthored a lengthy essay about everything that went on in the Gacy case from the facts to medical theories to the law that was used in the case.

Norgard leaned forward as one hand held tightly to the arm of his chair. "Yes, but you have a different standard for sanity in Illinois."

For hours each day, we went back and forth regarding the intricacies of Florida law, what medical insanity means and how it related specifically to the legal insanity case of Bobby Joe Long. Sometimes it seemed that we were going around in circles. And they continued to misunderstand.

O'Connor asked, "Do you think he is McNaughton insane?"

When they invoked McNaughton, the lawyers were referring to a theory of legal insanity dubbed the "McNaughton Rules." In England, over 180 years ago, Daniel McNaughton went to trial; he'd murdered the secretary to English Prime Minister Sir Robert Peel. But when testimony was heard, it was demonstrated that McNaughton was mentally disturbed. The jury in no way wished to send a sick man to the gallows. They refused to find McNaughton guilty, and he was immediately sent by the judge to a mental institution. Even today lawyers and judges use McNaughton Rules to determine legal insanity. Essentially, if a defendant is unaware of the distinction between right and wrong at the time he commits the offense or if he's unable to understand the charges against him, or if he's unable to assist in his own defense, he is probably legally insane.

"I sent you everything I wrote." In other words, I was saying, if you read the material, you should know by now how to proceed. I began to wonder whether they had prepared for the meeting at all and whether they had read what they should have read.

"You have never said that he is McNaughton crazy. In fact, you are the first person that I have ever heard say that even one of these yo-yos is McNaughton crazy."

Inwardly, I questioned if it was proper, even behind closed doors, for a lawyer to refer to his client as a "yo-yo." Instead I said, "I have said ever since the time I began working with these guys—since 1975—that they are McNaughton crazy."

"Okay. Well, maybe I didn't read it right."

It wasn't that I didn't like Long's team; I just didn't know if they could get the job done. Their lack of a clear strategy worked against them, as did the facts of the case. Then I heard that the lawyers and Bobby Joe had spoken to some other psychiatrists for his trial, and I felt that was not a good sign. As I found with Gacy, too many cooks spoil the broth. One doctor told Long that he must have wanted to be captured because he felt he had committed too many atrocities. Long responded to this when he wrote to me:

> As for McVey, I have trouble there too, in thinking I let her go because I "wanted to be caught."
>
> I let her go because I *could not* hurt her, even though I knew she would get me caught.
>
> A subtle difference. But a difference—I think. Don't you?
>
> I know, then theres the fact that I stayed in Tampa, and even after they pulled me over, and took my pictures, and I *knew* they would come for me. I didn't try to run.
>
> I still *cannot* say I *wanted* the police to catch me. I didn't *want* to go to jail. but I *did* want it to stop, and I knew if I ran, it would *not*.

He now wished to be secluded somewhere on a mountaintop, but Bobby Joe Long's dreams were trapped in a sixty-three-square-foot Florida jail cell, which he now was forced to call home.

And he did have dreams. Long, more than any other serial killer, wrote to me of dreams that were laced with fears. To Bobby Joe, they were vivid and horrible, a jail sentence of the mind in addition to a jail sentence of the body.

With all of the dream work that any doctor does, it's not the dream so much as the person's interpretation of the dream that matters. Despite the hundreds of books that have been published, there's no definitive dictionary that we turn to that explains to us, for example, that a spider means a mother or that a wolf means danger. That's a more popular psychology approach, which I like to avoid. But if I'm doing a real study of a person's dreams, I do it on the basis of what associations the person makes to the dream.

On March 31, 1985, at 6 A.M., Bobby wrote to me:

> I was in the death cell next to the execution room, waiting for morning to come and to be executed.
>
> My thoughts were of my family, my kids [his son and daughter],

and I was sitting on the bench smoking. (I don't smoke.) Two zombie-looking guards were outside the cell and they just stood there watching me the whole time.

Finally one of them who looked to be dead for a couple of weeks spoke to me in a real slow, low, death like voice saying the priest was on the way, it was almost time.

The priest showed up and came in and I told him I didn't want to talk to him.

He had on a brown monks robes with a hood on and I couldn't see his face.

He gave me the old "My son" routine and sat down on my bunk. I figured, what the hell, and sat down and could smell him. He smelled like whisky and cigarettes.

He asked me if I believed in God and I said "no."

He asked me, "why not?" but before I had a chance to speak he started laughing. He went hysterical, pointing at me and laughing.

I didn't understand. I thought it was all a joke. Then he threw his head back for a real good laugh and it was my mother's face under the hood, still laughing.

The two guards came in and were also laughing, but very slowly, they all left together, the two zombie guards and the priest mother.

I could hear them walking away down the hall, laughing all the way.

Then I was thinking again about the chair. I've had the idea before and in the dream I was convinced that when they fry you, it doesn't really kill you. It zaps your brain and nerves but your still alive.

I had visions in the dream that I was watching myself get zapped. Then the States Dr. comes and quickly pronounces me dead. But I am not. Then they rush me out on a stretcher all burned and smoking, and take me to a side room with an autopsy table and equipment in it.

They put me on the table and the State Dr. starts the autopsy cutting my chest open, all the way to my crotch.

Then he split the ribs with huge pair of scissor like things, opened me up.

My heart was still beating, my eyes opened real wide, the Dr. wasn't surprised. It was like it always went that way.

He cut my heart out while I watched and slowly was "going."

I opened my eyes one last time and there was the priest with my mothers face, and the Dr. looking down at me, both laughing again.

I woke up.

Other women made appearances in Long's dreams, women with zombielike features who seemed to be there to haunt him.

I'm not sure where this took place it was in a large bldg and there was a lot of us (different types—male and female) living in it, I think it was a prison. None of us liked being there and we were forced to sleep in old WWII Bomber planes' machine gun bubbles. Very small, had to sleep all doubled up, and woke up a lot to move and get blood flowing again.

Somehow me and one of the girls, nobody I know, nothing special, were leaving and I was going to give her a ride somewhere in my V.W. bug, where she wanted to go.

Next thing I know I'm asleep and she's driving, but she's skidding all over the road, so I make her stop and I drive.

But when we're switching and shes getting out and I'm allready in the drivers seat, she goes weird on me. Phases out, a total blank. She can't hear me talk to her or pays no attention, just looks off into space.

Then, she's half in and half out out of the driver's door and I can't close it. Then 3 or 4 other girls come up, and they're all acting like zombies, and go to the back of the car and are rubbing it and just acting very weird.

Finally I start driving with her half in and half out because I'm getting worried. It's not right. It was in Miami, I recognized the streets and I started to speed up to try to make her let go.

I woke up.

What's most important about these two dreams is that there's no emotional meaning connected to the appearance of the priest and the zombielike girls. Dreams can be very important in therapy and psychoanalysis because they can provide a window into the internal life of a person. But for a serial murderer, dreams to them are just things. They have no emotional significance. The temptation (which has to be avoided) is to ascribe meaning to them when to him there is no meaning. It's *so* tempting to say look at this dynamic, this connection, this link; it seems to say his mother is like the Grim Reaper, who wants to kill Long. So maybe it's because of his mother that he killed. But we can't make that leap. For Long, the dream happened and that was the end of it. He described it with the detachment of a reporter or journalist. There's nothing more to it than that, no symbolism, no connectedness, nothing. The dreams are nothing unless the dreaming person imbues them with meaning. As a psychiatrist, I can't endow what Bobby Joe dreamt with meaning. That's why you sometimes see a psychiatrist portrayed as someone who asks questions like, "What did that mean to you?" Had there been an emotional connection between Bobby Joe and his dreams, it would have been completely outside anything I had seen previously. I sometimes wish it were the case, but all data doesn't result in a "eureka moment."

On April 10, 1985, Long frantically wrote to me about Albert DeSalvo, the Boston Strangler. What he wrote had nothing to do with the serial killer from the 1960s himself, but with the movie he had seen starring a young Tony Curtis.

> I saw that movie once when I was young, again while I was doing all the "ad Rapes," on TV.
>
> The second time I saw it. It was the most scary fucking movie I ever saw. It was like watching ME in action. No, I hadn't killed anyone up until then, but when he was doing the things, grabbing the women, I could see on his face the way I felt when I did it.
>
> One I'll never forget was a blond he had from behind with his hand over her mouth. His face [Tony Curtis] was a mirror. He's an actor, but he had a grasp of it through his face . . . It hypnotized me. I'll never forget it. He was saying—No, not again! You'd have to see it to believe it, or understand it. I saw, and understood. It scared me. But

I thought, no way! This guy killed. I don't. I'm not like that. I could never kill anyone. I have more control than that.

I remember him tying one to a bed and she started fighting. I had been through the same thing. I knew how the guy felt. Like a mirror, I swear.

Would absorbing the violence he saw in entertainment lead Long to murder? Violence in movies has become a favorite subject in the media when incidents on film or in video games are described in cases before the courts as leading people to kill. A group called the Lion & Lamb Project makes it their mission to eliminate violence in entertainment because they believe seeing violence leads kids to violence. But unless the person committing the crime is susceptible or impaired, such as someone who's severely or profoundly retarded or if the person is reliving what he sees, it won't have an impact. Movie-initiated violence is rarer than people often presume. So Long may have had the flash of a moment from a scene during killing, but the movie or the scene or the moment from the scene didn't lead him to kill. Yet I think there was something in Long that wanted to believe that the violence he saw in the movie led him to kill. While I think a lot of today's entertainment goes too far, I don't think that televised entertainment or movies in theaters lead all people to real-life violence. Despite a plethora of theories and conjectures, there's just no real proof of the connection.

Long constantly complained about his once-injured head and the way it felt. It was not an ache exactly; if Long was to be believed, the formerly injured part had a kind of life of its own. Long wrote to me about his feelings, and of a mysterious woman called Barbara, whose acquaintance he could never later recall:

Even when its "normal" or what I'd call normal, "now." It's not like I used to feel. Used to be I never felt *anything* in my head unless I had a headache or something. Now I *always* feel the left side, it varies only in the way it feels. "Normal" for now, it just feels like its moving from time to time. It sounds weird but the rt. Side doesn't feel that way only the left. Its like if I sit here now, and look around, move my eyes radically from one side to another, or even close them and concentrate, I can feel it on the left side. Theres no pain, but a feeling in my brain that's absent from the right side. . . .

When I have the disoriented, confused, feelings, it's different. It's more like a blank feeling. Hard to concentrate, sometimes just hard to think at all. Cant organize my thoughts, cant read, its hard to even carry on a good conversation. Its like someone just busted me in the head real good. No pain, but slightly dizzy and disoriented. I feel like that right now. Even I notice it in my relating to people I talk to. Sometimes, like today, its hard to talk about anything meaningful, or deep.

Yes, Bobby Joe had had a head injury. But there was nothing in any doctor's examinations that said he had severe brain damage. Still, there is something about serial killers that leads them to complain about imagined illnesses. John Wayne Gacy claimed he had leukemia. Richard Macek felt he had a number of illnesses. I believe all this complaining is just a symptom of the serial killer disease. This kind of hypochondria is a disease, a manifestation of what a person may be feeling when they can't put that feeling into words. It's like a four-year-old who cuts his finger and thinks he's going to bleed to death. Of course, he isn't going to.

Long said that something in his head and even in his body changed when someone close to him, in this case, his former wife, did him wrong.

When Cindy lies to me, it makes my thought processes stop, I get mad, I hurt in my head, chest, everywhere. It's a feeling I've had with three people in my life: Cindy, Mother, and Barbara. All the same feeling, and I can't describe it better than "disoriented." I probably couldn't write my name at the time. It's a sick, terrible feeling, I hate it, it makes me feel *totally helpless,* and I hate that too. . . . it's frustrating, furiating.

The feeling that Long had is a little like the first feeling a worker endures when he's fired from his job or that sick feeling a lover suffers when getting dumped. The feeling is physical, like a combination of panic and the symptoms of a stomach flu. But what must be underscored is that it's only a little like those feelings. Long's reaction was so much bigger. He suffered an all-body attack that he could not halt or control. A serial killer's reaction to what he perceives as a problem is always on this kind of physical level, just like the all-physical reaction of an infant to stimuli.

And who was the mysterious Barbara that he mentions in the letter? He indicates she was important, but I found no reference to her ever again, not in any way, shape, or form. It's almost as if she were a passing mirage. She was not a fantasy or hallucination, but she was similar to part memories that people have. For a moment it looks like a substantial clue to something, yet it's nothing but smoke. I asked Bobby Joe later, What are you talking about regarding this Barbara person? He'd ask, "What are *you* talking about?" as if he'd never heard of her before.

Long wrote more about his thought processes, about the feeling he had when hitting his wife, Cindy.

> One time I was on the edge with Cindy. It scared the hell out of me. Another minute and I could have killed her. If her lip hadn't bled like it did, and made me see I was hurting her, my life, my baby, and I was ready to kill her, it just flat scared me. But then there were a couple of times like that with her.

More specifically, what was the feeling he had?

> It's similar to before I used to get into a fight, or just before I'd bust somebodys face. The anger. The blank thought. Its like I was void of thought. Like I left for a little while, then came back after. That's how it pretty much was with the girls, with the rapes too, now that I think of it. It was *all* encompassing, nothing else mattered. Just the target!

Like the fights, or the walls I kicked down, nothing else existed, or things I busted, nothing else existed, I had no other thought. Just the target.

No thought. Void of thought. Thought-less. A target. A thing. An object. The victims were dehumanized, as we have seen before. They were things that could be dismissed and even killed because they weren't human to Long.

Sometimes, Long said his head began to feel less tethered to his body. "The walls are still moving, and even when sitting still, it seems my head is moving." It was one of the difficulties with which I felt Bobby Joe himself had to deal. I told him he had trouble with distinguishing reality from nonreality. His mind was setting a perception of how things felt, and that wasn't necessarily the way that they really were. Basically, I told him he "needed to focus" so that we could work together to prepare for his case.

Then Long began to write to me only in capital letters. It was at this point that his letters about dreams stopped completely. I asked Bobby more than once why he changed and why the dreams stopped, but there were no answers, only the continued "shouts" of capital letters, as though he needed to get my attention.

Bobby Joe was increasingly confused, angrily confused, writing,

ITS NOT A GOOD FEELING TO KNOW MY LIFE IS OVER. TO KNOW THAT AT THE VERY BEST I'LL BE LOCKED UP LIKE AN ANIMAL THE REST OF MY LIFE. ALL BECAUSE *I* KILLED A BUNCH OF SLUTS AND WHORES AND I DON'T EVEN KNOW—WHY?

"What do you think?" Bobby often asked after posing a reason for his killing. It was almost as if he was trying to lead me to think, Well, this line might work in court in an insanity defense.

Even though he wasn't completely honest, Bobby Joe Long had done his best to open up to me. But what was disappointing was the way my work was treated by Long's defense team. After speaking to

Long, I felt there might be reason to believe the murderer was medically insane when he committed the crimes. After the long and exacting process of interviewing him and analyzing his letters, I determined his psychological state of mind during the murders. And I agreed to testify in the defense of Bobby Joe Long and appear at the murder trial of Virginia Johnson, his seventh victim. And then I wasn't paid. Because his legal team had begun to add more and more psychiatrists to the team, some of whom I thought lacked the necessary credentials, and because I wasn't sure Long's legal team could really do the job, I opted out. I had weighed the pros and cons. To me, it was a simple decision borne of a distinct feeling that the legal team ultimately didn't know precisely how to best try the case. After various trials for murder, Long was sentenced not to life in prison but to death row.

And there in Raiford, Florida, along with 366 others, a completely gray-haired Bobby Joe Long sits to this day, almost twenty years after his crimes, still dreaming of a freedom that will never come, of death that will indeed become reality sooner rather than later. But as my work with Bobby Joe Long wound down, the strange anger he had for his mother, Louella, made me look harder at the ties that bind serial killers to their famililes.

SERIAL KILLERS AND THEIR FAMILIES

Bringing a new life into the world is a weighty, awesome responsibility. Some people say you feel that responsibility to the marrow, but in a way, I feel it right down to the genes, at the level of the very building blocks of life itself. I consider the child's health: will he be sickly or healthy? Will he be emotionally stable? How do I protect him from the worst in the world without sheltering him from all the goodness? How do I teach him, nurture him, bring him up as a productive, caring member of a family in particular and of society in general? The questions I asked myself were endless.

Because of the horrific nature of serial killers, I have protected my own children from information about them. They have been kept out of the loop, and the subject material that you have read in this book has never been discussed in any way with them. They do know I have been on television, and that I do talk about people who hurt others, but it was not until our oldest child was in seventh grade that he knew I had spoken to John Gacy. This came from a friend of his who asked him about a TV show he had seen in which I talked about Gacy and others. I explained to my son and his friends that I am a "talking doctor," that I work with kids and adolescents. I keep my professional life as separate from them as is possible. And they rarely see me on television. TV in our house is not restricted per se, but my two sons are so busy with school, sports, and other activities that *Friends* or *SpongeBob* are afterthoughts.

Some of our friends think that I am too restrictive when I say I feel it is not necessary for kids to know everything about their parents' lives. This may be an old-fashioned idea, but kids need to be kids in their developmental phases. I feel the boundaries we have laid down have given my kids a sense of safety. There are so many examples of how we have failed our children because we were afraid to put limits on them, or failed to tell them not to do something because we wanted them to like us or to be their pal. Kids do not learn by osmosis, they learn by our being role models and by our active teaching. It is not essential for my children to know everything, especially about the violence and evil with which I deal, because it can be so pervasive.

I've certainly had an unusual perspective on the worst that parents can go through. From the devastated families of victims to the shocked parents and families of the serial killers in society, what I've seen is never a pretty picture. The guilt, shame, and denial of Marion Gacy, the mother of John, was only the tip of the iceberg. Other parents too experience a range of emotions about their ill-fated children, all dreadful, all sorrowful, all ultimately deadening of the spirit. And it is not only the parents who experience such wrenching emotions. It deeply affects the brothers and sisters, and the mournful, angry wives and the serial killer's children as well. You can see it by what's not said by the victims' children and wives. They usually won't talk to me because they're overwrought. And if I do eventually make contact, I'll often find on my next attempt that the phone number is disconnected and the family has moved away. One of the great mysteries of researching serial killers is how the families of the victims deal with their pain over time.

Graham Greene once wrote that "there is a moment in childhood when a door opens and lets the future in." As I've mentioned before, I believe there is something that happens in the earliest life of a baby that sets the stage for his future as a serial killer. At least there is something there that indicates the child will not be whole. It's difficult for parents to recognize this moment, so involved are they in the day-to-day activities of raising a family and earning a living. So it's no fault of their own that they often can't see it.

If it's true that a door opens in childhood to let destiny and free will lead the way, it's also true that a door closes on many dreams for the future when a mother and father begin to realize they have spawned a serial killer.

Then the parents sometimes can be painfully unpleasant to deal with. In 1985, Bobby Joe Long's defense team had asked me to attend his pretrial hearing. I stood outside the Dade City, Florida, courtroom, a nondescript building in a small town about half an hour outside of Tampa. It was a long day in a tiny, ugly courtroom, and I really needed the brief break the court had given us. As I breathed in the humid Florida air and relaxed for a moment, looking at the few tropical flowers placed outside, I felt someone approaching.

I looked up to find myself confronted by Joe and Louella Long, Bobby Joe's parents. It was instantly clear that they wanted to lash out at someone, anyone who had anything to do with their son's case. They were angry, boiling, and they needed to vent.

At the hearing, they had heard things about their son that went completely against what they believed about him. They had not merely heard about some of the unsavory details of his ghastly crimes, but they had also heard from me that in my psychiatric sessions with him in his jail cell, Bobby Joe had said he disliked his parents and his upbringing.

During the break, Louella watched a female television news reporter begin her story by saying that it was Bobby Joe Long's upbringing, particularly his lack of love from his mother, that led him to future life of rape and murder. Later Louella would say that she was so furious on hearing the reporter's words that she wanted to slap her. Instead of going after the reporter (who would have put it on the local news), Louella and Joe took it out on me.

The divorced couple, bonded by a firm disbelief regarding their only son's crimes, was livid. Joe, a tall man, was bending over and in my face, angrily taking me to task. They felt far too close for comfort, and it was almost like being mugged.

"We did the best we could with our son!" shouted Louella.

Joe got even closer to me than he had been. "You're making it look like we weren't good parents." He had managed to intimidate me. And I *don't* intimidate easily.

The confrontation had escalated in the blink of an eye, and I felt I was being pounced on. I was the enemy. If I didn't say something immediately, he'd be close to me as paint on canvas. At that moment, I wasn't sure if he himself would become violent. It's dark, I thought to myself. It felt like overwhelming darkness, like a shroud had been tossed over us. The Longs didn't believe their son had done anything wrong, regardless of what they heard in the courtroom. They must have thought, If only this woman had understood that their son couldn't have done this, then their son wouldn't have been in the mess he was in.

I realized that both parents were under a great deal of stress, but I was working to help, not hurt, Bobby Joe Long. Anger helped none of us. I said more than once that I was working "for Bobby and not against him."

They weren't having it. I made every effort to try to explain. "It is not me personally who is saying these things. This is what Bobby Joe said to me when I evaluated him. We are all trying to help him. He is not going to go free, you understand that, don't you? But what the lawyers are doing at this hearing is to try to get him a life sentence. And they'll continue that every step of the way. He'll be behind bars, but he'll have his life."

It all seemed to fall on deaf ears, though. I did not need to fight with the Longs; I needed their help. I needed details about Bobby Joe's life as a child, teen, and young adult, along with a clear picture of the lives of Louella and Joe. It was indeed a tightrope to walk; I needed information from them, yet I had to stand my ground as a doctor. I wouldn't be bullied by them, and the tête-à-tête ended in a kind of standoff.

Even before the hearing, on March 11, 1985, I sent the Longs a letter asking them to complete a lengthy child history document so that I could better assess Bobby Joe. On April 15, I sent another reminder letter, since neither Joe nor Louella had taken the time to post the essential information. It wasn't until May 3 that Joe returned his survey, but it was incomplete, lacking most information on the family medical history as well as other more minor facts like birth dates and occupations. Either they had forgotten or they didn't really want to know how Bobby Joe came to become what the newspapers in the Tampa area were calling a shameless monster who had killed nine women. I kept after them, though, trying to win their trust, as it was crucial to the research that was needed for Bobby Joe Long's upcoming trial. It meant writing a series of impassioned, single-spaced, three-page letters, but eventually I won them over.

Joe Long, an earnest man who was permanently injured while working in a paper mill, said he didn't see anything wrong with Bobby Joe throughout his son's childhood. But he and Louella separated before Bobby was a year old. The only odd incident he could recall from Bobby's childhood was that "Bobby was scared of snow and a snowstorm. He was young and flying here [from Florida to West Virginia] alone. Due to a very bad snowstorm, his flight was delayed in Cincinnati, Ohio, where he was put up in a hotel room alone all night." Joe did go on to say that his mother had had "seizures for as long as I can recall. Over a long period of time she has been tested by several doctors and they could never determine what caused them." Joe described these episodes as "she will slap her chest and stomp her feet and say there is a hot smothering sensation that overcomes her. There are times that she will pass out for a few seconds. . . . She is then perfectly normal." He also mentioned that his brother suffered from a "deep depression. During that time of the brother's illness his father-in-law was slowly dying of cancer." This family history really had nothing to do with the killings that Bobby Joe committed in the Tampa area. It's true that Bobby Joe's grandmother had seizures. It's true that Bobby Joe's uncle felt depressed. But nothing linked these illnesses to serial killing, so they were unrelated to Bobby Joe's problems. As the surgeons frequently say, "True, true, but unrelated." There were no signs that Bobby Joe had any kind of seizures or any deep depressions, either, and no signs of inheriting any type of genetic illness.

Though Joe was adamant in saying that his son had no health problems, he did reveal that the boy failed the first grade, "due to his changing school and that perhaps he was too young to become interested." Later, Bobby Joe also had trouble with insubordination in the armed forces at Homestead Air Force Base near Miami, Florida. He received a dishonorable discharge (which was later changed to an honorable discharge).

It was while in the Army that Bobby Joe suffered what his father called "the accident." To him, it was such a significant injury that he never even referred to the details of "the accident" in a many-paged handwritten letter to me. It was as if the result of the accident was too monumental to comprehend. Bobby Joe suffered severe trauma when his motorcycle was hit by a car and he was thrown forty feet from the vehicle, landing on his head (which was somewhat protected by a helmet). Joe said that it was after the accident that life changed for Bobby, and he offered proof in the form of a doctor's statement from the armed forces saying that Bobby Joe had indeed suffered brain damage resulting from the crash.

There are a few people who believe there is a direct link between serial killing and brain trauma. Psychiatrist Dorothy Lewis, in her book *Guilty by Reason of Insanity*, writes that a brain injury through accident or through physical abuse is evident in some of our most vicious killers. As an example, she writes about Arthur Shawcross, a vile murderer whom I have profiled. Shawcross took the lives of eleven women not far from the Upstate New York community of Rochester in the late 1980s. The sight of the mutilated bodies shocked the hunters and policemen who found them in and around the bucolic Genesee River Gorge. When more information became available, it was learned that with a knife, Shawcross removed and ate some of his victims' vaginas during his crimes. While these facts will hold some interest for fans of true-crime books, I had no real eureka moments with Shawcross or with police or lawyers during the case.

What engages me is this. Dr. Lewis states that under hypnosis, Shawcross told bits and pieces of his crimes, so Lewis theorized that he suffered incomplete temporal lobe seizures that wreaked havoc with his memory. She believed that the seizures occurred only when Shawcross was alone with the women, most of whom were prostitutes. After poring over the results of an MRI, she also found a cyst growing at the base of Shawcross's temporal lobe. Her partner, Jonathan Pincus, also found "two straight little scars" on both temporal lobes. While these are important findings, they are just not enough to prove that the growth precipitated or even influenced his behavior. What she hadn't proven was that one thing led to the other. That's not to say she was wrong. She needed to study the patient more fully, and more fully means attaching him to a machine that studies the brain while he is carrying on normal daily activities. Certainly, Dr. Lewis needed to examine more than one person who had a brain cyst and who murdered in a serial fashion. As I've detailed, John Wayne Gacy's brain had no tumors or cysts whatsoever. I do not believe brain trauma caused Arthur Shawcross to kill and I don't believe it caused Bobby Joe Long to kill. Again, it's true; true, but unrelated.

Letters from Bobby Joe's mother were more emotional and detailed than those from his father. Despite her various jobs as a bartender, a carhop, and a barmaid, Louella was an old-fashioned gal at heart. She claimed she drank alcohol fewer than fifty times in her forty-six years and that she never touched a beer or hard liquor. She said she preferred buttermilk.

She admitted that she had married far too early, so early that she didn't know how babies were born. Like many small-town girls of the time, she thought children "came out of the navel." After her father was killed in an on-the-job accident, Louella and her mother lived in what she frankly described as "a shack." Louella wrote, "Mom was a good person morally, but she didn't know how to raise children, and so we didn't know how to raise children (either)."

It was clear that Louella cared dearly about her only son, and the following letter is indicative of her doting nature. Louella wrote:

Son,

Do you realize, Bob, that until the other night, I'd never heard you talk dirty in your life. It ripped me to shreds. Have you become so hardened, son, that you just don't care anymore. Don't you know that I have planned and thought hundreds of times how I could get you out of there? I find myself doing this and I think, What's wrong with me, am I really planning this? Am I crazy? There's no way I could get you out and then I think more about it and I know I wouldn't want you out right now—in the shape you're in. Son, what's happened to you? . . . I remember your voice on the phone the last 2 or 3 times before all this happened. It's so unreal. I guess I've never really convinced myself you could've done these things—even though I know you did. It's just so impossible, seeing you with people and living with you, and knowing how you were with your children. I can still see you so many times combing Chris' hair for him, helping him put on his shoes and socks, brushing Bobby Joe's hair. Washing and drying the laundry. Folding their little clothes so carefully and putting them away. Taking them out with the dog and going to the lake. You were such an ordinary kind of person—what happened to him. Oh, son, don't let yourself become so hardened [that] no one can reach you. Be kind to people. Search for the good in them. You'll find more people wanting to help you. . . . Anything I ever did that hurt you or humiliated you, I'm so sorry for. I'm so sorry for everything I didn't do that I should have, and things I did that I shouldn't have.

Bobby Joe Long himself said he didn't remember enjoying all that much happiness with his mother, and on hearing this, Louella was aghast. She wrote about her feelings as if she had been stabbed through the heart.

I don't see how Bob could have blocked out every happy thing we did in our lives. The first 6 or 8 years we were in Fla., we went everywhere together. I have movies and photographs from all those places—monkey jungle, parrot jungle, seaquarium, porpoise show in the keys, Daytona, Spook Hill, and hundreds of pictures of many different days each year at the beaches. When he was small, we spent all our time together. . . . I never brought a man home and "kicked Bob out of bed." We lived in decent people's homes and I had to enter that home and come out of that home and I did not bring men home, as it was told at the last trial.

Whether Louella Long was telling mistruths or whether time led her to recall only good things doesn't really matter. Although she wasn't telling the whole story, as we'll soon see, nothing Louella did as a single mother bringing up her child made Bobby into the killer he became. To some, that may sound obvious, but it needs to be said because so many parents resort to self-blame, or are blamed by others for the serial murders of their child.

Millions of children are the products of terribly broken homes, and while they may harbor some emotional scars, they don't resort to the odious crimes for which Bobby Joe Long was tried. Whether or not Louella once asked Bobby to leave her bed so she could have sex with a boyfriend has no bearing on the crimes he committed later in life. As he murdered, he was never trying to lay retribution upon a society or a mother that he felt had dealt him a horrible childhood. However, Louella's overwrought emotions were indicative of the bottomless guilt and hostility a parent feels when her child commits the most morally and ethically repugnant crime of all . . . over and over again. Some parents and families never get over the weight of it all, condemning themselves to wallow in a past of shock and sorrow, constantly reliving the precise moments when they heard their son was accused. They pore over their past lives with their child, searching for clues as to where they went wrong. It's almost a twilight zone of regret, a self-made purgatory from which they never emerge whole and unscathed.

Louella (as well as Joe) was indeed suspicious of me early on, questioning my motives, as though I were working against Bobby Joe. But as I gained Louella's confidence, she began to open up, most specifically in a long missive in October of 1985. In the nineteen-page letter, handwritten and single spaced on legal-size paper, Louella detailed a few peculiarities in Bobby Joe Long's childhood that bear mentioning.

Louella's mother, Mamie, told her that "a couple of times she found him in the closet hiding and he told her something was after him and he was scared to come out. Naturally, she stayed with him 'til he went to sleep, I never knew of him being afraid." But in a letter to me dated November 30, 1985, Mamie wrote from her home in Shenandoah, Georgia,

> When Bobby was little and had to be by his self, he would hide in the closet with his ball bat crying his eyes out. Said Big Eyes was out to get him. I begged his Mom to get him help but she said she couldn't and then just before this [Bobby's crimes] happened, I told her their was something bad wrong with him. And her and Joe just would not listen. He acted like his mind was so troubled and didn't even look like his self. I ask God to please watch over him and give the judges the mind to not give him the chair.

Who was Big Eyes? Most monsters imagined are fully formed, not disembodied. Children see the monster under the bed, a shadowy figure, but a figure with a body nonetheless. But what Bobby Joe saw generally is a symptom that appears with people who fear being watched, kind of an early paranoia. Serial killers are suspicious folk, even before police are watching them. What Bobby Joe saw was an example of a very primitive psychological state, as though he had not moved emotionally from the earliest stages of infancy. Babies don't initially see you; they see shapes, forms, undefined types of pieces that lack wholeness. They see parts. It hit me like lightning striking. Like other serial killers I had profiled and interviewed, Long had never matured emotionally beyond infancy.

Additionally, Louella had written to me about a hormone imbalance that made him appear as though he had breasts like a woman. Called gynecomastia, it's a fairly common anomaly caused by either excess fat or glandular tissue. It can be somewhat embarrassing, since it gives the chest area a decidedly female contour. Louella gave a lot of thought to Bobby's dilemma, ultimately deciding on surgery. Said Louella, "A doctor gave him 6 or 7 shots hoping to decrease his chest, but it did nothing, so they suggested surgery. It wasn't that bad, but bad enough that it made him very self-conscious about his shirts and the doctor said for his mental sake, we should have the fatty tissue removed."

She also said she hadn't seen "Bob cry since he was hit by the car when he was 7 years old, except when the kids tormented him at school about his teeth protruding so much." There were also periods when "he was so cold and indifferent—days at a time."

Like many fifteen-year-olds, Bobby hid some pornography from his mother. But she also discovered his curiosity went far beyond photographs. "There were holes in the bathroom and in my closet which adjoined his (at the top as a separate compartment with sliding doors and he'd made a hole in his & could look directly into my dressing table mirror & see the entire room. I don't know how many years it had been there." Louella thought that Bobby may have played the voyeur and watched her with a boyfriend who lived with the two briefly. "Bob hated his guts. They had a terrible fight one night (over the placement of some shoes in the living room) . . . It was a bloody mess. I couldn't believe the hatred in Bob. He bloodied Jim's nose and beat him pretty pitifully . . . I don't know if Bob had watched us make love through that hole in the closet or not, but I feel in my heart he did, and that's why he hated Jim so much. . . . But Bob has never been able to forgive anyone anything. Why? He's hated my family for years & he wouldn't even speak to them. Why can't he forgive people?" Again, this boundless rage is the kind of reaction an emotionally immature person would exhibit. When children see their parents having sex, children often think one is hurting the other. Although Bobby was a teenager, he didn't have fully developed emotions. In fact, he never would.

According to Louella, Bobby began to imagine things that never really happened regarding the family. "He thought I was a mean, hard person who slapped people. Even said I slapped my sisters Luanne & Sharon right in the face. That's never happened in my entire life, but he really believes it—like he believes he very nearly drowned and they had to grab him in and resuscitate him. [But actually] he was holding onto a raft and the lifeguard went out & got him. We were up eating at the hot dog stand 5 minutes later." Bobby had posted two angry letters to Louella from jail chastising her about the near drowning that she adamantly believes had never occurred.

John Wayne Gacy's sister Karen was not as forgiving of her brother as Louella was of her son. Karen again and again acknowledged that Gacy's killings were a huge burden on her family. In early 1979, she wrote to John,

> You probably have wondered why I haven't written, but what does one say. I am shattered inside and out. I have not been able to function like I did before because the nightmare is always there.
>
> I was so proud of you, that you changed your life after Iowa [where he was incarcerated for sodomy], and then this. Why is all I ask? Why? Was sex that big a thing with you that you had to pick on innocent boys and then kill them because they would tell on you. God, why? Why didn't you come to us for help?
>
> My family has been torn apart by this; I only pray to God that the kids are not affected by this. Sheri was so torn up we had to get counseling for her. I'm still under doctors care, and Mom who know what its affects have been on her.
>
> What in God's name can I say to you. I am sorry I didn't get the chance to help you. Several times I got the feeling you wanted to tell me something and never did. You have been sick for a long time and I only wish I could have spotted it and helped you.
>
> We are going to try and piece our lives together the best we can as I know there is no way we can help you now. Only God can help you.

Mad Biter Richard Macek's wife, Sandra, was ambivalent about the misdeeds of her husband. She avoided going to see Macek at Central State Hospital in Wisconsin, saying, "I really haven't gone up to there myself or taken the kids up to him because I get very upset. He upsets me. He upsets them. I get all uptight. [My daughter] cries for days afterwards. At first I thought I wasn't going to make it through it, because all I did was walk around crying."

Unsurprisingly, she just didn't want to believe Macek was a murderer. She went on at length about how Richard helped the neighbors, repeatedly carrying a wheelchair-bound neighbor's mother down the stairs. "He even took days to make a lion costume for our daughter for Halloween. He brought animals home for the kids. A whole menagerie. I had four dogs. I had two cats. I don't know how many ducks. I had four birds. A tank full of fish."

But just as I detailed at the beginning of this book, Macek could change within seconds. Sandra related, "The day I went up to be with him for the lie detector test—he was boiling because he told me not to come unless I drove, and I felt I didn't want to drive. The weather was bad and I don't like to drive when it gets icy. So I took a train. They couldn't test him because he was so fired up at me. He was mad at me the whole day."

Worried, I recall leaning over to Sandra while we talked at Chicago's O'Hare Airport, saying, "I have concerns for the safety of several people he feels have crossed him if he ever got out. Do you think he would hurt you?"

She started by being somewhat indignant. How could he hurt her? They were married; they had a deep bond. But then she opened up. "I've never been afraid of Richard before now, and I'm not afraid of him now. But I do want a divorce. I've had girlfriends say, 'Well, how come your husband hasn't come around to see your new baby [who was born while Richard was in jail]?' I just say 'I don't know. He's in California somewhere.' I can't handle it any other way. If they ask about the Macek who's in jail, I say, 'I don't know who that is. Maybe it's a relative of Richard's family, but I don't know.' That's why I want to have my name changed. I don't want it to be Macek anymore. I don't want my kids to go through any more questions about their father being a murderer."

I can only imagine the trauma, the distressing combination of embarrassment and sadness, that a child can go through when harassed by other children about their father's murdering ways. They have to think about it every day of their lives. If they meet anybody new, the questions, formerly innocuous but now dire, inevitably come up. The innocent questions people ask when first meeting someone become dark and burdensome to answer. They echo loudly and persistently: How many brothers and sisters do you have? What are they like? Where's your family from? What do they do? Do you confess that your father had killed so mercilessly and fiercely? Never. You can only do one thing. You lie. You have to.

And imagine the ordeal of the divorced mother of the child, sitting alone at night at the kitchen table after everyone has gone to bed, trying desperately to make sense of something that makes no sense at all. Her friends have disappeared. They'll have nothing to do with her. If she testified for her spouse, she was immediately branded: she was as bad as he was. Kinship and loyalty are not supposed to exist with someone who has committed crimes so grievous as serial killing.

Friends and acquaintances sense that the family must have known that the killings were going on; therefore, the parents are guilty too. They have spawned this monster, and they must pay a price. Do townspeople march up to their houses with burning torches and raised pitchforks and scream "You grew a killer!" similar to the old *Frankenstein* movie? No. But there are more subtle and no less hurtful responses, like being shunned. If you haven't left town before the neighbors turn against you, you probably will when they do.

After thinking about all these things and more, Louella wished she could change not only history but also everything in her life. She had described herself as an "outsider—always aching for someone to love me" and had said that her life as a child was "a very scary time," for her and her sisters; as a result, they "suffered from colitis [the intestinal ailment] almost all our lives." At the end of her letter Louella wrote impassionedly, "It's such a shame that we can't live our lives over, after we've smartened up and come to realize the true values of life—like our precious children and our devotion to them & God, who gave them to us to bring them up in the right way." I truly wished that things had turned out better for Louella, but history can't be changed. Louella would eventually deal with the crimes of her son, yet somewhere in her mind they would always haunt her. It might hit her when she was making coffee or when she looked at a family photo or when she was at the beach or when she woke inexplicably in the middle of the night. She would be reminded of Bobby. She would be reminded of a killer. And though she shouldn't have, some part of her would always blame herself.

On the other hand, stewing angrily in his jail cell, there was Bobby Joe Long himself. He didn't blame himself. He couldn't. He had no remorse at all, not one molecule of it.

ELEVEN

THE SADISM OF ROBERT BERDELLA

Violence and sadism of the worst sort. Some people might think I enjoy studying it, that because I have been around violent people like serial killers for the past thirty-five years, I take morbid pleasure from all the evil things that humans do to one another. But that couldn't be further from the truth. I abhor violence, and deep down, I don't know why people are so brutal to one another. That's why the crimes of Robert Andrew Berdella Jr. literally made me sick to my stomach.

After being around Macek, Gacy, Long, and many others, I thought I knew violence as well as I could know it. I felt that I could function very well as a doctor and as a wife and mother even while I was immersed in analyzing the hideous thought processes that possess the mind of every serial killer. Yes, it's not easy. When I'm deeply involved in a case, I'm late for dinner parties and my children's extracurricular activities. It's just part of the job, though I find I'm usually able to focus on the work at hand, whether it's interviewing a serial killer or being a parent. But I recall that I was really thrown off-kilter by the savagery of Robert Berdella. His crimes were so intricate, experimental, and sadistic that they made me sick. I don't mean that it merely disgusted me or repulsed me. It got to me, deep inside.

In a way, Robert Berdella Jr. was like the child who pulls the wings off flies, except Berdella's deeds were exponentially more depraved. A boy might capture a fly with his hands or with an empty jelly jar. When the insect is weakened, the boy might pull off its wings or stick pins into it. When a child tortures an insect, he does it to see what happens. He can't hear the fly react in pain. If he could hear the insect scream, the boy might well regret his actions.

Robert Berdella, sometimes called the Butcher of Kansas City, simply "wanted to see what happened." Berdella lived a handful of blocks from Main Street in Kansas City, near historic Hyde Park, an area of beautifully restored houses through which the original Santa Fe trail cut a swath.

But Berdella wasn't like the proud residents who kept a neat house, maintained their lawns, and trimmed their shrubs. His house was full of clutter, everything from opened dog food containers to a colorful, embroidered robe from Afghanistan that hung oddly like a painting from his bedroom wall. This robe was likely picked from the inventory of a business he ran at a nearby flea market. He christened this shop Bob's Bazaar Bizarre, and it was full of oddities like African deity masks and books about the occult. It was from sales of objects here that the lisping Berdella made his living.

There was once a short article about Berdella in the local paper, about how the graduate (actually, he dropped out) of the Kansas City Art Institute transformed his house into a gallery showcasing primitive art from Egypt, Italy, and New Guinea. Tours, the newspaper item said, could be arranged by appointment. I don't think there ever were any "tours." And if the house was a gallery for a while, it soon became more of a warehouse full of Berdella's collections of weird stuff. Berdella was a pack rat the way Ed Gein was a pack rat, and the clutter in the house grew with every passing day.

The newspaper article, however, reported nothing about the strange goings-on inside the house. When Berdella tortured men in his unobtrusive three-story home at 4315 Charlotte Street, he often raped them "to see what happened." He even stuck his finger hard into the eye of a bound victim "to see what happened." And those acts were just the beginning of his coldhearted observations.

Berdella was an experimenter, but unlike even the most amateur scientist, he conducted his experiments as rote actions only. Berdella actually reminded me of another infamous experimenter, H. H. Mudgett, who killed during the Chicago World's Fair. Both drew no thoughtful conclusions from what they did. Certainly Berdella developed no theories based upon the confessed killing and mutilation and dismemberment of six men. (Actually, I believe he probably committed a lot more murders, since it was documented that there were at least twenty people whom he tortured, though these did not die. But six murders were the only ones police could pin on him.) Berdella chronicled his experiments in detailed bound diaries and in 334 Polaroid photographs that police discovered in his cluttered home. They were buried amid bric-a-brac, antiques, and curiosities, storage from Bob's Bazaar Bizarre.

It wasn't inside the shop that Berdella carried out his most heinous work. In his basement, but mainly in a second-floor bedroom, Berdella created a rudimentary torture chamber that included a bed, piano wire, a black velveteen rope, various animal tranquilizers, a wooden club, needles and syringes, cucumbers, carrots, a spatula, some copper wire, and a 7,700-volt transformer.

What he did with these tools was explained in his diaries, notebooks with a spiral binding at the top. They were dark and difficult to stomach, the epitome of man's inhumanity to man. The pages of Berdella's journal of murder were more like a madman's logbook than the secret musings and intimate thoughts of a human being. The grisly yet impassively described details made it too easy to imagine Berdella, looming over his victims with his six-foot-two frame and thick glasses, breathing heavily, experimenting, torturing, using, then killing. And as I reeled from this catalog of horrors I felt not only how blessed I was in my personal life but also a new resolve and a sense of purpose.

I looked most closely at the case of Larry Pearson, a sometime male prostitute who Berdella kept as a bound, frightened, and tortured hostage. He kept him not for a day and not for a week, but for six weeks. There is a photo of Larry Pearson, snapped by Berdella, that says so much about the torture that the killer inflicted. Lying on the thinnest of mattresses, the twenty-year-old is tied in Berdella's basement to a brick post, tied by his hands not with rope but with piano wire and handcuffs. The piano wire goes around his back, under his arms and into his mouth, tightly, so that it gags him, making him not only unable to talk, but also unable to make just about any sound at all, especially the sound of screaming. It is wrapped over his mouth and behind him three or four times so that his mouth is forced open. Pearson cannot close his mouth to swallow well. The wire digs not only into his skin but also into his facial muscle.

Also in the picture, a syringe and hypodermic needle stick at an angle just below his Adam's apple; in case the gag and piano wire did not work, Berdella had injected Drano into Larry Pearson's vocal cords so that Pearson would not scream. Pearson's eyes were shut and puffy. Berdella had taken a cotton swab and dabbed Drano into the victim's eyes as well. In the photo, he almost looks as though he is dead. But he would live like that—and even live worse, as he was tortured incessantly—for a month and a half.

Larry Pearson was Berdella's fifth victim, kidnapped and bound on Tuesday, June 23, 1987, not long after the two went to watch *Creepshow II*. When the two returned to Berdella's house, they began drinking. Berdella said they each had "twelve to fifteen shots," everything from vodka to schnapps. Berdella added some tranquilizers to Larry's drinks. Early in the evening, Berdella injected Pearson with four shots of chlorpromazine, a potent tranquilizer somewhat like Thorazine. Sometimes used for schizophrenia to stop the patient from hearing voices, the drug is nicknamed "the chemical straitjacket" because it can leave the user in a zombielike state. Like morphine, it is also sometimes used to ease the distress of the terminally ill. It's certainly not supposed to be in the hands of a nonprofessional of any sort. Yet chlorpromazine was fairly easy for Berdella to find. It is also used as an animal tranquilizer, and it was likely that Berdella bought the drug over the counter. And even if it wasn't, Berdella was no stranger to the world of drugs and to procuring them; he pled guilty to selling amphetamines when he was a sophomore in college.

On the rare occasion when Pearson became lucid, he tried to cry out but was unable to make more than a peep because his vocal cords were so damaged. But he must have mulled over the many horrors of his capture whenever his mind was clear.

Larry Pearson, a well-built, good-looking man with a thin mustache, met Berdella by chance when he stopped in to browse at Bob's Bazaar Bizarre. Later, when Berdella was driving along the streets of Kansas City, he would spot Pearson walking on the street and stop to offer him a ride. And without a thought, Pearson would get in. If the two weren't friends, they had become acquaintances. When Pearson was nabbed for indecent exposure a few weeks before Berdella took him hostage, Pearson phoned Berdella to post bond, which he did. Once Pearson was sprung from jail, the pair rode in Berdella's car to Ohio to visit Robert's family. Berdella felt it was peculiar that Pearson would call his own mother "Mom." After all, he had just met her. Odder yet was the fact that later, Pearson told Berdella's mother and stepfather stories about picking up a woman and how they "got into porno films together." When the two returned to Kansas City, Pearson moved in. He and Berdella didn't sleep in the same bed. Instead, Pearson stayed on Berdella's couch.

Something unknown built up in Berdella during those days in Ohio, and he felt that Pearson was exceedingly rude to his family. He wanted to have sex with Larry, but Pearson didn't give any indication that he wanted it or would have accepted any overtures. Long after his capture, when he decided to confess to avoid a death sentence, police asked Berdella if a comment Pearson made was the trigger for his capture.

Berdella reported that as they drove the streets of Kansas City shortly after seeing *Creepshow II,* Larry said, "I used to roll queers over in Wichita. Robbed 'em." Berdella let this pass without much debate, but it could have gnawed at him inside. Yet I don't believe Pearson's alleged prejudice was the trigger that made Robert begin his capture and torture. There was no evidence in the other murders that an emotion like rage played a part in Berdella's experiments. And Berdella did say about the comment, "I guess it was the trigger. I hadn't been thinking about it for days before or anything . . . I probably quickly formed the opinion 'This is somebody that no one's going to end up missing; they aren't going to know where he's at.'" His iffy answer seemed more like the response of someone who wanted to please the police, and to get the ordeal of the confession, then in its third day, over and done with.

Once Pearson was immobilized in the basement, Berdella brought five things down the stairs: two wires, two clamps of the sort that would be used to jump-start a stalled car, and a transformer, which he had purchased used at the flea market, one that emitted 7,700 volts. After sodomizing him with his finger and biting his nipple hard enough to draw blood, he attached the clamps onto Pearson, and over the next twelve hours, he gave Pearson a half-dozen ten- to thirty-second jolts from his rudimentary shock machine. During this time, he also whipped him, clubbed him, shoved a carrot into his anus, and then brutally raped him.

There were photos too of Pearson receiving the abhorrent electrical shocks. The victim would lurch forward, even though he was constrained so well that he shouldn't have been able to move. The look in his protruding eyes, eyes that looked ready to leave their sockets, was not one of fear so much as it was of pain and surprise. And there was Berdella, lisping away, commanding Pearson to keep quiet, all the while snapping photographic records of the poor man, Polaroids that he would later use to masturbate.

Though he was often drugged, some part of Pearson was lucid enough to understand that he was to be slave to Berdella's master. He was brought out to do his job and nothing more, and his job was to satisfy Berdella. Because he minded Berdella's commands for weeks, Robert moved the man upstairs to a bedroom. Berdella would sit and watch television with Pearson chained up next to him in bed, but Pearson wasn't allowed to comment or to talk or to make any noise whatsoever.

After five weeks, Berdella presumed that his slave was completely under his control. On Wednesday, August 5, Berdella made Pearson perform oral sex on him. At that point, perhaps fueled by hope for escape and an anger that had boiled over despite Berdella's efforts to tame him as though he were a wild animal, Pearson fought back.

"I'm not going to be treated this way anymore!" he cried, according to Berdella. In one swift moment, Pearson bit Berdella so hard, he nearly severed his penis. It was then that Pearson had his chance to escape. I'm positively sure the reason Pearson stayed in the room wasn't due to what Berdella theorized when he said, "I think more than anything else he bit me because he wanted attention." Was Pearson too afraid or too weak to leave? It's more complex than that. I don't believe Larry Pearson could make a choice to escape. There is the kind of person who has developed a victim mentality, and the unthinkable happens to him because he gets to the point where he no longer feels he has the free will to escape. Pearson may have thought for a moment he could make a run for it but then thought better of it.

Berdella then injected him with acepromazine, an animal tranquilizer, and began thrashing Pearson with part of a tree limb. It was thick, splitting Pearson's lip and knocking him out. Then Berdella, oozing a lot of blood from Pearson's bite, drove himself to the hospital. Upon examining him, doctors informed Berdella that he required immediate hospitalization, at least for a couple of days.

"I have to go home first to leave some food for my dogs," worried Berdella as he spoke to the doctor. "But then I'll come back."

Once home, Berdella looked in on the condition of Larry Pearson. He saw that Larry's face looked as though it had been put through a meat grinder. Berdella pulled a plastic bag over Pearson's head, secured it tightly, and went to feed the dogs. There's a kind of profiler who has studied behavioral science who believes that serial killers torture and kill dogs and cats in addition to humans and that torturing animals is a precursor to killing human beings. But I have not seen this to be true. Serial killers like Berdella can have pets, and they dote on them and treat them well—much better than their victims.

Berdella returned to see that the plastic bag had no more air and that his slave had expired after forty-three days of unthinkable torture. Without a twinge of human emotion, he turned away, locked up his house, and took a cab to the hospital. After an operation, he returned to the house on Friday, took a safety razor and boning knife to Pearson, and removed his internal organs and drained his blood. Because he was weak from the operation and still wearing a catheter, it took him two days to dispose of the body. Berdella used a chain saw to cut it up, then placed the body parts in dog food bags and then in plastic garbage bags. He cut off Pearson's head, some vertebrae still attached, wrapped it in a trash bag, and placed it in a freezer as a kind of keepsake. On Sunday night, he took the rest of the garbage bags and dragged them onto the street for sanitation workers to pick up on Monday. In the twilight on August 7, he retrieved the head from the freezer, dug up the head of another victim from his yard, and dropped Pearson's head in the same hole. He placed the other head in an empty, five-gallon pickle container and filled it with water to remove dirt and the remaining rotting skin and placed the container in one of the closets in his house. Why did he choose to do this? It was more like a repetition behavior than anything else. In a twisted way, it was kind of like planting a garden. Berdella may have thought, Well, last year I put cucumbers here, so I'll do the same thing this year.

Police suspected and even expected a much grander plan for disposal of the bodies. They deduced that Berdella would try to hide them carefully or in a place that would be unnoticed. To help solve the case, they brought in from Texas a dog called Junior along with his trainer, Sergeant Billy Smith, to search the backyard after they'd already found Pearson's skull. Smith, who had the words *LOVE* and *HATE* tattooed on his knuckles, had a plastic container of human flesh which he had the dog whiff to get him going for the hunt. At first, Junior found nothing. Then he began to growl and Sergeant Billy Smith said, "Junior smells death. The smell of death is strong around here." The dog began barking near Berdella's chimney and at the door of an old tool shed. Upon digging, the police did find some teeth . . . dentures disposed of by previous occupants of the house.

They even searched various nearby farms where Berdella traveled to visit friends. They *did* detect a body on one of the farms. But on closer examination, it was the body of a cow. The police never imagined it was as simple as it was; Berdella just threw the bodies out as trash. To him, it was just garbage. What do you do when you're done with your experiment? You dispose of it; you throw it away. Berdella murdered his other victims in a similar fashion, although with only one other person did he choose to keep the skull. One might ask why he kept the skulls. Were they totems, souvenirs, or something darker and deeper to Berdella? The simple fact is that I don't know. I've certainly asked Berdella and all of them over and over again. But serial murderers themselves can't explain these actions. And I cannot venture a guess or a theory when there isn't enough data to lead me there.

Berdella might never have been caught by police (who, as is usually the case, did not believe that the disappearance of drifters was a priority), but one of those whom he preyed upon escaped. The wily nature of his last slave, Chris Bryson, proved too much for Berdella. When Berdella left the house to attend to errands, Bryson, using matches left near his bed, burnt through the four ropes that bound him. Completely unclothed, Bryson then leapt from the second-floor window and ran to a neighbor for help. When Berdella returned home in his Toyota Tercel on the day before Easter 1988, police were camped out, waiting for him.

As the police took him away, the so-called butcher of Kansas City kept repeating, "This is not right. This is not right." He could not believe he had been caught. Moreover, he did not believe he had done anything wrong.

While in Kansas City for a conference for the Midwest Chapter of the American Academy of Psychiatry and the Law in the spring of 1988, I spoke to *Kansas City Star* journalist Tom Jackman, who was contemplating writing a book about Berdella. When I met with him at my hotel, it was clear that the serial killer's doings had rocked the city and frightened many of its 1.5 million residents. It was no help to the collective soul of the city that television personality Geraldo Rivera had swooped down and interviewed a woman who claimed that Berdella was a Satanist and that she had seen him attend various Satanist gatherings.

Jackman helped to arrange my face-to-face contacts with the jailed killer so that I could learn more about his mind. I was interested in the ritual experimentation that Berdella performed on each of his six known victims, and Berdella was happy to talk. After all, he was in jail for life and had nothing better to do with the forty hours we talked.

Berdella spoke to me wearing paper prison clothes and thongs on his feet. (Shoelaces have long been banned, because they possibly could be used as a weapon or in a suicide attempt.)

"Did you do all those crimes they accused you of?" I asked.

"Of course. I have already confessed to them."

He seemed somewhat annoyed, as though he felt I wasn't familiar with his case. But I had read the transcripts of his three-day, 715-page confession along with many other documents about him. I also had all of his school reports, most of which pegged him as a really good student who earned As and Bs without much effort. He was not unlike most serial killers in that regard. Many have IQs that are above average, though none are geniuses. Still, one English teacher wrote, "Very argumentative, sarcastic. Insists on his own way." And, of course, I had read those eerie Berdella torture diaries, written hastily amid the excitement of his experiments. He scrawled all of the words in capital letters, as though the writer himself screamed for attention, even though his words were abbreviated. He used "FRT FK" to abbreviate "front fuck," for instance. Beyond being perturbed at what he perceived as my lack of knowledge, it was clear that the torture to which he subjected his victims was no big deal to him.

"And why did you torture them?"

"I just wanted to see what happened. In fact, I tried to help these people recover from their infections with antibiotics. I tried to help them."

"But you did things like stick your fingers in their eyes and then shocked them and then injected them with Drano."

"They were experiments, nothing more, nothing less." Inside, I was taken aback by his languid attitude, even though I knew he fit the pattern of all serial killers. Like the other serial killers, he was an empty shell, bereft of most human emotion. Still, something here bothered me. As the hours passed and I talked with him, I realized this guy was probably the most heinous, most perfect clinical example of someone who lacked humanity and human emotion. He said repeatedly that he had tried to help the people, whom he considered to be his slaves. But it was just something he said, said without emotion, without empathy or sympathy, said just because he felt he was probably supposed to say something like that.

"You had all kinds of sex with those people. Can you tell me about that?"

"I kept them for my excitement, to do my bidding, so that they would not even think of doing anything without my permission."

When Berdella talked about excitement, it was not the kind of excitement that most people feel. It was not a pleasure full of joy, delight, or happiness. It was not the soft warmth a young lover feels after making love. There was no elation when Berdella had sex, nor did he feel any comfort when someone like Pearson lay next to him in bed. He had a person next to him, but he was not really a companion. It was similar to a young child manipulating his environment. He plays and plays and doesn't stop until he feels the object (in this case, the person) belongs to him. Whatever is his belongs to him and him alone, and he'll keep it as long as he can, like Charles Schulz's Linus and his security blanket.

Like a child, Berdella learned about his victims by doing things to them rather than by planning what to do. In other words, he had a more concrete relationship to the person he was hurting. The intent was not to murder, but just to experiment. When I use the word *concrete,* it's important to understand what I mean. Psychiatrists use *concrete* to indicate a thinking and learning style. Every young child has concrete thinking. It's why they don't teach math to children until the second or third grade; math requires abstract thinking, a way of thinking that goes beyond what the child can see. In kindergarten, for example, teachers use manipulatives, as they call them, like beans or coins to teach children to count. Kids can't picture in their mind the value of what "6 + 6" is.

I'm not saying that Berdella couldn't count well. I'm saying that he couldn't grasp the abstract ideas about life itself, ideas that every human deals with every day. Berdella, when it came to his victims, couldn't picture what the meaning of torture or even death is. He didn't know that it hurt. He didn't know that it caused irreparable harm. Even when Pearson bit Berdella's penis, Berdella didn't understand it. He felt the pain, but not enough to kill Pearson. Most people might immediately react to the pain by wanting to get back at the person who hurt them, a reaction that might lead to killing someone who did such a thing. Berdella did nothing to Pearson right away; he just left the house and went to the hospital.

So Berdella's torturing of Larry Pearson and the others was almost like a baby playing with a ball or one of those motorized playthings that hangs over a crib. He did not feel it was evil. He did not feel it was wrong. The only way to look at Berdella's failure when it came to emotional maturity is that he was a curious baby boy playing with a toy.

And when he masturbated while looking at the photos of his victims, there was no savoring of the moments past. For him, it was just a release without emotion. Some doctors have called Berdella a sexual psychopath. But even that moniker gives him too much credit for partially being whole and human. Psychopaths only experience a lack of conscience. Able to kill without experiencing remorse, psychopaths are otherwise humans like the rest of us, able to experience joy and happiness.

Yet another psychiatrist said that Berdella was lashing out at people who remind him too much of himself. But this psychiatrist acts as if serial killers are human beings gone astray and that psychiatrists and psychologists can explain them on the basis of any old theory. If that's the case, and if they're just old psychological structures that we know very well, then why can't we treat them? Why can't we simply give them medication to stop their killings? Why can't we use talking or behavior therapy, which works so well in other people, to help them? It can't be done, that's why. They are not treatable. They cannot be fixed and they cannot heal.

There was even one sensationalist-minded doctor who believed that Berdella got an erection when talking about his crimes during his three-day confession to police. And he said this without any proof from Berdella or from the police. But that theory is a lot of hooey; it's taking sex and aggression and making it human again. If it happened, and I doubt it did, it was an excitement but not a sexual excitement. Robert Berdella would not have confessed in order to become aroused.

He did it to avoid the death penalty, which he said to me directly. Just like Bobby Joe Long, he did not in any way want to die by the electric chair or by lethal injection.

I asked Berdella, "How did you feel when you killed Larry Pearson?"

"I put him to sleep. There was nothing else I could do. I had to go to the hospital. It was the best thing for him."

"What did you think of Larry Pearson after you killed him?"

"I didn't. Not that much. I put him out of his misery. He would have suffered while I was in the hospital. I didn't think of him very much after I disposed of the body. I had other things to do."

He sat there almost still, talking like a one-dimensional robot. In fact, he was less emotional than a robot from a 1950s B movie, less emotional than the pointy-eared Spock from *Star Trek*. As I listened to him speak, I kept thinking, There must be a motive here. This can't be all there is. Even after speaking to so many serial killers, it was still hard from me to believe. There wasn't any *there* there. I tried one more time to search for a motive. Police had discovered many things in Berdella's house. They found figures of many-headed dragons, odd windup toys that shot sparks from their mouths, raisin-colored faces with hair that looked like shrunken heads, scary plaster masks from faraway lands, a human skull replica carefully placed under glass . . . and twenty books on Satanism and witchcraft, including one called *Satanic Interpretations and Lifestyles*. Also found was a book called *How to Create Poisons*. And then there was Berdella's record player. On the turntable was a recording of Lucifer's Black Mass.

"Did you practice any kind of worship of the devil?"

"I had an interest, but nothing much more than that. I was not a Satanist, if that's what you're asking."

Satanism would have been a terrific motive for the killings. The idea of Berdella being a minion of the devil incarnate, which has struck fear in man since the dawn of religion, had spooked the eleven detectives assigned to the case. Those thoughts of the devil made them believe initially that Berdella was more complicated that he was. And the idea of devil worship had Geraldo Rivera and his television audience intrigued. But Berdella would read the books just like he would collect windup toys. He'd get them, peruse them, put them on a shelf, and pretty much forget about them. (Berdella was quite a hoarder; his lawyer once asked Berdella's mother if she wanted the criminal's papers, not his infamous notebooks, but clippings and things he collected. On hearing that he had four thousand pounds of them—two tons—she declined.)

"Did you have the Black Mass on the record player?"

"Yes, but I thought someone who came over to visit might get a kick out of listening to it. A lot of people came over to the house. These were individuals who didn't have anywhere else to go."

Like most serial murders, he wasn't killing all the time. Berdella was actively involved in his local neighborhood crime watch and with raising money for the city's public television station. He readily opened his door to the drug addicts, drunks, and prostitutes he met on the streets of Kansas City. People would stop by the house on Charlotte Street at all hours of the night to do drugs or to hang around. It makes some sense that Berdella would try to entertain them—whether or not he later chose to torture them. But the people who came by were too much chaotic stimulation for Berdella; he didn't know how to deal with them.

"Sometimes I think it was those people who did the killing."

Oh, give me a break, I thought. Though there was a theory that police toyed with stating that Berdella had help with the killings, it never came to anything. Berdella was constantly making excuses for himself. I knew it was a lie, a typical serial murderer lie, and I moved on to the next thing.

"Can you tell me anything about your family back when you were a child?"

Berdella averted his eyes. "My father died when I was sixteen. He worked at the Ford plant on an assembly line. Later he drove a truck. He liked sports a lot, more than I did. He bowled. He was just thirty-nine when he died. Too young to die."

"What else?"

"He used to beat me with a leather belt."

"A lot?"

"Yes."

"And your mother?"

Berdella stroked his big walrus mustache. "She still tries to help me while I'm here. However, we sometimes get into arguments when I call or when she travels here. I write to her often."

"When you were a child, were there any things you liked to do?"

"Orchids. I used to grow and sell orchids. I had a friend at a nursery who showed me how to grow them. And I liked to paint."

"Were there any incidents as a child that you remember, good or bad?"

"Not as a child. But at sixteen, I was raped where I worked, at a restaurant where I worked part-time."

I do not believe that Robert's murders had anything to do with his beatings by his father or with the homosexual rape he alleged he suffered as a teen. Berdella did tell me that he had gotten a gift of a chemistry set and that he was beaten by his father when he poured the remains of an experiment out the window, damaging the paint on the family's house. This says more about Robert's interest in experimentation at an early age (as did his love for growing orchids, plants that are difficult to keep alive) than it says about Robert's being forever emotionally affected by the strappings.

Unlike the other serial killers, Berdella had something of a problem with incarceration, screaming at social workers, complaining about the lack of hygiene in the prison, ultimately filing 175 grievances before being transferred to St. Louis's Potosi Correctional Center. Because Potosi was newer and he had access to TV and the library, he calmed somewhat (with the exception of a brief hunger strike, an action he took because the prison ruled that he could spend only forty dollars each month). After serving four years in prison, Robert Andrew Berdella Jr. died in prison of a heart attack at the age of forty-three.

I had learned a few important things from Berdella. The first was personal: though I had spoken with many serial murderers, I still could feel sickened about the nature of their crimes, no matter how detached I tried to be. The second thing was about the theory of experimentation and serial murderers. It was with Berdella that I began to believe that experimentation links many serial murderers, and this discovery was very compelling. I had long been intrigued by the killings of H. H. Mudgett in Chicago when I researched his case because his experiments became stranger and stranger as he killed; he sometimes cut up his victims to see what was inside. Some have called these autopsies, but there was no medical knowledge behind them. They were more like haphazard dissections. Ed Gein experimented by wearing a suit made of skin, as did John Gacy by putting the heads of his victims under water to see if they'd survive. It all was coming together. I could now say with assurance that at least some experimentation was part of every serial murderer's way of working. None of them could really pinpoint why they did these things, and that led me to believe even more that they hadn't progressed emotionally beyond the age of three to six months.

TWELVE

THE TRIGGER:
MICHAEL LEE LOCKHART

S erial killers take to the road as well. When I speak to a group of people, whether they're lawyers, doctors, or students, I sometimes joke that if it weren't for the interstate system of highways, serial killers would probably stay in one place (as did Ed Gein) and be a lot easier to apprehend. While they will occasionally take a plane, thankfully none of them has attacked anyone in the air. When they travel America's highways and byways by car, serial murderers don't do it with the manic glee of Woody Harrelson and Juliette Lewis in *Natural Born Killers,* nor do they fight with and claw at each other like the characters Mickey and Mallory did. That's fiction, and the movies rarely get it right (but then again, they don't want to; they need to entertain).

Like John Wayne Gacy, Ted Bundy, Richard Macek, and many others, most serial killers (with some exceptions I'll write about later) prefer to travel alone. They don't want partners and they usually don't want hostages. They don't have any appreciation for the mystique of the road, nor do they stop, get out, and appreciate the beauty of a waterfall along a creek or deer in a meadow along the way. And they really aren't using the car or the highways to make a rapid escape, like a bank robber might do.

Take the case of Michael Lee Lockhart, an Ohio native and high school dropout who logged thirty thousand miles in a Corvette and a Toyota on a spree that led him to brag about crimes in forty-five states. Lockhart was one of the smoothest, most charming serial killers in a murderous fraternity that is full of charmers. Adding to his allure was the fact that Lockhart was blessed by nature; he was an attractive man who took advantage of women throughout his life. (Even when he was captured and police moved him through a Gulfport, Mississippi, airport, he began flirting with an airline counter clerk, who was so moved by whatever he said that she didn't believe police when they burst her bubble by stating that Lockhart was a vicious killer. He was shackled and chained at the time, but she didn't seem to notice.) Michael told the women in his life exactly what they wanted to hear, and then, when they were hooked and he became bored or wanted something new, he'd move on.

Then, on one autumn afternoon, things changed.

In October 1987, the town of Griffith, Indiana, was a quiet little place about an hour outside of Chicago. It was the kind of place where there wasn't a lot of nasty news to report. The blue-collar workers who populated most of the town were good people who'd been though the unfortunate closing of factories in the 1970s, and they'd survived. Overall, it was a law-abiding town that was not ostentatious in any way. The town even had a curfew for teens between ages thirteen and eighteen—10:30 P.M. on school nights.

As Michael Lee Lockhart drove through Griffith, he spotted Windy Patricia Gallagher as she left school. A chatty sixteen-year-old cheerleader for the high school basketball and football squads, the pretty and likable Windy worked at the local McDonald's to make some extra money. Freckle-faced and skinny, she still seemed more like a girl than a teen, even when she wore lipstick. Lockhart followed her home. He quietly waited in the car and watched her go inside. Once she had closed the door, he waited some more, biding his time. After a few minutes passed, he got out of the car and sauntered up to the door to ring the bell. Lockhart said he needed to make a phone call, and when Gallagher saw the neatly dressed, handsome young man, she invited him in. When he lingered after the phone call, Windy initially thought nothing of it. She even gave him a glass of water.

Lockhart then dragged Windy up to the bedroom. He tied her hands behind her back and forced her bra up and over her breasts and stripped her from the waist down. With a knife, he stabbed her four times in the neck and seventeen times in the stomach. Windy's intestines were pulled up and out of her abdomen, as though they had been probed and examined, and a large pool of blood formed around her body as her life seeped away. It was such an evil murder that police began interviewing self-proclaimed Satanists in the area to see if Windy's murder had something to do with ritualistic human sacrifice (which the Satanists had bragged about on previous occasions).

The next fateful stop for Lockhart was a car dealership in Toledo, Ohio. During a test drive, Michael pointed a .357 Smith & Wesson Magnum revolver at salesman Rick Treadwell, took his money and credit cards, forced him from the red 1986 Corvette, and used its 230-horsepower engine to speed away, heading south to warmer climes in Florida. Later Lockhart would use Treadwell's identity as an alias. He also stole various IDs and a wallet from a man named Philip Tanner of Jacksonville, Florida, and used that name as well. Sometimes he would shorten his name and call himself Mike Locke.

Next came western Florida. East Lake Pladgett is part of the Land O' Lakes building project on Florida's Highway 41. Even though marketers boasted a familiar name for their new development (the famous butter is not manufactured here), real estate agents in the 1980s found it somewhat difficult to fill the homes they'd built. In a way, the town still felt like the small citrus farming community it had been prior to the building boom. Boasting one hundred lakes and a twenty-five-mile distance to Tampa, the new community allowed each of its homesteaders to feel he was well protected from the crimes of the big city, and at a good price to boot. Nice-size lots could be purchased for anywhere from four thousand to ten thousand dollars. Residents could boat and swim in the lakes, and spot the occasional heron as well.

Jennifer Lynn Colhouer, an intelligent fourteen-year-old girl, freckle-faced like Windy, enjoyed living in East Lake Pladgett. Like most Florida teens, she was fond of lying in the sun and talking with her pals on the phone, and she was excited about having her braces removed. Jennifer was the girl next door, bright, vivacious, nice. It was said that Jennifer did a terrific imitation of Cher, and she had a collection of soda pop cans, which she hung by ribbons from the ceiling in her bedroom.

The serial murderer made his way into Jennifer's house on the afternoon of January 20, 1988. Like Windy, Jennifer freely permitted the charming Lockhart access, as he posed as a real estate agent. He just seemed like such a nice guy. Most people who knew him couldn't tell that he was full of bull, at least not on the first few meetings.

Lockhart forced her quickly to the upper level of the duplex, just as he had taken Windy Gallagher. Jennifer shook from fear and panic. He pushed her T-shirt and her bra up over her breasts, and took the rest of her clothes from her. He left on her socks and sneakers. On that second floor, he sodomized her and slashed at her with a knife until she was dead. With such force and determination did he slash that Jennifer's liver was cut in two. Jennifer's intestines, like those of Windy's, spilled from her abdomen. Again, Lockhart was compelled to feel and touch Jennifer's warm blood and intestines. Lockhart was drawn to the flush of the blood and he pulled at, touched, and examined what was inside of her, but not in any truly sexual way. Also, when someone cuts open a human body, there's a warmth that rushes up that has been described by some as appealing to serial murderers, who, as I've said, have not progressed past infancy emotionally. Lockhart wanted to see what was there, what it looked like, what it felt like, what it smelled like. Police in Pasco County said the sight of Jennifer's eviscerated body was the worst thing they had ever seen in their years on the force.

Jennifer's brother Jeremy found his sister in a puddle of blood in his bedroom, next to his toys. A twelve-inch carving knife, the murder weapon taken from the kitchen, was found just beneath the wheels of a racing car, an STP decal on the toy's side. Lockhart probably had threatened her with the knife to force her upstairs.

Michael Lee Lockhart didn't stop to think about what he had done. Instead, he continued the trek in his stolen Corvette, this time heading west to the Lone Star State, getting as far as Beaumont, Texas, before settling on a place to stay for a few days.

Drugs were big in Beaumont, which had the questionable distinction of being on the country's most frequently used highways for transporting drugs. The city was trying desperately to emerge from its malaise, but it had one of the worst economies in the nation. "Dope Town" became an uncivil, drug-ridden area that most people chose to avoid.

It was drugs that Beaumont police officer Paul Hulsey Jr. was looking for when he spotted a local drug dealer and an unfamiliar man driving by in a sporty red Corvette in the early evening of March 22. Hulsey found and questioned the small-time drug dealer, who had been given a ride by Lockhart, but the Corvette had already sped away. In his heart, Hulsey felt some kind of a drug deal was going to happen sometime soon, so he searched for the Corvette in the parking lots of the local motels until he found it at the Best Western motel. When Hulsey approached Lockhart in room 157, there was an argument and then a struggle.

Lockhart found his Magnum and shot Hulsey.

"I need assistance," the injured Hulsey cried into his walkie-talkie. But those were the last words Hulsey had the strength to utter to his colleagues. Lockhart shot Hulsey again, and killed him.

Lockhart did the one thing you don't want to do anywhere, but especially not in Texas: he killed a cop. His hand bleeding profusely from being bitten by Hulsey during their clash, Lockhart ran out of the motel room and into the car, speeding away at a hundred miles an hour. As police caught up with him, he lost control of the vehicle and jumped from it before it crashed. Still, he managed to elude them, quickly cleaned up at a restaurant, and got a cab to agree to drive him to Houston, where he hoped to hide.

The Texas Highway Patrol, now involved in the manhunt, caught up with the cab. To their surprise, the cab pulled over on the right shoulder. As officers walked close enough to see into the windows, they felt Lockhart had evaded authorities once again—they saw only the cabbie. Still, they moved forward with caution. Then, close enough to look into the backseat, they saw him. Lockhart was there on the backseat. He wasn't hiding or cowering in fear. He wasn't taking aim with his gun.

He was sleeping like a baby.

But how could he have been calm enough to nap? Ordinary people would have thought, Gee, I have to get away and get away good. Adrenaline would have been pumping, and survival instincts would be at their peak. So I don't think Lockhart was simply exhausted. My guess is that he was lulled by the movement of the car, which can have a soothing, soporific effect, especially for someone like Lockhart, who wasn't emotionally developed. When babies are colicky and won't settle down, the old remedy used to be to put them in a car and drive them around until they calm. Some people now do the same thing by putting a baby, carefully strapped into a seat, on top of a clothes dryer. It's the vibration that seems to pacify them. Perhaps that's one of the reasons Lockhart drove around a lot. It wasn't that he drove to forget because he was worrying about his victims; none of them worry about the victims. Driving probably did for Lockhart what playing sports can do for others. It put him in the zone. It's like a baseball pitcher who, no matter what's going on around him, focuses on the task at hand. The thought here was singular, simple, and concrete: to drive and drive and do nothing else.

Once Lockhart was caught, he began to spill the beans to police. Animatedly, he talked with them about the crime of killing Hulsey, chatting casually, as though the cops were lifelong friends who would sympathize with his side of the story. He said the crime was Hulsey's fault, that he told Hulsey not to enter his Best Western hotel room, and he did anyway. Lockhart continued, "Why did he come into my room without a fucking backup, anyway? That was stupid!" The police held their tongues and began to become excited because they believed Lockhart was ready to confess. Yet they didn't want him to say too much without a lawyer, since that would jeopardize the whole case.

A day later, things changed. The same cops were called to Lockhart's cell, where he was screaming and raving. He swore at them repeatedly and vowed never to cooperate with them, ranting that he had seen a story in the paper in which the police called him a drug dealer. It was completely disconcerting for the authorities when Lockhart slipped from what they saw as giving a forthright confession to out-of-control raving. As we've seen, this is typical behavior for a serial killer. As if at the flip of a coin, their aspect, their external selves, change. Again, what Lockhart did was very childlike. At one moment, police were his best friends; at another moment he hated them, and for no reason at that.

Lockhart's impulsive nature went even further than his turnaround with police. It extended into the courtroom. After a break in jury selection for the case in Texas but before proceedings resumed, Michael leapt up from his chair, ran toward the window, and jumped through it. Shards flew everywhere.

To me, this dumb but dramatic performance proved that serial murderers are not the scheming people they seem to be. Lawyers for the prosecution give them a lot more credit for organizing and planning their murders than they really can muster. They *can,* however, organize simple, concrete things. Gacy had his ledger. Berdella had his notebook. During the investigation, Lockhart was said by a young woman he once dated to have kept a detailed but scruffy diary, held together by a rubber band. (This calendar book was never found, much to the disappointment of police. I believe it could have led police to other murders.)

Michael Lockhart didn't get far when he crashed through the window. He broke a bone in his pelvis when he landed, just one floor down, and was apprehended immediately.

The first time I saw Michael Lee Lockhart was at the request of the prosecutor's office in Porter County, Indiana, where he was being held for the Windy Gallagher murder trial. As is often the case when I become involved with the legal system, I was asked to examine Michael Lee Lockhart to gauge his mental state, his sanity or lack thereof. Lockhart was actually an attractive man. I've previously pointed out that many of the serial murderers I have met are average men who are overweight and doughy. They're charming but not handsome, with an underlying feminine air. Lockhart too had this noticeably feminine manner that almost imperceptibly manifested itself in his posture, his movements, and his voice. To me, it means they all have this kind of free-flowing identity that is sometimes male and sometimes female and sometimes something in between, pointing to the fact that they have a very fluid sexuality, which means they can function as heterosexuals or homosexuals. I can't say that it was his eyes or his bone structure or his hair that was appealing. Really, it was the whole package. Lockhart had something, and he could have used his assets for doing something positive. Instead he ruined his life, and the lives of many others.

On that day, Lockhart was antagonistic, and he was acting like a diva. One of the things I've seen with serial killers is that they tend to think they are stars of some sort. For Lockhart and all of these guys, the moniker "serial killer" gives them an identity, makes them feel special. After many years of aimlessness and floating around from job to job, Lockhart realized, That's who I am! I'm a serial killer. It was like looking in the mirror, seeing nothing for a long time, and then finally seeing a reflection.

Making a serial killer into someone who is respected and even revered because he, for some time, got away with disgusting acts of murder is something I will not accept or understand. Lockhart had been visited by the top brass at the local police department (people who never come down to see the average felon), but that wasn't enough for his massive ego. He demanded special treatment and privileges: better food than he was served; better treatment from the guards; better entertainment on TV. He couldn't stand being treated like the average prisoner.

"Why can't you help me out? You're a doctor. If you're so big, why can't you help me get better treatment here?"

"I'm not your lawyer, Michael. And I'm not a relative. And I *don't* want to be addressed with that tone of voice."

"I'm sick."

"You're not feeling well?"

"AIDS. I have AIDS."

"There's no evidence of that, Michael."

By now we know that most serial killers firmly believe they have some appalling disease. Strangely, they never follow up with anything reflective, such as "I'm scared I'm going to die." Their minds don't work in that way. Lockhart's statement about AIDS is like that of a child with whom I've worked who has cancer and says, "I have cancer and they're sticking me with all these needles and I don't like it." For both, it's far more about the immediacy of what they see as today's obstacle, not a plea for sympathy because the Grim Reaper is near.

Lockhart brooded for a while, and I made an effort to change the subject.

"Where were you born?"

"In Ohio. Wallbridge."

"How was that?"

"It sucked."

"What do you mean?"

"It wasn't good."

"What wasn't good?"

"The town sucked. My parents. People around me. The whole deal."

"How?"

"Assholes molested me."

I knew there was no evidence that Lockhart had been sexually abused. He continued answering my questions in short, clipped sentences that told me very little about how he killed and his reasoning for his killing, and I decided I was not going to accomplish much. I left the small jail where he was being kept and went about my business. Sometimes you can't push things with serial murderers. When they clam up like spoiled children, there's nothing I can do.

Nearly ten years later, I visited Lockhart again, this time in the East Texas city of Huntsville. It's a city in which many people are employed by the prison system, and the prison aura pervades most activities in the town. Until it was ended in 1986, the Texas Prison Rodeo, with horses and bulls ridden by inmates themselves, drew almost eighty thousand fans to Huntsville each October. To this day, a popular destination in town is the Texas Prison Museum, where the blood-red "Old Sparky" electric chair is the grim star of the show. Prison culture and prison lore are beyond popular culture in Huntsville; it spawns romance. Some of the guards at the prison have married former prisoners.

Twelve miles north of Huntsville, the Ellis complex itself was expansive and barren, made of big, thick brick and surrounded by fences and massive amounts of barbed wire. The redbrick building in which the executions themselves take place was known as The Walls. On its facade near the street was a large clock, slowly ticking away the moments of freedom that prisoners have lost. Although there were trees outside, the massive 11,000 acres of land itself was flat and uninspired, somehow already dead. Somewhere, I was told, there was a livestock operation and a prison farm, all for 2,200 inmates, 450 of whom were on death row. There was even a prison cemetery there, with simple white crosses and the prisoner's identification number. On one grave, the ground was freshly broken.

As I approached the doors of the prison, I expected the worst from the Texas Department of Criminal Justice. I had heard so much about Texas-style justice, and how the officials skirted the rules when they wanted to. People were hanged in Texas until 1923 and were executed by electric chair until 1964. Texas itself seemed to be enamored of the death penalty; the number of those killed increased exponentially in the 1990s. Back in 1977, about the time I began my work, death row in Texas was a simple row of cells holding two dozen people. By 1997 when Lockhart was to be executed, death row was six times as big (with each section holding three levels of cells); also that year, forty prisoners' lives were ended, each by lethal injection that used about $86 worth of drugs. Over three hundred people have been so injected since 1982. The Lone Star State leads all of the United States in the number of executions performed. Yet to my surprise everyone inside, from the burly, macho guards on up, greeted me in a friendly manner. They were respectful, gentlemanly, and just plain nice. The warden even booked a spacious office as the interview room for Michael Lockhart and me, far more appealing than the window with bulletproof glass, the plastic chairs, and the primitive telephone system usually employed by prisoners to talk with guests. Lockhart was permitted to be there without shackles, and there was no guard present in the room.

This time Lockhart, after years on death row, was in a mood to talk, and talk he did, endlessly. He talked like John Wayne Gacy in that "motormouth" kind of way. Michael had his reasons for speaking frankly; he was trying to appeal his death penalty ruling; he was used to prison and even liked it at times; and he didn't want to die by lethal injection. As I had been in Indiana when he proved to be uncooperative, I was there in Texas to try to gauge whether or not he was sane at the time of the murders and whether there were mitigating circumstances toward the formulation of an appeal. The lawyers would try to inject some of his medical history, but my guess was that there really wasn't anything there that could convince the court. Still, I felt he didn't totally understand his crimes, and there was a slim chance that he could avoid dying and live his life to its end in a small, sparse cell if that was explained to the court succinctly.

But it was not the terrible murder in Indiana which took the life of a Windy Gallagher (on what she called in her journal her "no worries day") that provoked the most important exchanges of our meeting. It was the murder of the young teen in Land O' Lakes.

I pulled up my chair close to the table and checked on my tape recorder to make sure it was working properly. "Can you talk to me about what led up to the murder of Jennifer Colhouer?"

"I was in Florida, and I said 'I am a real estate agent' to get into the house. It was easy to get in. She wasn't hard to convince."

"Why were you posing as a real estate agent?"

Lockhart sat back in his seat, relaxed. "It seemed like a good idea at the time. It gave me an excuse to go up to the house in the first place."

"Did you come up with the idea that day?"

"Pretty much. I think there was an empty house, next door or a few doors away."

"And the girl let you in?"

"Just like that. I still can't believe how easy it was. I could pretty much pick up anyone off the street, and they would follow me anywhere like a little puppy dog."

"It was that easy."

Lockhart leaned farther back in his chair and clasped his hands behind his head. "It was that easy."

I had seen it all too much in the past. Too many people just don't use their judgment; they don't take a moment to consider the consequences before they do something. Lockhart looked like a nice guy with a pleasant demeanor. Nothing set off a trigger that said "be careful," whereas if a potential victim saw a scruffy-looking guy standing on the doorstep, he or she would think twice.

"Let's go back in time a few hours. How did you start the day?"

"I got up, and I went to take a shower."

"Got up when?"

"Late morning or early afternoon, I guess." Lockhart kept the hours of a rock star or celebrity. He didn't have any kind of job, so he got up when he felt like getting up. And he enjoyed the nightlife, drinking and flirting with women at various bars in the area.

"Then what?"

"I was in the shower, washing up. And then it hit me. I had to go out and get me one."

It was as though at that moment, a lightbulb went on in my head. This really was one of those "eureka!" moments. I thought again about what he said: *"And then it hit me. I had to go out and get me one."* This simple, fourteen-word explanation was truly bigger than Lockhart had made it out to be. Lockhart had spoken it so casually and almost quietly that I was surprised I didn't miss it. *"I had to go out and get me one."* I couldn't stop thinking about it, even as I tried to continue my examination. It wasn't that he didn't like his mother or that his father had abused him, and that led him to kill. There was something deeper at work here, something that had less to do with nurture and more to do with nature. To me, there was a consequential, scientifically logical connection to be made here, a connection that no one, absolutely no one, before had made.

Part of my workaday life has been spent counseling drug-dependent youths. Those people, young men and women alike, were truly addled teens who really couldn't exist without their daily doses of cocaine or crack or heroin. Some consumed more than others, but they all had one thing in common: the habit. And the way those people described the frenzied need to feed their habits was quite similar to the way Michael Lee Lockhart described his sudden urgency to get a victim. It wasn't just a need; it was a drive, a compulsion. It came on like a flash and it came on strong. And when it came, it couldn't be stopped.

The question I had was as intriguing as it was challenging. Just as the kids I counseled were addicted to drugs, were serial killers addicted to killing? But in what way were they addicted? What caused it, and why? Certainly, if it were an addiction, an addiction theory would strike a serious blow to the prevailing thought, which held that serial killing was related to upbringing and abuse by the family.

I asked Lockhart a few more questions.

"What about the others?"

Lockhart looked around the room and then at me. "What others?"

"The others you killed."

Lockhart shrugged his shoulders. "Well, there could have been more."

"Where did they happen?"

"Where? All around. Not just one place. I been all around."

All around, all over the place, but now in one place, in one cell.

Years later, on December 9, 1997, after consuming a simple last meal consisting of a double cheeseburger, french fries, and a Coke, the thirty-seven-year-old Lockhart quietly received a lethal injection from the state of Texas for the murder of Officer Hulsey. I believe that Lockhart killed as many as ten more people, although police believe he killed as many as twenty more. The reason police open up the unsolved crime files when there's a serial murderer around is that it's very well known that they just kill and kill and kill. Lockhart wasn't prosecuted for the other crimes because he left no trace at the crime scenes. Sadly, the unknown people who have been murdered by serial killers could populate a small town. Somewhere, someplace, there should be a dignified memorial to the many unknown victims.

It wasn't Lockhart's death that had an effect on me. It was the addiction model of murder that I had discovered. In speaking to him for over one hundred hours, it was those few seconds, basically one sentence, that made everything jell. I looked at the people I had interviewed before. Gacy felt compelled to troll the streets in the middle of the night. Macek suddenly showing up in a Laundromat or a hotel room. Long turning off the highway to find the house of a young girl, a house he'd never seen before in a community he'd never before frequented. All the others before and all the others in the future: they all had this trigger moment prior to killing. They were addicted to killing.

THIRTEEN

ROSEMARY WEST AND
PARTNERS IN SERIAL CRIME

I looked carefully at her letters and remembered that she loved tea. Tea and teatime. That civilized, comforting ritual, when people take the time to sip and relax, gossip and converse, is one that's always associated with modern-day England. When Anna, the Seventh Duchess of Bedford, introduced her idea of teatime in the early 1800s, she partook, talked, and then walked with her friends through the pastoral meadows that were then still common in London. Before the introduction of these fashionable, late afternoon sit-downs to tea and cakes and chat, the Brits consumed just two meals each day. Many of the British think that most things can be taken care of with the help of a nicely brewed cup of tea (London protesters against the war in Iraq carried signs through London saying MAKE TEA, NOT WAR). Teas such as Earl Grey and English Breakfast are common at any time here in the United States, and I enjoy them on gloomy, rainy days in Chicago or after a difficult day at work.

But for the victims of Rosemary West, the dowdy partner in crime and wife of serial killer Frederick West, teatime entailed something far more sinister. It was after she and Fred had tortured and raped their quarry that the bespectacled Rosemary would brew some tea in a kettle in an effort to soothe and pacify these traumatized young people and children. These victims included the West's innocent daughters.

The ghastly story of what the Wests did and how they did it is the story of a particular kind of serial murderer called "partnership killers." Early in this book, I pointed out the case of Chicago serial killer H. H. Holmes (also known as Herman Mudgett), and his helper, the quiet, brawny Benjamin Pitezel. Pitezel was like a slave to Mudgett in Chicago during the time of the World's Fair, and he would ultimately be killed by Mudgett. The murders of French hero turned serial murderer Gilles de Rais included a small group of loyal minions in his inner circle. More recently, there was the well-documented Beltway Sniper case of John Allen Mohammad, a former U.S. Army weapons expert and his teenage accomplice, John Lee Malvo. Their actions, which frightened the whole country in late 2002, qualify as partnership killings.

But it's the husband-and-wife team of partnership killers that often forms the strongest bond. In this case, Fred West was the dominant member of the couple, and Rose was the submissive. Fred killed at least twelve over the course of two decades, from 1967 to 1987. It began with the murder of Ann McFall, the Scottish nanny pregnant with West's child, and ended with the murder of Heather West, Rose and Fred's first daughter. Information about as many as twenty more of the dead he held back from the police; West said he would offer the locations of the bodies at the rate of one each year, as though he still had the ability to control things, as if he were still the dominant one.

But one bit of caution before I continue: don't think of the words *dominant* and *submissive* as sexual terms. Though Fred and Rose indulged in violent sex, their relationship shouldn't be thought of as one that was based purely around Fred's fantasy world of S-M sex. It's no secret that there are those in society who indulge in such sex play, using whips and chains and rubber costumes. For these folks, such activity can let off steam or can be a kind of safety valve that releases some of the continual pressures of today's society. Both partners in S-M sex are willing, consenting adults. While many may not consider it "normal" sex, no one is seriously injured. No one is scarred for life. And no one dies.

I did not get to study the mangled mind of Fred West personally because he did not live very long in his English jail cell. While the guards were changing shifts, West hanged himself with strips of sheeting from his bed long before his trial.

I did, however, have a relationship with Rosemary West. I had been interviewed by the BBC television network about the case for a documentary about the Wests. After the broadcast, as is often the case, I received permission from Rose's lawyer, Richard Ferguson, to begin a correspondence in which she sent me letters in response to various questions I had about what had gone on in her mind and in her family history. Rose's lawyers felt that if we exchanged such letters, some fact or series of facts might emerge that would help Rose in her ongoing legal battles. The letters arrived secretly through the hands of messengers, so they would not be viewed by prison officials or anyone who might decide to open the mail. In a very rare development, Rose refused to sign the short document I require of most serial murderers with whom I deal, the one that permits me, for scientific purposes, to write about everything they say and write. Nor will she give permission now. While I can't reveal the particulars of those many letters, I can write about the murders themselves, murders that took twenty long years to discover. And I can write about the lives so secretly lived within Cromwell Street itself, in the gray fog of Gloucester, England, located on the ancient River Severn. I can analyze most of what went on in what the British press called the "House of Horrors" 114 miles west of London, but it would be unethical of me to write about or excerpt those most private letters from Rose West.

It would have been easy to miss. A casual passerby would have ignored that three-story home at 25 Cromwell Street, beige, nondescript, and on a side street as it was. But that passerby might have noticed the fancy wrought-iron sign that heralded its address in black and white. Bold and almost brazen, it showed Frederick West's pride in his awful little kingdom, as it seemed to say, "This is my property to do with what I want to do. The same goes for what's inside, including my wife and my daughters. My property . . . and no one else's."

The star-crossed relationship between Fred and Rose started off simply enough in 1969. Fred had the kind of square-faced, rugged appeal of a farm worker. He mastered the gift of gab early on in life and he used it on fifteen-year-old Rose Letts at a bus stop. Nervously waiting there, she looked even younger than her years, with her white dress, curly black hair, and short white socks. In fact, she looked like a little girl, cute and round-faced, and a little chubby. She had come from a poor family and began working at a bakery at the age of twelve, giving her mother ten dollars of her wages each week. Her father, Bill, ruled his family with an iron fist, and Rose lived in fear of him, although he treated her better than the rest.

By the time Rose met Fred, she had dated and lived for a short time with an older man with whom she had sex. Already well into his twenties, Fred played into Rose's love for children by saying he had two daughters, Anna Marie and Charmaine, from a previous marriage, who desperately needed minding. Rose soon moved in with Fred and obeyed his every order, as she thought a good future wife should. She did not know that Fred had already been arrested for impregnating a thirteen-year-old girl.

By the time the two were married in 1972, Rose had had a daughter with Fred called Heather, who would grow up to look much like her father. Also, Rose was pregnant with a second child, who would be named Mae June West. Immediately after their marriage and even while she was carrying Heather, Fred began prodding Rose to have sex with other men.

It was not just the goading to see Rose in bed with other men in which Fred indulged. He was up to far more unpleasant things. Fred had decided to dismember and murder his previous wife, Rena, and their daughter Charmaine, who lived with the murdering couple. (Charmaine was in reality the daughter of an Asian bus driver. Fred knew this, and Fred accepted the child, although he didn't like the idea of having a mixed race baby in the house. He referred to her as adopted.) Rose took part in the beatings of Charmaine that led up to her murder, sometimes whacking her with a wooden spoon, but likely not killing her.

Previous to this, in 1967, Fred had murdered and dismembered his girlfriend, Scottish nanny Ann McFall, who would have given birth, in one month, to their child. He also removed a number of Ann's fingers and toes before burying her in a field near his hometown of Much Marcle, a tiny farming community. Fred did the same with Charmaine, and chopped off her patella (the kneecap) as well. Later, he would kill the mother of his child again. When Fred had relations with Shirley Robinson, a lodger at Cromwell Street, she become pregnant and threatened to tell Rose. On hearing this, the enraged West killed Shirley by strangulation, cut her up with a serrated bread knife and a cleaver, removed her baby from her womb, and dumped the two into a hole in his backyard. Even the sturdy femur, the thighbone, had been chopped through, not one but nine times.

As for Rose, she gave in fairly quickly to Fred's ceaseless coaxing and began prostituting herself at the couple's new home at 25 Cromwell Street. Fred took a provocative snapshot of Rose in a bra and low-riding pants and placed it in a newspaper so she could readily hear from clients. The Wests installed no separate phone line for these services, and their children often answered the phone to hear the foul requests. The address became a kind of brothel and hostel with hippieish young white men and West Indian immigrants moving in and out at all hours of the day and night. It was a more liberal time in which the "do-your-own-thing" style of living was popular in Britain as well as in the United States. Yet what they were creating at Cromwell Street wasn't just about smoking some pot, making love, and listening to the music of Woodstock.

It was about savagery: savage rape, savage murder, and what in Western society is the most unspeakable savagery, incest. Unusual as it is for serial murderers to attack members of their families, don't forget that they were not all his biological children. It's not an unheard-of idea for parents to fawn over their biological children and mistreat their adopted children. On top of that, Fred believed that his daughters, biological or not, were his possessions and that he had a father's right to have sex with them before anyone else touched them. And Rose helped him. In one instance, she held down and used a vibrator on her gagged stepdaughter Anna Marie before Fred raped her. Rose told Anna Marie that this was a good thing, that she was fortunate to have such caring parents who would take time to prepare her for relationships with men.

The round-faced child was just eight years old.

After the attack, Rose gave her a bath to soothe her and probably made her some tea to sip. But poor Anna Marie suffered such pain from the rape that she couldn't attend school for some time. Rape such as she endured creates a tremendous amount of irritation of the vaginal walls, and sometimes vaginal tearing. Simply, if you have a small space and you're trying to enlarge that space in a forceful way, you can cause a lot of damage. What Fred did was severely painful for Anna Marie. It would have taken five to seven days for the inflammation to go down. If there was vaginal tearing, it would have taken a much longer time to heal.

Rape like this occurred many times with the West daughters, and lodgers in the house could hear screams and cries of "Daddy, stop it!" emanating from the damp cellar. Yet they did nothing about it. They didn't call the police. They didn't call social services. They didn't talk about it among themselves. They were silent. The way these transient people dealt with incest is really no different from the way others have dealt with it even in the more affluent suburbs here in the United States. It is not mentioned; instead, it is hidden away as though it couldn't happen, as though it didn't happen. This appalling silence was an indictment of all of those people. If you know and if you're denying that it has happened, then you're just as culpable.

At Cromwell Street, Fred West craved to have sex of any kind at any time. He had Rose pose as she urinated, and he videotaped the act. He poked a peephole in a door to watch Rosemary with her clients. After rigging up a speaker and wires, he blandly watched television and listened to Rose having sex while the TV was turned down. After touching Rose's genital area, he demanded that his progeny smell his fingers. After sizing up his preteen son, Stephen, West declared that soon he would be old enough to have sex with his mother. He told others that he had had sex with farm animals. At any moment, he might try to fondle any woman who passed by. With Rose in tow, he trolled the streets of Gloucester in his car, searching for unsuspecting targets, hoping they would be virgins.

In her quiet way, Rose served as a procurer for Fred. You're far more likely to get into a car with a couple than with a single man. Rose's function was not to be West's equal partner, not like *Bonnie and Clyde,* where Bonnie often helped to case banks, fire weapons, and drive the getaway car. Rose was Fred's loyal, almost simpering helper whose physical presence, whose very femaleness, made getting the girls much easier.

When they picked up a young woman, none older than twenty-one and most in their teens, they would take her back to Cromwell Street, gag her, bind her face tightly with packing tape, and rape her. For these purposes, Fred crafted his own tools of torture as well.

For Fred West, these actions weren't about getting and having sex per se. It was power and control that motivated West as he moved, seemingly insatiably, from one kind of criminal sex act to another. This horrific man wanted to rule everything and everyone he came into contact with. In his home and on the streets, he made his own laws and felt all should be subject to his decrees. But those whom he raped, from his daughters to hitchhikers he brought to his cellar, said the sex acts themselves lasted for a minute or two, even less. Fred, who wanted to control everyone else, had very little control over himself. In one instance, after he performed for a few moments and had an orgasm early, victim Caroline Owens reported to the courts and police that he began weeping inconsolably. It wasn't that Fred was sorry for what he had done, nor was he ashamed of performing so poorly. Fred's tears were a kind of autonomic release, almost a reflex, totally uncontrollable. It had nothing to do with heartfelt emotion.

Certainly he was devoid of any heart, soul, or conscience. What kind of human being would take his daughter's virginity? Then, when Anna Marie turned thirteen, Rose made her pose for a photograph in the nude, probably as a kind of advertisement for her to become a prostitute like her mother. But, while it might be impossible to believe, he became even more depraved. Fred's daughter Heather was not as compliant as Anna Marie, and she wanted more than anything to escape her father's constant fondling. She became introspective, silent, and as Rosemary said, "stubborn." Perhaps because of Fred's abuse, she shunned going out with boys, and Fred began to tell his cronies that she was a lesbian. When Heather told others that she had been abused, Fred beat her mercilessly. Then Heather announced that she was going to leave Cromwell Street. And the sixteen-year-old disappeared. Fred said she decided to strike out on her own. The reality was far worse.

Fred had confronted her in the laundry room, where she stood defiantly near the dryer with her hands on her hips. Fred confessed to police, "She had a sort of smirk on her face like you try me and I'll do the business. I lunged at her . . . and grabbed her round the throat." Within minutes, she was dead. Armed with what he described as an "ice saw," he cut his daughter up in the first-floor bathroom. He sliced around her neck and then began to twist off her head, no easy task. In the middle of the night, he placed Heather's two legs, her head, and her body in a hole in the garden. Later he poured concrete to extend a patio over her shallow grave. All of this was kept from Rosemary and the family for years. As a cover, Fred constantly lied to Rosemary, saying that he occasionally heard from Heather, who had gotten a job and was all right. I can't tell you why he lied. I said all along that these people aren't quite human. If I tried to say, Rose would have left Fred if she knew Fred had killed Heather, it would be explaining it as if Fred were an ordinary person like you and me. I can't say why he lied because I do not know.

When West completed one of these killing rampages, he sometimes had sex with the dead body. As I have pointed out in previous chapters, Fred West, like John Gacy, may have exhibited signs of necrophilia. But he was not a necrophiliac because, at its most basic, necrophilia refers to having sexual *attraction* to corpses, not having sex with them. I remember the case of a man who hired pale-looking prostitutes to have intercourse with him in a coffin. Another example was the case of a man who became sexually excited at funerals.

Nor was Fred a pedophile, because pedophiles desire to have sexual relations with children. Nor was he purely a sexual sadist, because a sadist doesn't always kill. Did he hurt people? Yes. Did he get sexual pleasure from hurting people, that same elation the average person gets from sex with a lover in the missionary position? No.

Fred West was like a robot when he was compelled to torture and rape and kill. Something clicked inside of him, something that even I have yet to fully comprehend. His humanity wasn't there any more as he acted. I can't say that he was a monster or an animal either. He was on a kind of autopilot that led him from one level of crime to the next until he succumbed to commit the ultimate crime, murder, over and over again.

But what of Rosemary West? She, I believe, was one step up from the empty shell in which the inhuman serial killer exists. She wasn't mentally retarded, but Dozy Rosie, as she was nicknamed at school, seemed as though she was as she dutifully fulfilled all of Fred's requests of her.

It wasn't so much that Fred brainwashed his wife. The best way to explain the relationship between Fred and Rose is to imagine someone sitting in front of a large television screen with a game controller in hand. That controller is linked to Sony's PlayStation II, and on the screen is, say, the bestselling video game Grand Theft Auto III. The video game is an alternate world, in the case of this game, a world of crime bosses and bloody death. Here, as the player frantically mashes the buttons to make things work on the screen, fantasies and adventures are experienced so enticingly that they almost feel real. Throughout the experience, there are prostitutes, tortures, maimings, guns, and murders. When people play this game for hours at a time, they often dream about the game at night.

For Fred West, his gift of gab was his controller and the star of his video game, the person who moved around to do his bidding in this world, was Rosemary West. He used her to realize not only his fantasies of the wife as prostitute as he watched her have sex with other men. But he also used her to carry out and consummate acts of abduction, rape, and incest. In the video game, there are various missions to complete before the user gets to the next level, which is always the goal. If the mission was to abduct a young girl to be picked up at a bus stop, Rosemary would help, perhaps by offering the woman some nanny work along with room and board at 25 Cromwell Street. If the mission was the act of rape, Rosemary would hold the woman down. If Fred directed Rosemary to abuse the victim as well, she would do so—without much fuss or semblance of protest. She would argue occasionally, but once she had this verbal release, she would always do what Fred wanted her to do.

And in Fred's strange world, reality merged with fantasy. Early in his life, he dated a girl who was an amputee. Later in life, he would make amputees of his victims. Early in his life, he worked as a skinner and a tanner. And later, he would use this knowledge to cut up his victims as if they were animals. Precisely how dreams melded into reality for Fred West and other serial murderers, I do not know. But I will tell you this: I am spending a good part of my professional life trying to find out.

Why was Rosemary so obliging about doing things that most of us would never consider doing, even if we were offered everything we've ever wanted? There is evidence that both Fred and Rosemary were sexually abused by their own families, that Fred was molested by his obese mother and that Rosemary was raped twice as a child. Fred may have convinced Rosemary, as he tried to do with his daughters, that there was nothing wrong with sleeping with his children. While Rosemary was not exactly a blank slate, she was naive, willing, and not particularly smart. It has also been said that because Rose's mother had electroconvulsive therapy—once more crudely known as electroshock therapy—when she was pregnant with Rose, Rose became somehow retarded. But a study done in 1994 of three hundred similar cases showed no such thing. The most common complication was one that occurred in twenty-eight of the cases, an arrhythmic heart rate, one that was brief and didn't recur once the baby was born. She wanted to do right by Fred, even if doing right by Fred meant doing wrong in the eyes of the law and society. Beyond this, Rose may well have been bullied by Fred into believing that what she was doing was perfectly all right. One of the things that psychiatrists know is that kids who have been sexually abused can become more active sexually. For them, sexuality becomes something that doesn't have a real "do and don't do" moral code about it. It's different when a couple like the Wests have no boundaries. It would have been easier for them to sink into the acts of incest. Throughout the years, Rose's loyalty to Fred was seemingly unshakable, even when the British constabulary showed up at Rosemary's doorstep after a child reported to her mother that one of the West girls told her there was a body buried in the Wests' backyard. Though the police didn't mention the tip, they asked difficult questions about the disappearance of Rose's daughter, Heather.

"When did you last see her?" "When did she move out?" "Why did she move out?" "What was the buildup to her leaving?" were the questions asked by Detective Sergeant Terence Onions.

And—

"Was there a row before she left?" "Who were her friends?" "Have you seen her since?" "What inquiries have you made (about her disappearance)?"

Rose took umbrage at the invasion of her privacy and at the many probing questions. "I can't remember" was her favorite reply to Detective Onions. And then, when she was hard up against the wall after being hit with question after accusatory question, this frustrated, confusing answer: "If you had any brains at all, you could find her. It can't be that difficult."

Their suspicions aroused, the police came back two days later to begin digging up the patio and garden behind the house on Cromwell Street while a nervous and sobbing Rosemary and the stunned children sat around the kitchen table, drinking tea. As the digging continued, Fred confessed to the police that they would indeed find Heather's body in the garden. After Fred was taken away to jail in late February 1994, Rose was arrested on suspicion of the murder of her young daughter Heather. Even when Rosemary was taken into custody, Stephen and Mae June, then in their early twenties, remained behind, still drinking tea as the excavation continued.

Yet once Rosemary realized that Heather had been killed and buried mere feet from where she slept, she wanted nothing more to do with Fred. The realization of the murder had quickly shattered her bond with him, and she was able to pull away from his Svengali-like power over her. The fact that police uncovered five remains in less than ten hours must have also jolted her into realizing that Fred had been much more than a player of illegal sex games. He was the murderer of her child. The murderer of others, yes, but mainly the murderer of her child. While she would never implicate Fred, she would never forgive him.

I believe Rosemary didn't participate in the physical procedure of murder. After looking at the evidence, it was clear to me that there wasn't enough of it to say for certain that she killed one or some of the victims. I have no doubt that she committed sexual abuse of others with Fred. However, after a trial full of high drama that included witnesses fainting from the strain of testimony, a jury speedily convicted Rose on ten counts of murder. Though there was no direct evidence presented in court, jurors believed the prosecution, which said she was not only an accomplice but also a partner in the murders. She, not the expired Fred, would be held responsible.

Fred's and Rosemary's deeds had severe repercussions far beyond the murders. Some say the town of Gloucester never really recovered from the blow it was dealt, not just to the economy but also to the collective psyche of its people. Fred's daughter Anne Marie (who changed her name from Anna—as if to rid herself partially of an unwanted tattoo) tried to commit suicide a few times, once jumping into the muddy River Severn and nearly drowning before she was rescued. Stephen tried to kill himself when the woman he loved left him. And Fred's brother, about to be brought to trial for allegedly participating in the murders with Fred, took the lead from his sibling, hanging himself in his jail cell. Rosemary, however, survives, still in her jail cell, serving ten life sentences. She never revealed any more about the murders, and remarkably, began a from-the-jail relationship with bass player Dave Glover from the 1970s British rock group Slade. They even prepared to be married, and Rosemary proudly announced their strange bond in the British press. And then, suddenly within a week, the marriage was off. Perhaps it had something to do with the fact that once Slade heard about the possible prison nuptials, Glover was un-ceremoniously fired from the band.

Of course, there have been other such partnerships: Paul Bernardo and Karla Homolka, well-off Canadians who raped, killed, and videotaped together, including the rape and murder of Karla Homolka's sister. Ian Brady and Myra Hinkley axed their victims, then buried them in Saddleworth Moor, a windswept part of England not far from the areas made famous by the literary works of the Brontë sisters. David and Catherine Birnie had their own "House of Horrors" in Perth, Australia. Gerald and Charlene Gallego kidnapped and murdered ten people, mostly teen girls, in and around Sacramento.

And then there was Alton Coleman and Debra Brown.

I spoke at length with Debra Brown, who with boyfriend Alton Coleman cast a pall of thievery, rape, and murder over Illinois, Indiana, Michigan, Ohio, Kentucky, and Wisconsin in the summer of 1984. The African-American pair traveled like the drifting Michael Lee Lockhart, but their reign of terror was more of a short, intense binge. It lasted fifty-three days and placed Coleman and Brown near the top of the FBI's most wanted list.

In his previous offenses such as rape, Coleman's handsome looks and nice-guy attitude on the witness stand turned juries in his favor, and he often escaped the grasp of justice. With his mustache and long, carefully trimmed sideburns, he looked more like an R&B star of the day than he did a criminal. In 1983, he was charged with sexual assault after his sister accused him of attempting to rape her eight-year-old daughter. But the case never went to trial, as Coleman's sister dropped the charges. Coleman felt he was protected against all crimes he could commit, not by a guardian angel, but by a Haitian voodoo god called Baron Samedi he had heard about from his grandmother. Called both the god of eroticism and the lord of death, Baron Samedi is a mythical figure often depicted with a stovepipe hat and a formal coat with tails who zealously guards the entrance to the afterlife. Said to drink rum steeped in hot peppers, the dancing, laughing god is also seen as a protector of children and the critically ill and is the latter's last best chance at regaining health.

On June 18, 1984, Coleman and Brown spied bright-eyed and carefree seven-year-old Tamika Turks and her nine-year-old aunt, Annie, in Gary, Indiana. They were heading back from a candy store when the pair coaxed them into taking a walk in the woods under the ruse of playing a game. Away from witnesses and covered by the silence of the woods, the two bound and gagged the children. When Tamika whimpered, Coleman jumped up and down on her chest. In an even more depraved turn, the pair forced Annie to carry out acts of oral sex on both of them. Coleman cut and raped Annie, and the two choked her until she passed out. When Annie came to, alive despite tremendous blood loss, she found Tamika's body tossed in some shrubbery, strangled and dead.

On July 13, Coleman and Brown bicycled to the home of an elderly couple, Marlene and Harry Walters, in Norwood, Ohio, near Cincinnati, claiming they wanted to purchase a camper in the yard. The Walters invited the two in to have lemonade on that hot July day. Once inside, they ransacked the place, stealing things they saw of value. Coleman beat Harry and took to hitting Marlene with various items, including a magazine rack, over twenty times. He also used a pair of Vise-Grip pliers to disfigure her face and scalp before she died. With the couple bound and tied, Coleman and Brown made off with the Walters' red Plymouth Valiant.

By the time they were apprehended, Coleman and Brown had committed what amounted to a laundry list of crimes, including eight murders, seven rapes, three kidnappings, and fourteen armed robberies. After a tip from one of Coleman's acquaintances, police spied the two in the bleachers of Mason Park in Evanston, Illinois. They were casually watching a street basketball game.

But what were their excuses?

On the day he was born, Alton Coleman's mother didn't want him and gave him up to his grandmother. (Another account says she threw her baby into a garbage can.) Coleman's grandmother wasn't the most stable influence a child could have, since she ran a brothel and a gambling parlor. She also beat him more than occasionally. Alton developed slightly feminine mannerisms and the embarrassing habit of peeing his pants. So the local kids, who constantly bullied him in Waukegan, Illinois, came up with a nickname for him: "Pissy." Later, he would enjoy dressing in women's clothing.

In an interview with Ohio Public Radio just weeks before his execution in April 2002, Coleman blamed the Walters murder on Debra Brown, claiming that she was "speedy, a little bit high . . . We was drugged up." He asserted that they ransacked the Walters' house because the pair wanted items to sell to buy drugs, and that Brown hit Marlene repeatedly with a candlestick because Mrs. Walters kept fighting back. While Debra was no innocent bystander, it was extremely cowardly but typical of Coleman to protest his innocence and blame Brown in a last-minute effort to escape the death penalty.

Like Rosemary West, Debra Brown was considered a slow learner, so that her intellectual ability was the equivalent of that of a child. Like Rosemary West, she was very much under the thumb of the dominant Alton Coleman. If he told her to go out and get a bag of potato chips in a downpour without a raincoat, she would do just that. And if he told her to kill, she would do just that.

Before my conversations with Debra, I had seen a black-and-white photo of her. She wore a Pennzoil baseball cap placed at an angle on her head, her face tough and hardened, albeit youthful. She would tell a judge that she "had fun" killing, then tempered the statement by saying she was kinder, more understanding and "more lovable" than people believed her to be. On the surface, she seemed very cocky, even brazen, but I found Debra to be a very quiet, relatively passive, yet occasionally hostile person.

"Why are *you* here?" she whispered. "I'm not crazy."

I could tell that she indeed was not crazy. Instead, she was in love. "I just want to ask you some questions. Can you tell me a little bit about Alton?"

Her eyes immediately brightened, almost as if thinking about him made her free of prison. "There's nothing wrong with Alton. Alton's the best thing in my life. From the minute I met him."

"Are you in love with him?"

Softly, she said, "You bet I am. I'd do anything for that man."

"Anything?"

"Just about."

"What about the bad things you did?"

"If I did anything, I did it because Alton wanted me to."

"People were killed."

"Alton took me everywhere. We went all around. All kinds of cars. It was fun. We had fun."

"How upset are you about what's happened to Alton?"

"What do you think? I'm upset. Damn upset."

"Why?"

"What we had was . . . different. It was exciting. He took me everywhere. He took care of me. Now, who's gonna do that?"

"What about Marlene Walters?"

"Well." There was a long pause and she lowered her head a bit. "I did that."

"You?"

"Not Alton. Me." She was so small and subdued, and so very much in love that I did not believe her. I felt she was covering for Alton because she didn't want him to die by lethal injection. Psychiatrists could call the partnership of Alton and Debra one that was "enmeshed." She felt she couldn't function without the other person, or at least what she saw as the vivid memory of how well they seemed to work together. Somehow she could deal with his incarceration, but she couldn't bear to think about his death.

It was the kind of thing I've seen in little kids when they're clinging so much they can't be independent from the parent figure. In addition, Debra was like the mousy person in a relationship who can't even seem to move without the permission of the other. Recently *Zits,* the comic strip about the misadventures of a mom and dad with one teen and one college-age son, ran a series about a couple in a relationship who breathed the same air. They were constantly on each other. Each could not and would not survive without the presence of the other person. That was what the love between Alton Coleman and Debra Brown was like. Not unlike Rose West, Debra accepted what was going on around her. When something like the legal system threatened that relationship, she got very upset about it. But she wasn't about to do anything about it—because someone else, Alton, had always been the aggressor.

In my mind, the only way Debra could have committed the violent killing of Mrs. Walters (remember, there were over twenty powerful blows that pummeled her) was if she had been doing crack at the time of the murder. Crack is one of the very few drugs that has been known to have the potential to increase the level of violence a human may do. Debra may have had a little speed and some marijuana on that fateful day in Ohio, but that wouldn't have led her to carry out such a vicious crime. She would need to have been far more irate, and much stronger. Yes, I saw that she had been described as a mean little witch who could lash out verbally, but she was not a brutal murderer.

To me, the partnership killings are like a transmogrification of what John Gacy and even Michael Lockhart had said, that there was always someone there in the room helping them kill. For Gacy, it was Bad Jack. For Lockhart, it was Jamaican people involved in illegal drug deals said to have been in the hotel room with Officer Hulsey. For us, these demons are clearly figments of the imagination, but to them, there really was somebody else there. To some, delusions are real. In the instances of the helpers of Alton Coleman and Fred West, the partner was no imaginary being. She was real, a warm, submissive body there to be directed in living color, not an enabler who stood by and let it happen or a disciple as if she were part of a cult. She was as real, close, and attached as an arm or a leg. But though they were attached in that way, serial killers don't make terrific husbands. They're not really loving, caring, or understanding. They don't share in the hopes and dreams of their spouses. And, with the exception of Rose West, the marriages don't last long at all. The comment I often get from the wives and former wives is that the serial killer husband wasn't around that much or didn't care that much. That's why these marriages ended. So these were no mystical bonds that could last an eternity. If they hadn't ended before, they certainly ended when the murderer was convicted in court. So why do some of them, like Debra Brown, say they were deeply in love? It's probably due to a combination of adequate sex and cold experimentation that was misinterpreted by the partner as the wild adventure of two people together against society. And that misinterpretation may well have become the partner's idea of love. It didn't matter that the serial murderer came home late at night or ignored them completely or put work or murder or feeding the dog before love. The stark reality? There was no love at all.

Why didn't the partners become victims themselves? If they were concrete extensions of the murderer like arms or legs, the murderer wouldn't see them as potential victims, just as part of himself. But one thing is certain about the partners. There was a hole to be filled inside of Rosemary, Debra, and the others, an emptiness, and it was filled by these dominant murderers. It's almost as if they were reaching out to grasp in their partners something that they didn't have inside of themselves. It's not that they were looking for someone to treat them badly, not at all. They felt they had found a stable force, a man they could, at any time, come to for fulfillment. They may have even made a preconscious decision that the badness in their men didn't override the comfort they felt in being sheltered and protected. But the women involved in the partnership killings were beyond sad; it's tragic that Rose or Debra or any woman could feel complete only with a lying serial murderer by her side.

FOURTEEN

THE INTERNATIONAL
PHENOMENON:
CHILD KILLER IN RIO

I t was Thanksgiving 2002. I usually go all-out for the holidays, inviting twenty or more people over to our place in Chicago. For weeks before the big day, I take care to prepare all of the food myself, crepes with mushrooms and chives, salmon rolls, homemade cheddar cheese sticks, butter patties in the shape of turkeys, homemade gravy, and, of course, two twenty-five-pound turkeys. It's a great feast for everyone, and with the combined demands of my medical work, family, and the food preparation, I don't get much sleep from Halloween on forward. But all the work is worth the effort once everyone sits down to enjoy the feast and just talk.

But in 2002, Thanksgiving was very different.

A few days before the holiday, I received the long-distance call I was waiting for, only I had expected it to come in September around Labor Day, not during the Thanksgiving break. The call came from Brazil, and my intermediary there reported that Brazil's most notorious serial killer was ready to talk to me. Although I had spoken to him before in the 1990s shortly after he was captured, I had been waiting a decade to sit down again with the killer of fourteen young boys. And so, when the call came, it didn't take long to make a decision: for me, there was no other choice. I forgot about "over the river and through the woods" and the bracing chill of the Chicago wind that's perfect for the holiday, and I used up a hefty chunk of our frequent-flier miles to make quick reservations for a trip that would take us to São Paulo and Rio de Janiero. Since the kids were home for the holiday, I packed them up, and my husband too. We'd all make the best of it, I thought, and I'd have a working vacation of sorts.

The kids knew nothing of the real purpose of the trip and they'd occupy themselves by exploring the islands, swimming, and fishing. By now, they did know that I sometimes talk to murderers, but I've told them nothing more specific than that. At the age of fifteen, my oldest son had actually seen me on television speaking about the abduction of Elizabeth Smart, but he didn't ask any further questions. And I won't offer answers. I trust he'll let me know when he wants to know more details about my career, as will my younger son.

On the plane, I read a story that quoted a true-crime writer who said that there has been a conspicuous increase in the incidence of serial murder in countries whose political landscape has recently changed. He pointed to Russia, Brazil, and South Africa as examples where regimes had evolved into more democratic, more open, more permissive societies and where serial murderers have been on the rise. But this is a lot of bunk. Regimes, presidents, and policies aren't the reasons for serial crime. Serial murderers are everywhere, but in some countries, we just don't hear about them. It may also be true that the lack of a free press in China or Russia diminishes the number of reports about serial crime. In any event, serial murder is an international phenomenon.

In the village of Rostov in the Ukraine beginning in 1980, for example, Andrei Chikatilo ate some of the sexual organs of the people he murdered. All of Russia was horrified. It's interesting to note that it was fairly common during World War II (and even before) for everyone from children to grandmothers to consume the bodies of the dead to prevent famine. During the height of the famines, people were even killed for their flesh. There simply was no food anywhere to be found in the more rural areas, whose landscapes were white, frigid tundras. Chikatilo witnessed and lived through these times; in fact, his mother told him that his brother was eaten for food. Of course, Andrei himself did not kill because he longed for a politically different time in the Soviet Union, when he could eat people without fearing that the authorities would crack down. Nor did he kill and eat to avenge his brother or as vengeance for his sexual inadequacy (though the latter was his explanation in court). There were many people in Russia who had to resort to cannibalism just to keep from starving, and none of these became serial murderers. So it can't be said that what Chikatilo saw, horrible as it was, led him to kill or to eat the sex organs of his victims.

As the crude killer watched from a cell in the courtroom, his accusers screamed at him, chastising him. On his face was not the look of repentance. Moreover, during the testimony of witnesses and officials, he looked up at the ceiling as if to ask, Why are they oppressing me? Then he dropped his drawers and underwear to expose himself and said, "Here, take this if you want it." I believe Chikatilo was medically insane, and society was not to blame. However, during a lengthy trial from April to August 1992, the point was driven home again and again: Chikatilo was ruthless and sane; he knew what he was doing, and he even took pleasure in what he did. Two months later, the Russian judge found him guilty of fifty-two murders. Chikatilo's life was taken by an executioner's bullet to the head in early 1994.

I thought about the many places to which I'd traveled to learn more about serial murderers, particularly India, and its Golden Triangle, which includes Delhi, Agra, and Jaipur. From the colorful mosaics near the vibrant bazaars in Delhi to the historic marble minarets to the lush green gardens at the tomb of Akbar to a ride on the back of an elephant, every inch of India is full of romance and mysterious, ancient history, and, yes, poverty. In India, I heard the story of a beautiful lower-caste woman known as the Bandit Queen (though she was not royalty) and also as the Rebel of the Ravines. Phoolan Devi carried a rifle and wore a red bandana and a belt of bullets slung over her shoulder . . . and killed twenty-two politically influencial landowners in an uprising in the town of Behmai in 1981. It was one of the biggest slaughters modern-day India has ever seen. Devi's sometimes considered a serial killer here in the United States, but she killed for political reasons, stealing from the rich and giving to the poor like a female Robin Hood. After serving an eleven-year jail sentence, she became a much-loved politician in the Indian Parliament, fighting for the rights of the lower castes. She was not insane at all, as her motive included vengeance to punish the upper-caste men who gang-raped her, and the men of Behmai who watched them do it. She was in no way a serial murderer. In 2001, Devi was murdered herself by a man wearing a mask outside her house, killed by a man who later said the murder was retribution for the massacre in Behmai. In India, many consider Devi to be a great hero to this day.

In the late 1990s in the Punjab city of Lahore in Pakistan near the Indian border, Javed Iqbal took an iron chain and choked, sexually abused, cut up, and threw the remains of a hundred street kids into vats of acid. He is said to have had three accomplices. The paunchy, giggling Iqbal, who wore a preppy-style pullover sweater and geeky-looking glasses when posing for cameras, turned himself over into the hands of editors at a local newspaper, proclaiming, "I could have killed five hundred." Like Robert Berdella, Iqbal kept a detailed diary of his deeds. He also kept many of his victims' shoes, eighty-five pairs of them, probably as souvenirs. An adamant, angry Judge Allah Baksh offered up an eye-for-an-eye sentence in which Iqbal would be cut into one hundred pieces and put in acid before a crowd of people. But it wasn't to be. Like Fred West, Iqbal killed himself in his cell before Pakistani justice was served. Serial murderers rarely commit suicide. Could it have been that the structure of prison life led West and Igbal to experience some kind of coming together in their personalities to make them more humanlike? And when their personalities came together, could they have seen the horror of what they'd done? Could this "new human-ness" have led to their suicides? I have no real answer, but it's an interesting question to think about.

The Japanese are reticent about many things, including cancer.

Until several years ago, they considered even speaking the word to be taboo. A Japanese friend of ours who was stricken with the disease refused even to utter the word, as did the family around him. It was as if by merely saying it, the cancer would spread further. And this friend might have known better—he was a physician. The Japanese are also silent about serial killers. The 1988 case of Tsutomu Mizayaki stunned the residents of Tokyo. He abducted, mutilated, and killed little girls as young as four years of age and no older than seven, and called the killings a dream from which he had never really awoken. Five months after killing one child, he burned the body and dropped the remains, enclosed in a cardboard box, in front of her parents' house. He consumed the flesh from the roasted hands of another victim, and claimed he began murdering after he saw visions of "rat people." Like other serial killers, he at one point professed that his confessions were obtained forcibly by members of a violent police force. Mizayaki, whose voice never rose above a whisper in court, complained that police kept hitting him on the head to coax a confession. While his lawyers tried to convince the judge in Tokyo that Mizayaki was insane at the time of the killings, in April 1997 he was sentenced to death.

One country that is terribly ill equipped to identify or admit to the presence of serial killers is China. Some reports in magazines like *Time* have suggested that the reason (again!) for the upsurge in serial crime is related to the slight loosening of restrictions in a post–Chairman Mao era that seeks to open society a bit more than the old hard-line Communists permitted. Hua Ruizho, for instance, found prostitutes near the Great Wall Sheraton Hotel in the capital of Beijing. Ruizho spirited them away in his van, raped them, killed them, and took the bodies to garbage dumps. He was executed in 2002. Another killer, security guard Duan Guocheng, murdered thirteen women, cutting off the breasts of some. On the run, Duan evaded police for months in 2001 by sleeping in flea-bitten hotels that cost a few dollars each night. *Time* reported that the network of communications among cities to which police have access was less than stellar. The idea of miscommunication among Chinese authorities is not a problem exclusive to the Chinese. It happens to this day in the United States to a lesser extent, possibly because China's communications infrastructure isn't as advanced as is ours. I'm quite sure that China always had serial killers in the time of Mao; they just were not reported to the police or to journalists, or officials kept the murders quiet and they weren't talked about. Wherever serial murders occur in the world, it's important for all governments and law enforcement agencies to be completely open and to share information, so citizens can learn more about this ever-present danger. Otherwise, the problem will continue . . . and grow.

Once we got off the plane and took a cab to the city, we were immersed in the dusty, noisy chaos that is always São Paulo, the world's second largest city. Nearly seventeen million people live here, many of them in the favelas, the ghettos within the cities of Brazil.

Shortly after we settled in, the phone in our room rang: Marcelo Costa de Andrade, the serial killer, was having second thoughts about talking with me. He also made the request for ten thousand dollars for his time, which staggered me. I was crestfallen. Great. I had made the five-thousand-mile trip to Brazil, and I was expected to wait at the whim of a serial killer, at that. Why did I even begin to believe that he would be forthcoming? After all these years, why did I think anything would be different? Serial killers specialize in manipulation. While he sat in his cell making his grand decision, we decided not to wait around. Packing up the kids, we drove to Paraty, a little-known but beautiful fishing village on the ocean about two hours by car from Rio. We found that Paraty has sixty-five islands and three hundred beaches in the area to explore. Fishing and eating, we had a fine Thanksgiving time, Paraty style.

Occasionally, among the colorful tropical parrots and chirping tanagers, I would sit alone in the courtyard of our *pousada* and think about Marcelo Costa de Andrade. Nearly a decade ago, when I was in Rio for a neurology conference, I had seen a dramatic headline splashed across one of the tabloid newspapers about a twenty-five-year-old murderer who sometimes drank the blood of his victims. Because my Portuguese isn't very good, I asked a colleague to translate for me.

I began to hear a startling story of the downtrodden favela in Rio called Rocinha where Marcelo lived. The word *Rocinha* means "little field," and it's located on a mountain called Two Brothers, but the place is far more ominous than the names would indicate. From where I was staying, I could look up on the impoverished city within a city made up of dwellings haphazardly constructed of drab concrete blocks, tin roofs, and wooden shacks. It was like a medieval town, without running water, plumbing, and often without electricity (unless someone illegally tapped into it). Back then, the only time a member of the upper or middle class would venture into Rocinha was to buy drugs or sex. But they can't or won't stop the drug lords that rule high in the hills, nor will they clean the canal reeking with raw sewage that constitutes the area's main water supply. In Rocinha, it's as though the nearby famous tourist towns and beaches of Ipanema are a planet away. Like many of the children in Rocinha, Marcelo lived a life full of violence, abuse, and hunger. Like Alton Coleman, he was beaten regularly by his relatives, sometimes so hard that he was dizzied and stunned by the blows. By the age of fourteen, he had begun to work as a prostitute. Soon he began a long relationship with an older man, with whom he eventually resided, but it was a utilitarian relationship during which his life became easier and better than what he had in the favela. He was fed, clothed, given gifts, and went to movies occasionally.

At the age of seventeen, Marcelo would listen endlessly to tapes of his brother crying (why, I don't know), and then tried to rape the same ten-year-old brother, with whom he lived. When the relationship with the older man ended, Marcelo returned to his mother and began an honest, if badly paying, job handing out flyers advertising various items for sale in a Copacabana shop. Marcelo seemed to be making every effort not to stray from a straight and narrow path that might eventually lead out of the favela. Attending church regularly, he and his mother now lived in the more rural but still downtrodden town of Itaborai, twenty-four miles from Rio, where horse-drawn carts are still common. It's horrifying but not so strange that parents of abused children refuse to believe such abuse could happen. She may even have had her own need, whatever that was, to keep Marcelo around, so she let the abuse pass.

The churchgoing became more frequent, as often as four or five times a week for four hours each night at the Brazilian-founded Universal Church of the Kingdom of God, a sect that claims evil spirits are the roots of all troubles. They believe that depression and fear are caused by demons, and exorcisms are not uncommon within the church. Among their tenets is the notion that the church can cure illnesses like AIDS . . . and the "illness" that the church calls homosexuality.

The Universal Church of the Kingdom of God had been called suspect by many since its inception in 1977 because of its unusual practices. Leaders of the church have been investigated for alleged links to Colombia drug cartels. In Brazil, the group controls well over a dozen TV stations, over thirty radio stations, even a soccer team named Universal, and members of the church hold high political office. Also in Brazil, some church leaders under came investigation by the government for possible fraud. None of the group's teachings, however, preach murder in the name of God in any way.

As I've indicated, religion is a major part of growing up in Brazil, and it infuses everything people do. It's more than merely following certain rituals for an hour or so on Saturday or Sunday. In Brazil, practicing religion is considered to be as essential to life as is breathing the air. I wouldn't say that de Andrade was overpowered by religion, however. No church—in fact, no religion of this earth would have been able to stop Marcelo from acting on the catalysts that lurked deep within his own afflicted mind.

The Brazilian tabloid press began to call de Andrade a vampire because he drank the blood of the children he murdered. They had begun to call him a "monster," making him bigger than life. It was clear to me that Marcelo was about to become Brazil's most infamous serial murderer. Yes, later there was São Paulo's Francisco de Assis Pereira, who was charged with murdering nine women in 1998, and Larete Patrocinio Orpinelli, a drifter who was said to have killed ten children over a twenty-year period and who confessed in 2000 after having repeated nightmares about his crimes. But Marcelo killed quickly over a nine-month period in 1991, and he raped the children, had sex with the bodies, and sometimes drank human blood. It was like nothing that the good people in modern-day Brazil had ever seen before.

The boys whose lives were ended by Marcelo were kind of like The Runts gang portrayed in the sad and violent Brazilian movie *City of God,* which was based on a true story. These children lived on the streets of the favelas, hustling and begging, holding up little stores or mugging passersby to make their wages or, if they were "lucky," running about as messengers and lookouts for the drug lords in an effort to become drug lords themselves one day. Their lives, in a sense, were dead-end lives, but they were precious human lives nonetheless. Children do end up missing in the favelas of Rio (which hold one and a half million people), sometimes at the hands of vigilantes who have had enough of the robberies, sometimes at the hands of drug lords during turf wars. But these children, poverty stricken or delinquent, deserve better. These children, one of whom was just six years old, deserved to make their way in life, whether it was in or out of Rocinha.

One thing that continued to annoy me was the way the press focused on the blood drinking. Earlier in this book, I pointed to the life of Elizabeth Bathory, the Hungarian countess who drank and bathed in the blood of her servants in the 1500s in a bizarre effort to remain young. In his fairly dry but still widely published 1886 book *Psychopathia Sexualis,* German neuropsychiatrist Richard von Krafft-Ebing profiled over two hundred cases of such sexual oddities—including blood drinkers like vampires and werewolves. Krafft-Ebing made clear that the primitive need to drink human blood has a history, a long history dating back to the caveman and cannibalism, and it certainly pre-dates the publication of Bram Stoker's *Dracula.* But Marcelo was no vampire. In reality, only twice did he drink his victims' blood.

In early 1992 in Rio, I lost no time in trying to arrange a meeting with Marcelo. I didn't really believe it would happen while I was there, but I felt it was important that I give it a try. What if Marcelo could tell me something the others hadn't? What possibly might be lost if I didn't get to him? By sitting down with de Andrade, could I possibly find another significant piece of the serial murderer puzzle? I had to find out.

It took a few days, but through an affable go-between who was a well-regarded and well-connected doctor in Rio, I got word that Brazilian officials would indeed permit me to speak with Marcelo. Still, there was one looming problem: my difficulty with the Portuguese language. My trusty intermediary helped me in tracking down a translator, and we set off for the prison in Rio, a run-down two-story stucco affair with wooden shutters over the bars that, compared to American prisons, wasn't particularly secure. Additionally, vigilance wasn't as high. Guards were not watching Marcelo's every move (and in later years, he did make an escape, although he was reapprehended) as they do with serial killers here in the United States.

The sprawling country of Brazil imprisons more people than any other country in Latin America, and its prison population has doubled in the last five years. As I was led through the halls, I saw no visible signs of abuse, although the conditions were less than what Americans would call sanitary. Overall, the jail I visited was not a hellhole by any means, but within its humid interior I would see the occasional centipede creeping or cockroach scurrying by on walls whose paint was peeling.

The officials in Rio were a bit taken aback by my presence, wondering, "Who is this blond woman from the North, and why is she here?" But they were fairly polite and led me to de Andrade without hesitation. In a small, windowless room, there he sat at a rough-hewn wooden table, shackled, looking younger than his twenty-five years. While Marcelo was marginally younger than other serial killers, people in Rio don't have the extended adolescence that we have here. They go to work sooner and don't stay in school as long. Marcelo grew up more quickly than a serial murderer in, say, Illinois would have. So it wasn't exceptional that his rampage came a bit early.

De Andrade himself was dark and round-faced, but calm, reserved, and almost resigned to his circumstance. His brown eyes appeared earnest as he tried to answer questions through the translator.

"What was it like growing up in Rio?"

"We were very poor," he answered softly.

"It must have been difficult."

He hunched forward and looked at the table. "We are so poor that we must do anything we can do to survive."

"What does 'anything' mean?"

Marcelo sat silent for a minute. Then he scratched the back of his head and said, "I made money on the streets," he said, referring to working as a prostitute. Prostitution is close to being a sanctioned occupation in Rio, a place that's much more open about sex and sexuality than we are here in the United States.

It may have been difficult for Marcelo to prostitute himself initially, but it was difficult for him to live at home as well. "And then, after I worked, when I would come home, I was hit. My stepmother sometimes would not give me food."

"What about going to school?"

He thought for a moment, stroking the light, few-days' growth of beard on his face. "There was not so much school for me in the favela. There was just the street and everyone would try to make some money on the street."

"What was fun for you?"

"We all make things for Carnival. It takes a long time. It is not fun always. It is work." The people of Rio are obsessed with Carnival, the entertainment-filled festival that precedes Lent, especially the great parade with its grand costumes and floats that passes before at least 85,000 in the open-air Sambadrome. But I could see that for Marcelo, the making of costumes for Carnival was not something that he took much pleasure in doing—though everyone did it.

"What else do you like to do?"

"I like to ride a bike. Sometimes soccer. I like the sun. I would like to see the sun again."

It was a challenge for me to try to keep up a conversation because the interpreter had to translate everything I would say and everything Marcelo said. I felt I lost a bit of the rapport I usually have when I can speak directly to a serial murderer. And I wondered whether the translator was being accurate, especially as we moved into the more serious parts of the interview. Yet I didn't have time to be distracted. I forged ahead and looked straight at de Andrade.

"Marcelo, you have done some bad things."

"Bad," he agreed.

"Do you know why you did these bad things?"

"The children have bad lives here. If they are children when they die, they go straight to heaven. A better place." I wasn't buying it. I knew there were cultural differences between the United States and Brazil. I knew about his connection to the Universal Church. It's no secret that Christians are taught to look forward to an afterlife in heaven. But no religion, certainly no Western religion, advocates murder, let alone the murder of children. I didn't make my feelings known and continued.

"Why did you take young boys?"

"They were prettier. To me."

"What did you use to kill?"

"My hands. Once with a machete. My mother had it. I would say that I was going for bananas. I cut off the head." In this incident, Marcelo had already killed and raped an eleven-year-old boy called Odair Jose Muniz dos Santos, who he picked up while the child was begging and who resisted his advances on a soccer field. He returned to the scene to cut off the dead boy's head.

"Why the head?"

"I wanted people to make fun of him in heaven."

"Can you tell me more?"

"People used to make fun of me too. I did not want to hurt anyone. Sometimes I do not know if they are dead or alive. It was . . . I could not stop myself." Again, it was like Michael Lockhart had described: something went awry and he was driven to kill.

"Why no one older than sixteen?"

"The adults, if they had sins, would go to hell. I did not want to send anyone to hell. Children when they go, they go to heaven." I found all this ironic because he himself had killed so many people and, according to the tenets of his religion, would be bound for hell once he died as well. On the surface, his "logic" sounds reasonable, and Marcelo would tell this story over and over again to police and to journalists. But Marcelo had no real concept of religion. It was a complex concept too abstract for him to grasp.

In a way, de Andrade's use of religion as an excuse was like John Wayne Gacy saying it was Jack Hanley who made him kill thirty-three people in Illinois. Both were giving something to us so that we "normal" humans can remark, "Oh, yes. That's why he did it." They hear us desperately trying to make sense of their crimes, so they offer reasons, excuses, defenses. In general, people cannot deal with not knowing the whys and hows.

How did Marcelo's string of murders finally conclude? On December 11, 1991, ten-year-old Altair and six-year-old Ivan Abreu received permission from their mother to walk to a friend's home to eat a meal of fried fish and bread. As they strolled, the two were as excited about eating as a child here would be to get a gift like a new toy. But when they stopped at a bus terminal to ask passersby for spare change, they met Marcelo. He promised that if they helped him light candles in the church of St. George, he would give the boys 4,000 cruzeiros (then about $20). It was a huge amount of money for boys who didn't even have a bed to sleep on. Marcelo made small talk as they walked and even lifted Ivan and perched him on his back when he tired. Then, when they reached a deserted beach, Marcelo grabbed Altair and began kissing him. When Altair tried to run, Marcelo pushed the boy down onto the sharp pebbles on the beach, where he hit his head and began to bleed. Then Marcelo turned on Ivan, choking, raping, and killing Ivan as Altair watched. Altair stood stunned, unable to move or comprehend what he saw unfold before him. Then Marcelo moved toward Altair and opened his arms wide. Altair felt he was about to die, and he could literally smell his brother all over de Andrade. Surprisingly to the young boy, Marcelo hugged Altair, as though nothing wrong had occurred.

"Why?" asked Altair.

"I have sent Ivan to heaven." De Andrade never used the words *kill* or *rape* or *death*.

"I love you," announced Marcelo, who then took Altair by the hand. They spent the night together outside, on the ground in a thick forest behind a gas station, away from any people, their presence obscured by plants and shrubbery. The next day, the boy was taken to

Marcelo's workplace, a jewelry outlet in Copacabana. His heart beating fast, Altair was able to escape when Marcelo was distracted. Recalling the right buses to board, he returned to his mother, who informed police about Ivan's disappearance. Meanwhile, Marcelo returned to the scene of the crime and placed Ivan's tiny hands into the pockets of his pants. He said he did this to save the boy's hands from the gnawing teeth of rodents.

When the police arrived at Marcelo's shop a couple of days later, de Andrade seemed to expect them, wondering aloud why they took so long to arrive. Initially, Marcelo confessed to killing Ivan but no one else. It took two months in jail, but de Andrade then told police about thirteen more murders.

We had trekked back to São Paulo and dealt with the massive traffic jams on the street and the smell of fuel emissions that intruded even through our closed windows. Once we were back in the lobby of our hotel, the desk clerk handed me a message from my intermediary, and the news was not so good.

De Andrade had come down in price, but he still requested five thousand dollars for a talk. Nearly hitting the roof, I was livid that I had been duped and that I was gullible enough to have made my way to Brazil for nothing. When I calmed down, I resigned myself to the fact that at least it was a nice Thanksgiving vacation.

A five-thousand-dollar request from a serial killer is an obscene amount to me and it borders on extortion. Yes, it has always been my policy to make every effort to follow up with the people I have profiled and interviewed to see how the prison system has changed them. Has the person adjusted to prison life? What kind of life had the prisoner made for himself within the prison, such as Gacy had made with his paintings? Had he lashed out at another prisoner? (That's a rarity; serial murderers rarely attack others in prison unless they themselves are first set upon.) How was the confining structure of a Brazilian prison beneficial or detrimental to the murderer?

But five thousand dollars! It was obvious to me that Marcelo thought he had become a celebrity. Like the serial killers stateside, he had gotten a kind of fan following, groupies who had written to him and fawned over him. Probably, the people who run Internet Web sites had gotten to him too. It's ghoulish, but they sell everything from locks of hair to handwritten letters procured from the murderers.

I have never paid to speak to a serial killer and I vow that I never will. It's not just the principle of the thing, it's the questionable honesty and candor I would get by greasing a serial killer's palms. He may say something dramatic that he thought I wanted to hear just to earn his wage. Another important consideration was this: offering any kind of remuneration is never an ethical thing for a doctor to do. It's the kind of thing that could ruin a reputation, and it was silly for Marcelo to think that I would agree to his unscrupulous demands. Finally, the idea of paying money to someone who has taken the lives of children is repugnant to me.

I knew I would encounter more obstacles before I really could discover what makes a serial killer tick. And I still felt that, somewhere down the line, I would get to de Andrade again. I'm no manipulator in the way serial murderers are, but I do stick with things over time and that tends to wear them down. With some of them, I have requested interviews for over ten years. I just don't give up . . . until they're executed. Constant research is key in this business, and things have changed dramatically since I started back in the 1970s. It was time to consider the various advances in science that could well be used to help the world discover who isn't a serial killer . . . and who is. And who can be stopped.

FIFTEEN

DNA AND THE
GREEN RIVER KILLER

J ust as medicines and technologies change, so does the intricate science that helps us to track down serial murderers. Over the course of the next decades, that science will only become better and more refined. To understand what I mean more fully, we have to backtrack somewhat.

I remember that I stood in my beige raincoat on the precipice of a deep ravine in the ever-present Seattle-area mist, cold and wondering how and when the Green River Killer would be found. Carefully, I walked around the crime scene, as I do with many of these cases, to try and collect any missing pieces of information, and I peered over and into the rocky abyss. This was one of the locations where he disposed of the body after he killed. Could another body be near here?

I looked around for other clues the police might have missed in the tall grass, but I saw nothing.

I *did* have my ideas regarding who the killer might be. My theory held that the suspect was a white male who was married, and he was in his thirties. He would be found working at a blue-collar job as a truck driver or a factory worker, or some position that gave him the opportunity to take time off pretty much whenever he desired to take a break. The suspect would not be someone from very far outside the area. In other words, the person knew Seattle and wasn't a drifter. Additionally, he would be someone who wouldn't stick out in a crowd: he wouldn't look like a killer. He would look like a normal guy, the same kind of normal-looking guy that I have described throughout this book. That normalcy would provide him a cover, like a cloak of powerful invisibility.

The Green River itself twists along a sixty-five-mile course that begins just to the southeast of Howard Hansom Dam inland and pours into Elliott Bay just to the south of Seattle. To local fishermen, the river is known for its rainbow trout, steelhead, and salmon. To the police and the FBI, it became known as a dumping ground for corpses.

On July 15, 1982, in Kent, Washington, two boys stopped their bicycles on the Peck Bridge to horse around, talk about fishing, and look out over the water. As they chatted, they glanced down into the Green River. There they saw the bloated body of sixteen-year-old Wendy Lee Coffield, floating naked with a pair of her own jeans tied around her neck. Police immediately deduced that she had been strangled. A few weeks later and just to the south of the Peck Bridge, an employee of a meatpacking plant discovered something lying on a sandbar. Thinking it to be a dead animal, the worker slowly moved closer to examine the find, only to realize the unmoving hulk was the nude body of twenty-three-year-old Lynne Bonner. She hadn't drowned: there was no water in her lungs. An autopsy revealed that Bonner had been choked to death. Other similarities between the two murders included these facts: both Bonner and Coffield were young prostitutes who had tattoos.

The killer wasn't finished. On August 15, 1982, a man enjoying a Sunday respite leisurely rode on an inflatable raft down the Green River's slow current. He discovered not one but two more bodies in the river. Once police arrived on the scene, they found yet another body in the tall wispy grass on the riverbank, a body that was likely placed there only a day before. Two of the five victims also had a rock inserted into their vaginas. I wondered whether this was done to weigh them down. Was there a sexual meaning that no one, not even the killer himself, could comprehend? Whatever the case, there was little doubt in the minds of authorities that a serial murderer was the perpetrator of the crimes.

The FBI's top people from Virginia jetted to Seattle to try to help. One felt the killer was very close to the police, not necessarily a cop, but someone who had an interest in the doings of law enforcement. The same person then said the killer was a fisherman or a hunter. Another felt the killer was a sexual psychopath. There were agents who speculated that there was more than one killer. Another thought the murderer was a military man trained in intricate special operations. A psychic even got into the act with her predictions.

The Green River Task Force was created to track down the murderer ASAP. With a team that included not only members of the FBI and local detectives but also the specious from-the-cell "insight" of serial killer Ted Bundy, the task force sounded auspicious on the face of it. But they were bogged down by infighting and rampant ego. Similar chaos had reigned over Seattle's Ted Bundy investigation a few years before. Ironically, though the Green River Task Force was created to avoid the same mistakes, one could argue that the quality of information retrieved by the Green River group was inferior to that gathered for the Bundy investigation.

I thought I could help the task force and I gave one of the leaders of the group (who had also worked on the Wayne Williams case) a call to offer my help. The conversation was very short, the answer was as abrupt and brusque as it was startling: "Not interested."

One of the problems I've often seen with law enforcement is that they become too territorial. They don't want anyone messing around or flying in to add new ideas or theories. And they don't want anyone else getting credit for the capture except themselves. Additionally, they don't understand how sitting and talking something through might be helpful. They generally see a forensic psychiatrist as someone who's involved only in the trial aspect of the case, someone who's extremely biased as part of the defense or prosecution teams. They couldn't imagine that I could be objective. Plus, I was seen as a civilian and not as part of their closed circle. Did this narrow attitude affect the investigation of the Green River Killer? It certainly didn't help. I went to Seattle to dig around anyway.

After I began profiling serial murderers, the FBI created its Behavioral Science Unit (and some members of the unit went to Seattle to join the task force). But their goal was to assist law enforcement people in *apprehending* perpetrators. Behavioral scientists don't do the medical work that I do to discover what makes a serial killer commit murder after murder. They'll look at the external characteristics of the person, and sometimes they get into a false way of "psychoanalyzing" the serial murderer. They come up with ideas like: he hates his mother and that's why he murdered. But the ideas have no basis in scientific research. They believe in simplicities like "wet the bed, start a fire, and kill an animal, and you'll become a serial murderer.*" It's just too easy an assumption to make.

Opinions about the Green River Killer's profile varied widely within the task force, and there were more and more of them as time went by. At the same time, more and more dead bodies were found in 1982 and 1983 in locations beyond the Green River—closer to Seattle itself. Leads increased exponentially, but the task force had only one primitive computer—and the information on it was lost when there was a power outage. Over time, the FBI and the police proved they could not track down the killer and the task force was scrapped. With renewed hope, another task force was created in 1984 with over forty people assigned to it. By then, skeletons and remains were found as distant as forty miles away from Seattle. Later, authorities began to believe the killer had murdered people as far away as Vancouver and Oregon. While the task force had amassed thousands of pieces of evidence, only one percent of it had been properly analyzed. The need to find the killer reached a fever pitch as months turned into years. But the baffled authorities had no definitive answers. Some even

---

*An agent from the FBI told CNN about the serial murderer conundrum plaguing Baton Rouge, Louisiana, in 2003. The generalities the agent used in his profile after months of investigation were almost of no use. He was "too smart to be caught," "able to lift 175 pounds," "wore size ten or eleven shoes," was "impulsive," "determined," "nonthreatening," and "white." So much for the vaunted depth of behavioral science.

thought Michael Lee Lockhart from Florida might have been the Green River Killer.

Amid much media hoopla, King County Police Captain Frank Adamson predicted that the Green River Killer would be brought to justice in 1986. But the year came and went. With little success to show for the years it had been in existence, the Green River Task Force closed up shop in 1990. It wasn't until 2001 that police apprehended a suspect, after forty-nine murders had been committed. The beady-eyed, mustached man was a Caucasian in his early fifties, Gary Leon Ridgway of Auburn, Washington, a town a little over twenty miles south of Seattle as the crow flies. The tagline the Auburn chamber of commerce came up with for the sleepy town of forty-five thousand is "More Than You Imagined." Indeed it was—especially with a serial murderer living there.

Ridgway was a quiet man, a journeyman painter who toiled at the same company for thirty-two years and loved rooting around at flea markets. He also occasionally bragged to friends about his exploits with local prostitutes. In fact, members of the task force had picked up Ridgway for soliciting a prostitute as far back as the early 1980s, but they were never able to pin the murders on him. Though he was considered a suspect in the murder of seventeen-year-old Maria Malvar in 1983, there wasn't enough evidence to charge him. In 1986, Ridgway even passed a lie detector test.

Over the course of twenty years, however, science has evolved in breathtaking fashion. Perhaps the most important discoveries in the last few years have come in the field of DNA and the mapping of the human genome. Advanced DNA testing was what helped crack the case of the Green River Killer in a way no law enforcement officer could. A sample of saliva that had been retrieved from Ridgway by court order in 1987 came up for DNA analysis in 2001 by using a method called PCR, polymerase chain reaction. The groundbreaking test was invented by University of California chemist Kary Mullis in the 1980s. In 1993, Mullis won the Nobel Prize for his work, and since then, the test has been refined and perfected enough so that forensic experts now trust it more implicitly than any other current investigative tool.

What PCR testing can accomplish is nothing short of amazing. Using a machine with a price tag of more than $50,000 and often about the size of a small cube refrigerator, chemicals are used to separate the DNA's double helix into two distinct pieces. These delicate strands are placed into a solution of enzymes including the polymerase and the nucleotides adenine, thymine, guanine, and cytosine (molecules containing nitrogen that are the building blocks of DNA). The two strands of DNA, the polymerases, then act like a kind of superadvanced copy machine. Under the right conditions, the chemical recreates the DNA and makes a copy of it so there are a pair of double helixes. Within a few hours, the PCR chain reaction can produce billions of copies of the original DNA. The repetition was necessary because many copies were needed to create a kind of map of Ridgway's genes. Once the map was in hand, comparisons could be made.

The DNA within Ridgway's saliva sample was compared to the DNA found on the dead bodies. Hearts skipped when researchers were able to match up sequences of nucleotides that were unique to Ridgway and only to Ridgway. The possibility of a mistake was minuscule, since the error rate for the test is one in three trillion. It wasn't that authorities didn't find DNA on the dead victims along the way. They did. But the amount of DNA wasn't enough to have been used in the fairly unrefined tests that were available at the time.

So the authorities finally nabbed their suspect. Three heroic scientists worked a total of 640 hours obtaining the right DNA samples to test and then used PCR to resounding success. When the news was announced, one Seattle journalist told me, "There was a lot of excitement—it seemed like a movie script, really. Here were these seemingly ancient murders, and suddenly the legendary killer was unmasked and the whole country knew about it. It was hard to believe, but little revelations kept pouring out, and it became more and more real." In early November 2003, an unemotional Ridgway pled guilty, one by one, to forty-eight murders in exchange for a life sentence. Reading from a statement before the judge and some of the families of the deceased in a small courtroom, Ridgway said, "I'm sorry for killing all those young ladies. I have tried to remember as much as I could to help the detectives find and recover the ladies. I'm sorry for the scare I put into the community. I want to thank the police, the prosecuting attorneys, my lawyers, and all others that had the patience to work with me and to help me remember all the tragic things that I did and to be able to talk about them.

"I know the horrible things my acts were. I have tried for a long time to get these things out of my mind.

"I have tried for a long time to keep from killing any ladies. I'm sorry that I put my wife, my son, my brothers, and my family through this hell. I hope that they can find a way to forgive me." That admission made him the worst serial killer in United States history, and families were up in arms. Most relatives of the murdered still wanted death for Ridgway (one stated, "I'll kill him myself"), but the state of Washington has only performed a handful of executions since it initiated the death penalty. You might ask, Well, if serial killers are addicted to killing, why did Ridgway's murders seem to stop in the 1980s? The fact is, they didn't stop. Ridgway probably killed many more. If you look closer at the interviews he gave to authorities, Ridgway actually admitted to killing sixty women. But authorities could pin only forty-eight on him. Shortly after his plea of guilty, Snohomish County police announced that they were looking at twenty additional unsolved murders to gauge whether Ridgway may have been involved—especially because Ridgway admitted he didn't stop killing in the 1980s. Police forces from San Diego to Canada are now looking at Ridgway as a possible connection to their unsolved murders of women.

We have made much progress in understanding the mind of the serial murderer. In 1975 when I began my research, serial killers were considered no different from mass murderers. But in my work on such cases as the worst massacre in Australia, where thirty-five people were killed (and eighteen injured) with a semiautomatic rifle in Port Arthur, I've found that the difference is quite distinct. Port Arthur was a historical site in Tasmania, the location of a former penal colony. On the afternoon of Sunday, April 28, 1996, Martin Bryant lunched at the Broken Arrow Café on the grounds of the tourist attraction. After sitting down and eating, he removed an AR15 semiautomatic shotgun from a blue gym bag and began shooting people. Twenty people died and fifteen were wounded in the restaurant and fifteen more were shot and died outside of the café and in locations nearby.

The mass murderer is a human who has a personality structure, whereas a serial murderer really does not. As he readies to kill, the mass murderer regresses from that personality to a very paranoid state. Becoming suspicious, angry, and revengeful, he develops clear motives for his murders. As he begins to shoot from a campus tower, from inside the halls of a high school, or in a seaside cottage to kill many people at once, he feels he's getting back at somebody. Unlike serial murderers, who are seen by neighbors to be nice and helpful, a mass murderer is often said to be unusual, different, or odd. And the mass murderer often dies in a battle with police or kills himself to avoid police (although Martin Bryant stayed alive and currently is serving a life sentence in Risdon prison). Serial murderers never commit suicide before being apprehended, and they rarely kill themselves in prison. The mass murderer has blamed society for his woes.

As I've written, my belief, my theory, is that society and parenting and even accidents that injure the brain have little to do with creating a serial killer. John Wayne Gacy's father continually called him "dumb and stupid." Bobby Joe Long hated his mother. Ed Gein was obsessed with his mother. Gilles de Rais had a thug of a grandfather who never set the boy on the straight and narrow. But we humans are an adaptable species, tougher and more resilient than we think we are. The majority of people do not break down in the way serial killers break down. People may be hurt or emotionally wounded by parents or society, but they move on, some to become CEOs of large corporations, some simply to have a family that is far more stable than the upbringings they endured.

I am firmly convinced that there is something in the genes that leads a person to become a serial killer. In other words, he is a serial killer before he is born. He is a serial killer as he grows during those nine months of nurturing in the womb, not yet influenced by the words or deeds of parents, teachers, and caregivers. He is a serial killer when he is a fetus, even as soon as sperm meets egg to create the genes of a new person. Those genes will create a disordered brain, a "diseased" brain that is predisposed to serial murder.

It's almost too facile to say the brain is the most complex of human organs, but it's true. Franz Joseph Gall, the German-born scientist who worked in the early 1800s, was considered the Newton of intellectual physics and the creator of phrenology. He stated that "each of our feelings, our instincts, our intellectual and moral principles has, in the brain, its own specific organ which can be seen on the surface in the form of either a prominence or a Fossa, according to whether it is highly developed or not, and the skull, faithfully reproducing the outlines and sinuousity of the brain, also reproduces the configuration of these various organs." While the writing itself is a bit obtuse, the eccentric Gall was on the right track in assigning specific activities to specific parts of the brain. He did mistakenly believe those with a big brain were more "powerful" than those with a smaller organ, and that bumps on the head indicated what was going on inside the brain. Today in my office, I keep a ceramic head that phrenologists used to use. It reminds me not to go too far off in speculation without having a good basis in fact.

With the discovery of the brain's Papez circuit in 1937, science really began to show the connection between emotion and bodily response. Simply put, the Papez circuit is the brain route senses take, the result of which colors your emotions.

One of the first things a medical student learns in neuroanatomy courses is that this Papez circuit affects part of the brain called the hypothalamus, which is a kind of a minibrain in itself. The hypothalamus releases chemicals and hormones to the pituitary gland, which then releases them to the blood, where the chemicals have their effect on the human body. In addition, the multitasking hypothalamus helps to manage body temperature and the cardiovascular system. Many serial murderers will complain or talk about being hypertensive or having multiple autonomic symptoms, from sweating to rapid heartbeat to vomiting to passing gas at the time of or just prior to the act of killing. But not all people who have brain disease are violent, nor are all persons who are violent suffering from brain disease. While there's not space enough to detail the intricacies of the neurological functions of the brain, I believe it's important to understand that one of the primary keys to understanding the serial murderer lies within the hypothalamus and in the limbic system. To put it very simply, these parts of the brain regulate emotions and moods.

Created by Professor Zang-Hee Cho in the 1970s, the process of PET (positron-emission tomography) scans the brain to detect changes in blood oxygenation and blood flow. After the patient is injected with a radioisotope, the PET machine watches for the emissions of particles called positrons from the decaying radioisotope in the brain. When the positrons meet with electrons, photons are emitted, and the computer is then able to create an image for study by researchers and doctors. These pictures can tell quite a story.

In studies using PET, researchers induced emotions in patients by asking what people thought about movies they had just seen. When the brain patterns were studied, it was seen that happiness, sadness, and disgust are associated with increased activity in the hypothalamus and various areas of the brain that we can specify and target. I'd detail each of the areas I mean, but truly explaining places in the brain like the occipitotemporoparietal cortex would take a course of study in school, not just a book.

Again, without becoming too technical, there are various chemicals in the body that instigate emotions and lead to actions. For instance, I've said throughout the book that one of the clues to understanding a serial killer is that he has no social or psychological attachment. Killers such as Fred West or Michael Lee Lockhart are like infants emotionally. Two substances, oxytocin and vasopression, have been seen as being involved in attachment. Receptors have been located in the limbic system and in the brainstem. Could a serial murderer have an imbalance of these substances or a lack of receptor attachment in the brain? These are just two of many substances that can lead a human being to human action. Will we, sometime in the future, find one particular chemical that is the serial killer chemical? I certainly hope so.

In the mind of the average person, decision making occurs at several levels of the central nervous system. At the highest level, the individual uses past experience and future predictions to choose a course of action. At the lowest level, conscious decision making does not occur until after the actions are performed. The latter is the state of mind of the serial murderer. He is completely unaware of the process leading up to murder.

In addition to the Papez circuit, there are various other "switches" within the brain that create a cascade of events that lead a serial killer to kill. In the mind of a serial killer, something goes wrong in the switching process of these circuits. A multitude of factors, not the least of which are these circuits, keep the neurochemicals in the brain usually at levels that lead a person to function normally. To keep the brain on an even keel, the circuits strike a very fine balance, but what tips that balance? What makes that limbic system, the center of affect, emotion, and action, go berserk? I am convinced that it's in the genes. In addition, there have not been any murders from serial killers until they have become adolescents. I believe that the changes in adolescents that make them become serial killers are in the neurochemical and neuroendocrine changes that go along with puberty.

What we did initially in looking at the DNA and the genetics of these people was very primitive. In the 1970s, I remember taking the blood of Richard Macek and passing it on to a geneticist to analyze. On reflection, how unrefined that process was. You could almost compare what we did in looking at early gene patterns with phrenology, because we were saying, "Wow, look at the shape of this gene, does this say anything?" We did not know how incredibly complex the internal structure of each gene is. We were trying to do some pioneering work, but look how far we've come since the 1970s. In thirty years, we've made mammoth strides.

There are now ways to monitor the brain's function that psychiatrists used to believe could be observed only through analytic exploration like talking therapy. Being able to single out a chemical like oxytocin in the hypothalamus is only the very beginning. It doesn't define anything or answer anything, but it gives me a clue. Finding that clue is a little bit like finding a clue when I'm on the trail of a serial murderer—it's exhilarating and exciting. But much more work is needed.

Scientists know a good deal about brain metabolism and function, but then, where can these clues lead when it comes to serial murderers? What in the brain and in the genes makes them addicted to killing?

Overseas in the Netherlands, geneticist Hans Brunner from the University Hospital in Nijmegen has made a fascinating discovery. One day, a young woman approached Brunner and said she was concerned about bearing children. During her conversation with Brunner, she confessed to a history of brutal behavior in her family, like attempted murder. After testing, Brunner found that the woman's family carried an unusual gene mutation, a preponderance of the substance monoamine oxidase A. This enzyme stopped transmissions in the brain that are essential in maintaining tranquility and contentment, and the presence of the enzyme led the brain to refuse to break down serotonin. An excessive amount of serotonin may well cause a person to lash out with destructive behavior. Hans Brunner's discovery is just another small, important piece of the puzzle in the picture of the causes of violence.

I've attempted to run various tests with the permission of the serial murderer and of the government. Consistently, I'd like to run the whole gamut of genetic, biochemical, neurological, and neurochemical testing—including some cerebrospinal fluid–sampling studies. Cerebrospinal fluid guards the brain and spinal cord, and it takes chemicals on their rides through the central nervous system. Testing is a relatively easy process in which a local anesthetic is rubbed onto the area between the third and fourth vertebrae on the lower back and the doctor takes a needle to remove samples of the fluid. The pain involved is minor, but there may be a headache after the procedure is completed.

The testing would also include the implantation of deep brain electrodes, the output of which I would follow over periods of time. This does require surgery, which includes placing electrodes in the brain that are joined to a battery via a wire placed underneath the skin. In most cases, the battery is turned off at night. The risk of any possible bleeding in the brain is low—between one and two percent. Data suggest that the implantation of electrodes has no long-term side effects, and the electrodes can be removed at a later date.

In other words, this is long-term testing that would be conducted with the prisoner within the prison system. Some might say, well, you've said the serial murderer acts different within the structure of prison than he does in the less structured environment in which he commits his murders. But even if he were in a structured prison situation, such tests would give me a good baseline as to how an individual reacts to certain situations, from work in the kitchen to prisoners that don't particularly like him to dealings with visitors like family. If I see an external change, has there been an internal change to go along with it? Long-term testing is the way to find out.

Testing doesn't mean the prisoner would be constantly tethered to anything. But I would want to monitor electrical patterns and neurochemical patterns in the brain. Doctors already do this on patients who aren't incarcerated. Again, I'm not suggesting cutting into his skull to operate on his brain in an effort to change the way his brain functions. I just want to gather important information that the brain is telling me, information that occurs naturally in the course of the prisoner's everyday life.

I would be remiss if I didn't explain that there are legal obstacles to overcome with all of this. They're not obstacles that stem from the serial murderers themselves. Usually the murderers are all for testing, as they often express how exploration will help them to understand themselves and their murderous deeds, deeds they sometimes cannot remember. Over the years, I've approached lawyers, judges, and legislators to gauge their opinions over coffee or at fancy fund-raisers. I've even suggested that a law be passed to allow testing of serial killers. Sometimes I've received blank stares. Sometimes I've been laughed at. Sometimes I've dealt with angry responses. Sometimes they've cited a litany of case law.

The courts themselves have been very clear on the subject. Judges in many states have ruled that the prisoners don't have the free will to participate in the studies I propose simply because they are prisoners, thus incapable of exercising free will. Therefore, the state thinks for them in these matters, and the state says no to testing. The American Civil Liberties Union would likely pitch a huge fit even if the states agreed to testing, saying that the individual's freedom to agree or disagree would be impinged upon.

Yet when I look at a movie like *Minority Report,* I wonder what the future might hold. In the film based on a short fiction by Philip K. Dick, Tom Cruise is a kind of detective in the year 2054 who is able to use technology and psychic beings called "Pre-Cogs" to capture killers before they kill.

I sometimes wonder whether our knowledge of DNA may someday prevent serial killings, but not in the dramatic way the characters in *Minority Report* prevented killings. Any person can already submit a DNA sample by simply brushing some skin from the cheek or by giving blood samples to companies like Kimball Genetics. They can diagnose predisposition to illness in the average person for a fee, everything from inherited mental retardation to periodontal disease. A Florida company called Applied Digital Solutions offers the VeriChip, a tiny device about the size of a grain of rice. Implanted under the skin, it is full of information that becomes known and can be disseminated when scanned into a computer. The company is also working on a device to track children and wandering Alzheimer's patients via satellites and the Global Positioning System.

What if we were able to know, from something that was flagged deep within in the genes, that a person was predisposed to serial murder? Could we track him with an implanted device currently used by companies such as Applied Digital Solutions? Under what circumstances would it be ethical to do so? Would the legal system or the United States government ever permit even an experiment involving such a system? It's important to create a discussion of these questions now because the day will come, sooner rather than later, when doctors using DNA analysis will have the ability to reveal whether or not we will have a serial murderer in our midst—even before the murderer is born.

When that day comes, I'll know my work is done.

WHERE DO WE GO FROM HERE?

Down in my basement, past bicycles, hockey equipment, and the rhythmic sounds of the furnace, there is a dog-eared cardboard box. In it is a large plastic container. As I pull out and carefully open it, the odor of formaldehyde hits me. What's inside doesn't look like much, sliced up into segments as it was years ago, but there it is: John Wayne Gacy's brain. I know it sounds a little gruesome, but as I've mentioned, Gacy's family permitted me to keep it for scientific research purposes. I lift the container to eye level, and as I look at what was once living gray matter, I wonder to myself, What will you be able to tell me when I have the proper tools? How soon will the secrets inside you be revealed? For me, it can't be soon enough.

As I look back over the past thirty years of my career, I know I have moved forward in beginning to understand the unusual minds of serial murderers. Still, there are many questions to be answered, and sometimes I think there are far more questions than answers. I do feel that in the next twenty years, staggering progress will be made, progress that will make the genetics that helped to capture Green River Killer Gary Ridgway appear primitive. That being said, not nearly enough has evolved in the way psychiatrists, profilers, and law enforcement types approach the serial killer phenomenon. In the mid-1970s, for instance, the FBI's Robert Ressler is said to have coined the term "serial killer." Prior to this time, a series of unsolved murders with similar facts across the cases were often called stranger murders. Ressler, who believes that those who are cruel to animals may become serial killers, continues to label serial murderers as monsters and demons, which is the kind of thing that promotes fear in the general populace, not knowledge and understanding. In his most recent book, Ressler even cites pornography as leading to serial killing. But as I've pointed out in chapter after chapter, it is not a perceived weakening in the American moral fiber but a genetic anomaly that probably causes serial murderers to kill.

After so many years, I almost expect the FBI's investigators not to understand because their ideas based in behavioral science haven't changed much over the last few decades. And whenever I learn of their work, I still feel that they treat women as outsiders, just as I was when I worked on my first case, that of Mad Biter Richard Macek. Now I'm used to it and it bothers me much less. But in 2002, I heard of a committee meeting held during a national conference at which a psychiatrist had presented what he called a startling new theory about the development of the serial killer and why they killed. His theory of development of these killers was not new—I had presented the material at the same annual conference, years earlier! He was trying to say the theory was his own, when it clearly was my theory. I called the psychiatrist and confronted him with this fact and said, "I presented this entire developmental theory in 1990, have been working on the theory for many years, and here you are in 2002 representing that your theory is brand-new. How can you do that?" He stopped our conversation, and to this day will not discuss this with me. Any conference that promotes the free exchange of new ideas is fine by me. However, it does the psychiatric community as a whole no good when a colleague makes another's theory his own. It reminded me of a time when some Hollywood producers came to me, asking to pick my brain. They had big ideas about a show about a profiler and said that if I cooperated, I would be, in some way, a consultant for the program. So I spoke with them for days. They left, and they did the show, but I never heard from them again. I would almost expect that kind of spin from wheeling-and-dealing producers, but when a fellow psychiatrist does that, it really irks me. Even worse, what he was also trying to do was to shoe-horn serial murderers into current theory, which states that serial murderers are developmentally disabled and perhaps even autistic. What he was trying to do was to find some commonality between children's developmental disabilities and the way a serial murderer acts, but as we've seen, it's not as easy as shoehorning one theory into another.

There are some very specious theories out there about what makes a serial killer. Perhaps the strangest is that of psychologist Joel Norris, who in his book *Serial Killers* infers that diet, malnutrition, and vitamin deficiencies cause a serial murderer to act. Norris suggests that anything from lead to cobalt poisoning to consuming too much sugar can lead to killing. I was surprised he didn't say getting heartburn from eating pepperoni pizza ends in serial murder. Those who espouse other theories say that trauma, childhood abuse, and being treated badly—everything from a hated teacher to being fired at a job—causes a serial murderer to kill. We've also seen in this book that Dr. Dorothy Lewis believes that a cyst or injuries to the brain can result in a person turning to serial killings. But no one has been able to prove successfully that these societal or medical injuries lead to murder. That's why I've proposed the kind of careful, serious testing of the patient outlined in the previous chapter and presented with more detail below.

Why did Marcelo de Andrade feel the need to listen to tapes of his crying brother? Why didn't Englishman Fred West ever attack his wife and partner in crime, Rose West? Why didn't she become one of his dismembered victims? Why did Robert Berdella cut the head off only two of his victims and not all? Again: more questions than answers. The fact is, these people don't fit the profiles of the other murderers that I know. And they don't fit templates or equations, such as if you have someone who chokes cats, wets his bed, and has an overbearing mother and a violent father, you will eventually have a serial murderer. The upshot is that I don't yet know all the answers.

A major question that I am often asked regarding my research on serial killers is, How do their brains work? Here too more questions than answers have arisen, and no wonder. Today the brain is being studied as if it were made up of individual trees, and often researchers don't have the foresight to see the forest, the whole. If that's the case with research into the brains of average people in general, we haven't even looked at the leaves of the trees with serial killers, and it isn't just the forest we haven't understood with serial killers, it's most of the ecosystem.

I've dissected brains and the information I get when I look at those gray pieces provides less knowledge than I had hoped to obtain.

And this process is being repeated not only by me, but also by many others as well. So I ask questions again and again. Is the brain prewired at birth? How do I find out what influences the developing brain, especially in the serial murderer? Are the influences limited to environment, genes, and culture or just to genes? Scientists estimate that there are 300 million feet of wiring in the brain, and 10 billion cells. So discovering precisely which areas of the brain influence particular behavior or emotion is no easy task.

How are the brain regions connected so they end up specializing in certain functions like taste, sight, smell, or in a serial killer, the act of constant murder? Again, it's difficult to say with precision.

Emotions are known to originate in both the body and the brain. This recognition is the result of research in the area of the brain called the frontal lobe. Long known as the focus of the integration of thought and cognition, body sense, volition, and a sense of self, research into the frontal lobe is beginning to unravel a mystery that has plagued neuroscientists, ethicists, and religious scholars over time. Most of this scientific research basically points to the fact that there is truly no fine line that differentiates brain from body, and that makes it harder to pinpoint what makes a serial killer kill.

The aim of detailing my journey in this book was not to sit back and spin tales about my dealings with serial killers, but rather to explain that we are indeed slowly getting closer to answers. The electrical system of the brain was initially studied with external tools, such as brain-wave study. Thirty years ago, firing patterns of the brain were measured by attaching electrodes to the head, electrodes that could measure what was happening in a single cell. Three decades later, we have the capacity to see images of the human brain as it functions, and we can see how it works while people do anything from making ethical judgments to playing a hand in poker.

Where we face real difficulty is in answering how the brain is involved in the concept of free will. Some of our thoughts, behaviors, and actions are conscious. Many more are not conscious. All of us make decisions and choices, including the serial murderer. Are his choices those of free will, or are they already somehow predetermined? Neurotransmitters work with neuronal systems, and the combination of these yields the underpinning of thought, feelings, and behavior. Neurotransmitters and enzymes are also involved in cognition in the prefrontal lobe areas of the brain. If there are weaknesses in the system, then there will be weaknesses in what the person thinks, shows, or feels.

To understand what makes a serial murderer murder, it's important to know how all of us develop. Brain circuits actually begin developing prior to birth. They continue to develop, and males do not reach their brain maturation until their middle or late teens. Brain circuits change and grow through a person's life as a result of the influence of cells and genes, and of culture and environment. Anyone who has had an infant knows that each baby is born with a temperament, be it easy or difficult. Even though each child has the same parents, each child can be completely different. So parents could have ten children, each with wildly different characteristics, and none might grow up to be a serial murderer. And even if parents have no ancestral history of violence and most of their children have no violent streaks whatsoever, they still might have a child that is a genetic anomaly, a serial murderer.

The Human Genome Project, begun in the 1980s and completed in the first years of this century, explained the genetic sequences in humans. It is hoped that being able to define and delineate the sequences, especially of known disease, will assist in the management of those illnesses. Molecular genetics will help us to identify genes that are susceptible to causing certain diseases. Once this procedure becomes accurate and common, I may be able to answer with some finality this question: is serial murdering a disease? I feel it is, but I need to prove it.

I often wonder whether both the newest and future technology will help me to identify the potential for criminal acts. If we do identify that potential, what are we ethically and morally permitted to do to the potential criminal? It's a fact of the American justice system that Americans do not imprison people for what they think. Would you or I feel different about a neighbor if we knew without a doubt that our next-door neighbor Tracy's baby would become a serial murderer? Would we be frightened? Would we try to jail the baby and make pariahs of the parents?

Can we predict, with certainty, that a person will commit an act of violence? That's been the question posed by the courts to me and forensic clinicians before making a decision regarding whether a person must be hospitalized against his will, whether an order of protection must be served, or whether a serial killer should be executed because he will kill again. It's somewhat easier for juries to decide guilt if someone has killed thirty-three people. But what happens if we predict that a person is at a high risk to commit the most violent of acts, what do we do then? Though we can't imprison a person based on thoughts he may have, we should have the protection of the public as our goal.

When I wrote about John Wayne Gacy earlier in this book, one of the defenses was that he may have had a so-called criminal gene, the XXY chromosome of Klinefelter's syndrome. Actually, it's been found that it's not always the case that someone with this chromosome arrangement will become violent. A promise of early identification was followed by the recognition that the gene did not invariably produce a person who engages in criminal behavior. On the other hand, a controversial professor from Canada believes there is no criminal gene. Rather, he believes that a murderer might have inherited too few genes that regulate social responsibility. This gene deprivation, he says, may cause violence and murder.

Whatever the theories, I believe it's just a matter of time before we're able to isolate genes that contribute to major problems, like constant, murderous violence. Right now, it's clear that genes contribute to many domains of cognition in the brain where thinking occurs and to some processes of thinking.

For serial murderers, my experience has shown that once they kill, they can never be completely rehabilitated. They must be imprisoned and they can't be freed—again, for the protection of the public. Does this mean that serial killers should or should not be subjected to the death penalty? Will every doctor who participates in the death hearing for a serial murderer be castigated by physicians' organizations like Physicians for Human Rights that do not believe in the death penalty? Though they have not condemned me at this point in time, PHR may lash out at forensic experts, similar to the way in which PETA goes after people who wear fur coats.

PHR mightn't like it, but I have a plan to go about testing a serial murderer. If I use MRI, I might try to have one of them recall something about one of their murders under focused attention. (Of course, I would make sure the situation is far more controlled than the small room without a guard in which we hypnotized Richard Macek long ago.) If I'm able to trigger a feeling like rage by giving him a cue or a task that would relate to homicide, I'd not just be searching for how he would react outwardly. With MRI, I'd be looking to see what part of the brain would "light up," to see which area of the brain is most active during these times. Then I would relate these to encephalography, radiography that produces X rays, results to see if there were any similarities between the two tests. I would hope to be able to see whether there was an abnormality in the electrical system of the brain or neurotransmitter system of the brain.

As MRI continues to get more sophisticated, I believe I'd be able to pinpoint something important in the brain function of a serial murderer. Then I might be able to plan an intervention on that area of the brain. Would it be careful stereotactic destruction of that area of the brain or the use of a proton beam to dissolve that small part of the brain involved in serial killing? Doctors do use these technologies now to treat brain disease, and they do work.

One of the neuropsychology tests I perform on serial murderers is a paper and pencil test that serial murderers take, and some are like the one I gave to John Gacy, which dealt with throwing the ball into the woods. In the early days of neuropsychological testing of serial murderers, the tests were so long that many were unable to finish them; they can take up to twelve hours to complete. A serial killer just cannot focus on a structured task for that length of time. Forget a written test, it's difficult for him even to talk for that long. He'll have many false starts and he'll try to change the focus of the conversation because he wants to think he's in charge. Today, I can use a new kind of neuropsychology test that allows for shorter assessments that are just as accurate as the longer tests. This neurocognitive profiling helps to clarify the subtlest deficits in functioning. In addition, the interpretation of these test scores is being updated almost constantly, so I can compare the results with a very wide base of results from others on a private Internet site reserved for doctors who are qualified to interpret tests.

There are more tests that I'd use when dealing with a serial murderer. There's an IQ test, of course, which measures general intelligence. Then, there's the q test, which measures many different ways of thinking rather than a numerical score and tells me that there are common differences in these abilities among people. The results of this standardized test let me offer an educated guess about what kind of person has the ability, say, to work in a management position. A serial killer might function well in school and in the workplace, but with the q test, I might find he has problems personally. Here, I can also measure attention, the capacity for a person to receive irrelevant stimuli in the environment around him. I also measure working memory, which is how a person uses his short-term memory.

The brain takes one function—anything from problem solving or motor function—in the frontal lobes and connects this with the area that stores long-term memory, the parietal lobes, which are located toward the back of the brain. Problem solving happens in these connections, and I would like to see what differences there may be between a so-called normal person and a serial murderer. How distinct are the thought processes that lead up to the task and what are the thought processes afterward?

Memory in general has two parts. There's procedural memory, or the ability to recall past skills that have been learned, and memory that has the ability to remember past events. Language and reading can be influenced by genetics, and it is usually the left side of the brain that's involved such tasks.

But how does a person use information once he gets it? Information has to be processed or passed through the cognitive system. The brain reacts with its electrical response to stimuli, and that can be measured by something called event-related potential, or ERP. A doctor interprets the results of continuous electroencephalography from the electrical patterns of all brain areas and looks at the results, which come in graph form. What's measured isn't simply the fact that some sensory stimuli are being registered, but also the meaning of what's being registered. What I would like to do if I was allowed to test serial killers is to find out whether murders mean nothing to them.

In addition, I'd like to try brain imaging and see what results those tests bring. You can imagine how those in charge of correctional institutions react to the suggestion that a serial murderer be moved to a nonsecure facility for "just testing." They just wouldn't do it, not right now, anyway. But I believe tests like imaging could help me to learn much about a serial killer.

In the mid-1970s when the CAT scan was developed, this computerized axial tomography allowed doctors to see how brain structures looked. When MRI was developed and put into use, magnetic resonance imaging took the process a step further, allowing doctors to see the brain, not just gray matter, but white matter as well, which allows the various gray-matter areas to communicate with one another. Now, fMRI, or functional MRI, helps doctors understand how parts of the brain function when a person is given a range of tasks like reading or mathematical problem solving. It can even indicate the part of the brain that feels rejection when one person is shut out of a game and two others continue playing. If I tried fMRI testing with a serial murderer and re-created the task of murder, I might possibly see the area of the brain involved in killing. But if I asked Gary Ridgway about the killing of, say, Marie Malvar, and I brought in another murder in which he played no part, what would be the outcome? The theory would be that he would not react to the murder he hadn't committed, and that he would deal with the results of the reaction to this murder as if it were a placebo in a clinical drug test. Would the serial murderer even be able to find enough working memory to deal with completing the test of the murder he *did* do? Even if he didn't finish the test, would part of the brain "light up" even if he couldn't verbalize what he'd done? These are some of the questions that intrigue me, questions I would love to begin to answer.

Further, I might try another imaging test, called DTI. Diffusion tensor imaging is another magnetic resonance test that would allow me to differentiate among white matter fiber tracts in the brain. Would there be any abnormality in those tracts that I couldn't see through any other means of testing? DTI would also allow me to see in three dimensions on a computer screen the microstructure of tissue. As if I were looking through a powerful microscope, I could see aberrations I cannot see with the usual MRI tests. Even more incredibly powerful is the newest of the new, four-dimensional brain imaging, which provides breathtakingly detailed and precise views of the brain. Positron-emission tomography, or PET, measures the energy found when radioactivity is released in brain tissue. This involves very expensive equipment and an extensive staff but would allow me to make inferences about a serial murderer's neural activity if the activity were different from that of a normal person. Single photon emission computed tomography (SPECT) is a bit like PET because a radioactive tracer is taken up by the brain, tracers that can be active in as few as two or three minutes. Here, by interpreting different superbright colors in parts of the image, I could see what blood-flow changes to the brain look like.

As I've mentioned in various parts of this book, there are at least nine things that are common among serial killers:

—They do not have motives for their murders.

—They have no personality structures and do not fit into the usual theories of development espoused by people like Freud or Kohut.

—They are not psychopaths because psychopaths can have the ability to control what they do, think, and feel.

—They are not mentally retarded; most of them have an above-average intelligence.

—They are not psychologically complete human beings, even though they can mimic and play roles.

—They have not all been sexually abused, nor have they all been physically abused.

—They are addicted to killing and they cannot control their actions.

—Serial murder is not a phenomenon only of Western society. It happens around the world.

—Serial murder is not a new phenomenon. It probably began with the most primitive of societies thousands of years ago.

I keep these in mind wherever I happen to be when I profile serial murderers. If you, the reader, remember some or all of these points when watching frightening reports about the latest killer, you too will be able to keep the strange phenomenon of serial murder in perspective.

I place John Gacy's brain back in the box because my kids are calling for me upstairs. As I walk up the stairs, I'm not sure that I'll ever show them this book, at least not until they ask and definitely not until they are adults. It's been difficult, but I feel I've done a good job in keeping them separated from the ultraviolent world of serial killers.

It's time to pile into the family car and go to a hockey game and, speaking of violence, watch our son play. After all, I shouldn't think of serial killers all the time. My bet is that I will not hear of a new serial murderer case today. No lawyers will call to aggravate me, and no one will ask me to leave town to puzzle over a crime scene.

But I *will* leave my cell phone on . . . just in case. The cell phone is *always* on.

ACKNOWLEDGMENTS

How does one acknowledge the many people who have assisted in making the book that you hold in your hands? Always, someone may be inadvertently left out and any lapse on my part is just that, just a lapse. I apologize to all of you. To our agent, Chris Calhoun, who always came up with answers immediately, and Diana Thorn, his assistant, who never lost her cheerfulness. To our editor, Mauro DiPreta, for his incisive, clear vision of what we needed to do to refine and explain our topic; to Joelle Yudin for managing the reams of paper and e-mails, and never losing anything, including us. To all those on the William Morrow team who sat patiently through meetings and left their mark on those meetings with their enthusiasm and curiosity. Especially to my cowriter, Harold Goldberg, who waded through boxes of documents, and managed to have innumerable telephone conferences during which the book took shape and meaning. I truly appreciate and thank you all.

I must also acknowledge those in my life who have given selflessly, with true, honest, and ethical behavior. They understood the scope of this and assisted me in the research I continue to conduct. To Dr. Richard Anderson, mentor and friend; dedicated geneticists, neuropathologists, neurosurgeons, physicians, psychologists, law enforcement and correctional personnel, and lawyers who are mentioned in the book. Some wish to remain anonymous due to the often negative lessons they have learned from those who have tried to sensationalize and therefore minimize their work and scientific contributions. To those peers who have been obstructionists at best, and pernicious at worse, I also thank you. You taught me that no one can derail the pursuit of true collegiality in search of scholarly knowledge.—Helen Morrison

To Helen Morrison for being smart, strong, and brave enough to make the leap. The genius and keen eye of Helen J.P., always helping to weather the storm. Chris Calhoun, friend and agent, for making it happen literally overnight. Maer Roshan for the thoughtful tip. The hip craftsmanship of Mauro DiPreta, which put it all into perspective. John Saul and Mike Sack for simply being cool. Andrew Lee, Chris Tennant, Drew Kerr, and Steven Kent for their honest enthusiasm. Joelle Yudin for being organized. In the Queen City of the Lakes, Aunt Alexandra, Aunt Mary, Paul, John O., and Rud for being themselves. Catharine and Jeffrey Soros for the witty nights on their porch in sea-sprayed Nantucket. Diana, Tracy, and Nancy at Bar 6 for brightening this work on Wednesdays. Patrick Porter, David T. Bazelon, and Adam Moss for knowing what writing really means. Big Indian, the bear, the beaver, and even the mice there, for being the escape from the darkness.—Harold Goldberg